# Deductive Databases and Their Applications

For Thea and Rosie

# Deductive Databases and Their Applications

ROBERT M. COLOMB
*The University of Queensland, Australia*

**UK**   Taylor & Francis Ltd, 1 Gunpowder Square, London EC4A 3DE
**USA**  Taylor & Francis Inc., 1900 Frost Road, Suite 101, Bristol, PA 19007

**British Library Cataloguing-in-Publication Data**

A catalogue record for this book is available from the British Library

ISBN 0-7484-0796-0 HB
ISBN 0-7484-0797-9 PB

**Library of Congress Cataloging-in-Publication Data are available**

Cover design by Jim Wilkie

Typeset in Times 10/12pt by Graphicraft Typesetters Ltd, Hong Kong

Printed by T.J. International Ltd, Padstow, UK

# Contents

# Preface

This book is intended as an advanced undergraduate text, conveying the main ideas in the design and use of deductive databases in information systems applications. It assumes that the reader is familiar with the main concepts of relational databases. Some familiarity with Prolog is also an advantage, although not essential.

For those readers familiar with expert systems, a link is established between the production rule formalism and deductive databases, opening the way for the employment of techniques derived from information systems in the development of expert systems.

Major examples are drawn from bill of materials, CASE tool repositories, federations of databases, university course rules, and semantic data structures encountered in information retrieval.

The text was developed for a third-year Information Systems subject offered in the Department of Computer Science at The University of Queensland each year since 1991.

R.M. Colomb

## CHAPTER ONE

# Introduction

Deductive database technology is a name for a technology which lies between database and logic programming. It has a close relationship with the production rule formalism used in expert systems. This chapter is an introduction to the field, with some motivating examples sketched. Key terms are emphasized in **bold**; many are discussed in detail in the remainder of the book, as outlined in the plan of the book in section 1.5.

## 1.1 THE ORIGINS OF DEDUCTIVE DATABASE TECHNOLOGY

Databases are at the core of Information Systems technology. Originally, the data in an information systems application was held on decks of cards and on magnetic tape. The programs read the files, made changes in their contents, then wrote them out again as a new version. When disk technology became available, it was possible to make changes to the files without copying their entire contents. The structure of the files to achieve this updateability was still, however, embedded in the programs which did the updates.

The next advance was the introduction of database technology, first hierarchical then network databases. This technology provides a way to describe data independently of the application programs, so that the database can be seen as a separate resource, and many details of the procedures required to access and update the data are hidden from the applications programmer.

The most significant conceptual advance came with the introduction of relational database technology. With earlier technologies, the structure and content of a database record is described independently from the way it is stored, accessed and updated. However, the connections between records are represented essentially as pointers, so that the application programs need to know how to navigate around these complex data structures. In relational database technology, all records are identified by their contents. Furthermore, relational databases are organized according to the mathematical theory of relations, which is very close to being a subtheory of the first-order predicate calculus.

Since the data in a relational database is organized according to a large-scale mathematical structure, it is possible to transform queries from one expression to another, so that the second expression can be proved to have the same result as the first. This algebra is the basis of query optimization. When a complex query is made using a navigation-style database, the program must know the access paths, etc., and must contain a strategy to find the right data in a computationally economical way. In an optimized relational database system, one of the tasks of the database management software (**database manager**) is to construct a reasonably economical access strategy on the fly given the query expression and statistical information held in the system catalogs.

A query processing program written in COBOL against a hierarchical database is a program, while the same query written in SQL is essentially a specification of a program. The actual program is constructed by the database manager. Navigation-style databases are more declarative than native file systems, because details of record structure and content are declared to the database manager and managed independently of the applications programs. Similarly, relational database systems are more declarative than navigational database systems, since access strategies are largely determined by the database manager rather than the application programs.

The simple and regular structure of relational databases has led to a number of ancillary facilities, for example:

■ Views, which are standard queries stored in the database rather than in application programs.

■ Integrity constraints, which are enforced by the database rather than application programs (navigational databases also support integrity constraints).

■ Fourth generation languages, which take advantage of the structure of a relational database to make applications programming much easier than with third generation languages such as COBOL.

■ Triggers, which enable many business rules and more complex integrity constraints to be enforced by the database manager irrespective of which application program makes the relevant update.

A view is a derived table. The database manager stores both the schema for the derived table and the rules by which that table is derived. It is quite possible to have a large number of views, and to have views built upon views in complex ways, possibly involving negation and aggregation. One deficiency of database technology is that a database can reason *with* views, but not *about* views. One of the advantages of deductive databases is that **metaprogramming techniques** are available to reason about views, and to rewrite them for various purposes, including optimization.

A second deficiency is that relational databases do not permit **recursive view definitions** (nor the recursive queries from which views are constructed). This is a computational deficiency which prevents many interesting applications from being implemented using relational database technology. Several such applications are discussed below. A very important one is the bill of materials central to the manufacturing industries, which is a database of assemblies which are themselves composed partly of assemblies. There are many bill of materials based software packages available, with the recursive structures manipulated and managed by applications code written in third generation programming languages.

Integrity constraints supported by database systems are of two types:

- simple structural constraints such as keys, mandatory roles and foreign keys which are supported in the core of the database manager;
- more complex constraints which are implemented by view definitions which must never generate any tuples. (If a tuple is generated, then the constraint is violated.)

Since deductive database technology permits much better tools to manage views, and also permits much more powerful views to be defined, it can do a much better job with complex **integrity constraints**, including optimizing their computation.

Fourth generation programming languages are used for two broad purposes: to implement user interfaces and to implement business rules. Since deductive database technology is essentially a better means of building and managing views, it is just as easy to incorporate a deductive database into a fourth generation language as it is to incorporate a relational database. In addition, since it is easier to manage complex views, it may make it practical to remove some of the code from the application program into the view definitions, thus simplifying the job of developing and maintaining the information system.

Finally, the power of triggers in current databases is limited by implementation considerations. The limited ability of a relational system to reason about queries and views has meant that triggers can generally be defined only on base tables, and generally only one trigger may be activated at a time. Deductive databases permit the implementation of the much more powerful concept of **active databases**, in which triggers may be defined on views, and which have the ability to manage many interacting triggers.

## 1.2   SKETCH OF THE TECHNOLOGY

Database technology may be caricatured as in Figure 1.1. A database system is intended to allow a user to store and retrieve data. The data is organized into tables described by schemas. The user provides the schemas to the database system via a **data description language** (**DDL**), and makes retrieval requests to the database system via a **data manipulation language** (**DML**). Relational systems commonly use SQL DDL and DML respectively for data description and data manipulation. Retrieval operations are complex, so the database system generally translates the user's request from the high-level data manipulation language into some lower-level host language for execution.

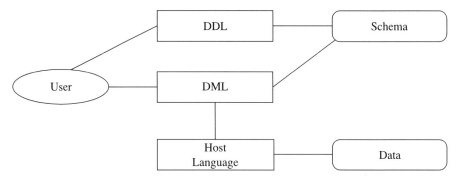

**Figure 1.1**  A database system.

The integration of more aspects of the application into the database system, and particularly the new capability of recursive views, introduces considerable complexity into the software which implements the deductive database. Deductive database systems therefore focus more clearly on what is analogous to the host language in a database system. This software is referred to as an **inference engine**.

The design, construction and maintenance of information systems is generally assisted by a number of modelling methods supported by **Computer-Aided Software Engineering (CASE)** tools. From the database point of view, deductive database technology presents a uniform formalism for expressing database schemas, queries and view definitions, integrity constraints, and derived relationships. It also permits recursive views. These aspects of information can be **modelled** by natural extensions of the modelling methods used in database systems such as Entity-Relationship Attribute analysis or Object-Role Modelling.

Quality of design is very important in any sort of system development. Since deductive database technology combines the description of data with specifications of complex computations, **quality criteria** from database design and from software engineering can be represented in a uniform manner.

With the publication of the recursive SQL3 proposals, the forthcoming availability of platforms such as Illustra (POSTGRES) and STARBURST, and the extensions to CASE technology, it will be natural to build information systems into a deductive database framework.

We can expect the trend towards replacement of procedural code with declarative statements in very-high-level specification languages to continue. For example, updates are an aspect of an information system which is still outside the scope of well-understood deductive database technology. An **update** may take the form:

> If a query is successful, then construct some new tuples based on the results of the query. Taking the integrity constraints into account, delete some tuples and add others.

Elements of the updates, such as the query and testing the integrity constraints, are part of the deductive database, but the whole transaction is still somewhat problematic, so is still in the province of applications code.

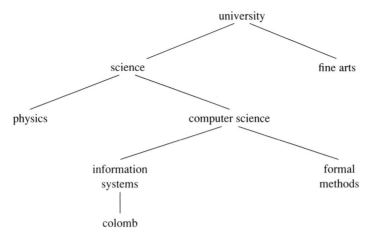

**Figure 1.2** A directory structure.

## 1.3  SKETCH OF SOME APPLICATIONS

### 1.3.1  Information systems

Since recursive queries and views are the main increased expressive power of
deductive databases, it makes sense to consider some applications where recursion
is an essential, or at least convenient, feature.

A familiar such application is based on a directory, as modelled in Figure 1.2.
An entity *colomb* is a member of the *information systems* group of the *computer
science* department of the *science* faculty of the *university*.

This application might be implemented in two tables:

subgroup(Wider, Narrower)

member(Entity, Group)

Both attributes of *subgroup* are drawn from the set of group names (*science*, *physics*,
*formal methods*), as is the second attribute of *member*. The first attribute of *member*
is drawn from the population of individual members of staff. A recursive search
through the *subgroup* table is required to determine whether for example *colomb*
is indirectly a member of the *science* faculty. The **X.500 standard** is a net equivalent of the telephone white pages for the location of people and resources in a large
communication network. X.500 is a good example of a directory structure with a
database flavour, since it is detached from an individual operating system, and must
be updated and searched by software which is visible to the user.

As noted above, the **bill of materials** application is a very common instance of
a recursive data structure. An assembly is composed of subassemblies, which are
composed of subassemblies, etc. until the whole assembly is decomposed into its
elementary parts (screws, pieces of sheet metal, gear wheels, etc.). Typical queries
which could usefully employ a recursive strategy include

How many elementary parts are required for one instance of assembly X?

To what assemblies does subassembly Y contribute?

Bill of materials problems often require extensive use of aggregation (COUNT, SUM, etc.).

Both the directory and the bill of materials are examples of tree structures. The techniques used to structure and retrieve information from tree structures can be generalized to graph structures, either directed or undirected. A clear example is given by a rail system, where the main data structure might be the set of station adjacencies

   adjacent(Line, Station_1, Station_2).

A query might be how to travel from one station to another, and would have in its response the lines used and the stations at which the passenger would change lines. In general, any system of referential links can be modelled by a graph.

Another sort of graph structure is a subtype lattice, such as is commonly encountered in conceptual modelling. (Banks have *products*, which may be *deposit accounts* or *loan accounts*. A deposit account may be a *cheque account* or a *savings account*. A savings account may be a *basic*, *classic* or *special* account. And so on.) Subtypes and inheritance of properties are also central to object-oriented technology. Since deductive database technology provides a coherent mechanism for representing and reasoning with view definitions, it is a good formalism for defining subtypes with complex derivation rules. The evaluation strategies used in deductive database technology are a good way of implementing the more straightforward aspects of object inheritance which are supported in the proposed SQL3 standard.

CASE tools can be seen as information systems whose content is the specification of aspects of an application system according to a particular method. Nearly all software engineering methods are based on visualizing the system in some way, involving the connection of components in a graph structure. The core of a CASE tool is the data structures which store the specification, and from which the visualizations are constructed. These structures are often called **repositories**, and can be implemented as deductive databases.

The examples sketched so far are fairly explicit applications of graph or tree structures, and might seem to be fairly specialized. This would be a misconception: the conceptual schemas of advanced information systems are generally becoming more abstract in response to the need for flexibility. For example, organizational information systems often include many similar kinds of relationships between similar kinds of entities, as in Figure 1.3.

A particular project is developed by one organizational unit and maintained by possibly a different unit, and is sponsored by a responsible company officer. A particular instance of user training is conducted within an organizational unit by a particular class of officer, and is authorized by a different company officer.

The abstract enterprise model of this kind of situation is often as in Figure 1.4.

In this more abstract model, the relationships of Figure 1.3 are recorded in the *Role* entity, the organizational units and company positions generalized in the *Party*

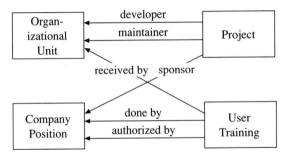

**Figure 1.3** Example of similar relationships between similar entities.

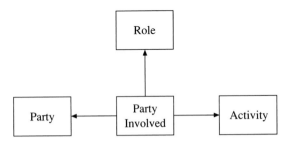

**Figure 1.4** Role abstraction enterprise model.

entity, and the projects and user training instances are generalized in the *Activity* entity. The *Party Involved* entity is an association which ties all three together.

Using this kind of data structure, it is possible to formulate recursive queries, such as

List all the direct and indirect relationships between two organizational units U1 and U2

Using these **generalized structures**, it becomes necessary to remove constraints from the data model. For example, the functional dependencies of Figure 1.3 disappear in Figure 1.4 if at least one possible relationship is many-to-many. It is much more suitable to express constraints on, for example, the number and types of roles required for a particular kind of activity in terms of rules in a deductive database.

A particular place where these constraints become visible is in **federated data-bases**, where an information system is composed from the inter-operation of a number of autonomous information systems, either in different organizations or different parts of a single organization. A widely used architecture for such systems is the **five-schema architecture**. These schemas are

- **local schema**: the underlying schema of the component database system;
- **component schema**: the translation of the local schema into the canonical data model of the federated system;

- **export schema**: the portion of the component schema which the component database chooses to make available to the federation;
- **federated schema**: the integration of the several export schemas for the component databases;
- **external schema**: a view of the federated schema defined for a particular user or application.

The component schema is defined as a series of views on the local schema, and it is often necessary for the federated schema to be constructed as a series of views on the component schemas. The federated database manager must translate queries on the federated schema into a collection of queries on the component schemas, then assemble the results. It is necessary to check these views for redundancy and for gaps in order to know how to process a query. Such systems invite recursive queries, such as might be used to track a message through a number of information systems.

A federated database manager must enforce global integrity constraints. The constraints control not only updates to individual information systems, and updates in one information system generated from another; but also the management of the global state of the integrated system. In particular, the constraints are necessary for management to have a global view of the organization.

Further, as information systems begin to inter-operate, often across organizational boundaries, it becomes necessary to express constraints not as business rules but as restrictions on what kinds of programs the programmers are allowed to write. For example, there may be data items which are not to be made available to queries which can go outside the organization. It is much safer if these constraints are managed by the database manager and by the CASE tools which support the development of applications.

A closely related technology is **data warehousing**, where *ad hoc* reporting and computationally intensive processing such as data mining is removed from the operational information systems of record, and performed on a derived database containing all the globally relevant information. The derived database is called a **data warehouse**, and is conceptually very similar to an eagerly computed federated database. (An eager computation is done as soon as its data is available, as opposed to a lazy computation, which is done only when its result is required.)

The argument that these considerations are becoming important in information systems generally is strengthened by the development of the SQL3 proposed extensions to SQL. The **SQL3** proposal includes

- temporary tables and views, so that more complex queries can be easily constructed;
- inheritance, so that more specific data structures can share properties of more general data structures;
- recursive expressions in joins, so that recursive queries and views can be described;
- stronger quantifiers, both existential and universal, so that complex integrity constraints and conditions can be more easily expressed.

One way to view this text is as suggesting how to both design applications for and to implement essential aspects of SQL3 systems, although for historical and practical reasons, the proposed SQL3 language is not used in it.

### 1.3.2   Knowledge-based systems

Artificial intelligence research has its origins in the early days of computing, contemporaneous with information systems. It took many years for techniques to be developed with commercial significance. What emerged was expert systems. A major technology used in expert systems is **production rules**, which considerably predate, but are very similar to, active database rules. A production rule is a statement of the form "if the following set of conditions is true, then perform the following set of actions". The set of conditions is very similar to a view definition, and the action performed can use the tuples generated from the view. As the technology has become better understood, much of its mystery has evaporated. At present, systems with large numbers of rules are often referred to as knowledge-based systems, whether or not the system is intended to emulate the behaviour of a human expert.

Classical production rule systems such as OPS-5 are grounded, although somewhat weakly, in the same logic from which deductive database theory has arisen. Therefore, most of the facilities of production rule systems are available in deductive database systems. This allows many expert systems to be expressed in a deductive database framework. The global optimization, program analysis and transformation mechanisms from database and logic programming allow much more reliable programs to be written and for programs to be executed orders of magnitude faster. This applies in particular to the important class of expert systems which use **propositional reasoning**. A proposition is a statement which can be either true or false, something like the WHERE EXISTS clause in an SQL query. These programs can be transformed to decision tables and decision trees, simplified, verified, re-ordered, and made suitable for real-time execution; all using automatic transformations which provably preserve their computational meaning.

A good example of a propositional expert system is **Garvan ES1**, which constructed clinical interpretations from the results of thyroid hormone pathology tests. It was in routine clinical use from 1984 to 1990, generating more than 6000 interpretations per year. It was built as a propositional production system and was in fact a deductive database. It had 661 rules at the end of its life. Garvan ES1 has been replaced by a system called PEIRS, which generates interpretations for a wider range of chemical pathology tests, and which has upwards of 1700 rules in a different structure which is equivalent to a propositional deductive database.

**SIRATAC** is a non-propositional system which is used in Australia to give cotton farmers advice on pest management. Each farmer periodically inspects his crop both for its stage of development and for the presence of 25 or so insect pests. This information is entered into SIRATAC, which maintains a historical database of this information and also has a small database of 25 or so chemicals used for pest control. Using pest and crop models and more than 100 production rules, it first determines whether the reported insect infestation is economically worth controlling; and if so, with what chemicals. SIRATAC could profitably be implemented using deductive database technology.

SIRATAC is an example of a class of expert system designed on the **endorsements** paradigm, in which there is a set of possible treatments (the chemicals in this case) and a set of considerations (in this case, efficacy of the chemical in controlling observed pests, cost, persistence in the environment, possibility of the pest developing resistance, etc.). Each consideration is implemented as an **agent**, which computes an **endorsement** for each possible treatment. An endorsement is similar to a vote. A supervisor agent combines the votes for each treatment from each of the endorsement agents, and selects the best endorsed treatments as the system's recommendation. Endorsement-based systems can generally be implemented using deductive database technology.

Garvan ES1 and SIRATAC are both classical expert systems which have many rules but relatively little data. There are knowledge-based systems which have much more data, which can be implemented as deductive databases with a database flavour. One such system is CAVS, which was a prototype system developed by the Australian Wool Corporation to demonstrate the feasibility of computerized assistance to wool buyers to help them assess the stocks of wool offered at auction.

The main database in CAVS is the sale catalog, which consists of a set of 80 or so measurements made on each of the several thousand lots of wool offered for sale. It also had available the same measurements together with the sale price for the 50 000 or so lots of wool which had been sold in the previous year. The measurements provided by the Wool Corporation were based on the properties of wool in its raw state. The buyers, on the other hand, act as agents for wool processors, and make their assessment of the quality and value of wool offered for sale based on estimates of the properties of the wool after various stages of processing into yarn.

CAVS contained knowledge about the relationships between the raw wool measurements and the processed wool characteristics in the form of decision tables, regressions and price forecasts. It also contained a linear programming package. A buyer purchases wool towards an order from a mill. This order is much larger than an individual sale lot, so that many sale lots are needed to fill the order. The linear programming package allowed CAVS to accept a buyer's requirement in processed-wool terms and a required price and to suggest an optimum strategy for bidding on the wool offered at a particular sale.

There is also a very close relationship between active databases and production rule systems.

## 1.4  SKETCH OF THE MATHEMATICAL BASIS

Deductive database technology stands at the intersection of database, logic programming, and expert systems technologies. Its unifying principle is logic. There are several logical systems which can be used for this purpose, notably

- the propositional calculus;
- first-order predicate calculus;
- higher-order logics.

Each of these logics is a language for expressing knowledge, but each also has a technology of automatic theorem proving so that it can make deductions based on the knowledge. These theorem provers can be adapted to function as inference engines in deductive database systems.

The relevant aspects of these logical systems are described formally and in detail throughout the text, but their main structure is sketched below to give their flavour.

The propositional calculus is concerned with logical propositions, which are statements that can be either true or false. Elementary statements are combined into complex statements using the connectives *and*, *or*, *not* and *implication*. The main inference rule, called *modus ponens*, says that if we know the proposition $p$, and also that $p$ implies the proposition $q$, then we can conclude that we know $q$. The database in these systems consists of the truth values assigned to the various elementary propositions known to the system.

The first-order predicate calculus is a propositional system with the addition of variables and quantifiers. The propositions, which are analogous to the tuples in a relational database system, are grouped into predicates, analogous to relations. Quantified formulas are analogous to queries or integrity constraints in relational databases. First-order predicate calculus is a very powerful and somewhat unwieldy system, so various subsets of it are in use, notably for our purposes **Horn clause logic**.

First-order inference is based on the principle of **resolution**, in which one disjunct of a true formula must be true if all the others are false. Resolution applied to Horn clause systems leads to the various inference strategies used in logic programming, including that used in **Prolog**.

Deductive databases are generally identified with **datalog**, which is a restriction of logic programming to systems which are much like databases, with possibly recursive views and integrity constraints. It is therefore much more computationally tractable than, say, Prolog. It allows database-style set-at-a-time reasoning and consequently potentially very much faster evaluation of queries. Since a deductive database program is a logical theory in the same way as a Prolog program, all of the machinery available for reasoning about logic programs is available. In particular, this allows programs to be transformed into forms more suited for execution purposes, while guaranteeing preservation of input/output behaviour.

### 1.5  PLAN OF THE BOOK

The book first reviews Prolog (Chapter 2) and explores the relationship between Prolog and databases, including a discussion of the properties of a number of standard complex data structures (Chapter 3). These chapters motivate and provide the language for the description of datalog, the main technology used in deductive databases (Chapter 4).

Attention then turns to design issues. Chapter 5 presents a design method which is an extension of well-known information systems design methods, and uses it to develop a small example. Chapter 6 serves two purposes: one is to show how a deductive database can be designed with the support of a CASE tool, and the other is to examine the CASE tool repository as a larger example of a deductive database. Quality of design is addressed in Chapter 7.

Having established what deductive databases are, and how they might be constructed, we consider some advanced aspects of the technology. Query optimization is covered in Chapter 8, and a very useful metaprogramming technique in Chapter 9. The metaprogramming technique is applied to the important special case of propositional expert systems in Chapter 10.

In Chapter 11, we examine the formulation and optimization of complex integrity constraints, while in Chapter 12, we consider the problem of updates and of maintaining consistency in complex data structures.

There are exercises at the end of each chapter, with solutions provided at the end of the book.

## 1.6    FURTHER READING

The present book is intended as an introductory text in deductive databases and their applications. As such, it covers the main points in an expository manner, omitting proofs. The interested reader will wish to explore the finer points, including the mathematics. The first stage of this exploration will be the world of research monographs, which give a coherent view of major segments of the field. Further exploration will bring the reader into the research literature: journal articles, conference papers and compendia where specific results are presented and criticized. At the end of each chapter will be found a brief sketch of the territory to be found in the next stage of exploration, with a mention of key references. These will be to monographs generally, but where necessary, to the research literature. The monographs and papers in the references for this text will open the deep literature to the keener student.

The reader is expected to have a good background in databases, such as would be gained in courses using Elmasri and Navathe (1994) and Nijssen and Halpin (1989) or Halpin (1994). The reader is also expected to have some familiarity with logic, and with Prolog, such as might be gained in a course based on Clocksin and Mellish (1987), Bratko (1986) or Sterling and Shapiro (1986). It would be an advantage to have some awareness of knowledge-based systems, such as might be obtained in a course based on Winston (1992), Genesereth and Nilsson (1987) or Rich and Knight (1991). Some of the issues in generalized data structures mentioned in this chapter are addressed by Batini *et al.* (1992). A widely cited survey on federated databases is by Sheth and Larsen (1990). Finally, a contemporary survey of deductive database technology is given by Ramakrishnan and Ullman (1995).

## 1.7   EXERCISES

The reader is expected to have a knowledge of relational database technology sufficient that these exercises be easy.

1.1   Given two relational tables:

| A | B |  | B | C |
|---|---|---|---|---|
| a1 | b1 | | b1 | c1 |
| a2 | b1 | | b1 | c2 |
| a3 | b2 | | b2 | c1 |

What is the schema and population of their natural join on the attribute B?

1.2   Add the table

| A | C |
|---|---|
| a1 | c1 |
| a3 | c2 |

What is the schema and population of the natural join of AB, BC and AC on
all shared attributes?

## CHAPTER TWO

# Summary of Prolog

The reader is assumed to be familiar with Prolog to some extent. The purpose of this chapter is to summarize the material about Prolog needed for the rest of the book.

## 2.1  BASICS

Prolog is a branch of logic programming. A Prolog program consists of a collection of logical formulas which form the set of axioms of a formal system. The axioms are turned into a program procedure by the Prolog interpreter, or **inference engine**, which is a type of theorem prover.

Formally, Prolog statements are Horn clauses. Horn clause logic is a subset of the first-order predicate calculus defined as follows.

A **constant** is a string of characters beginning with a lower-case letter, a digit, or enclosed in quotation marks, for example

a   alpha   aNB_vx456   42   "Arbitrary text string"

A **variable** is a string of characters beginning with an upper-case letter or the underscore (_) character, for example

X   _   Xact_43   _22

An **$n$-ary function** is a function symbol with $n \geq 0$ arguments, each of which is either a constant, variable or function. A **function symbol** is a constant beginning with a lower-case letter. A 0-ary function has no arguments, and is indistinguishable from a constant. Examples of functions are

f(a)   f(X, y, Z)   f(g(h(X), Y), a)   first_person

A **term** is either a constant, variable or function.

An **atom** is an *n*-ary predicate consisting of a principal functor and *n* arguments consisting of terms, with $n \geq 0$. An atom looks very much like a function. In fact, a predicate is a function whose range is the set {*true, false*}.

Predicates are sometimes described by their principal functor and arity. For example, the predicate *p* with arity 2 is described as predicate *p/2*.

A **literal** is either an atom or the negation of an atom. An atom is sometimes called a **positive literal**, while the negation of an atom is called a **negative literal**.

A **clause** is a disjunction of literals. It can be shown that any formula in the first-order predicate calculus can be transformed into a clause. We can eliminate existentially quantified variables by substituting unique constants for them. We can then transform the formula into a clause in which all variables are universally quantified by quantifiers whose scope is all the literals in the clause.

A **Horn clause** is a clause with at most one positive literal. Using the definition of implication $A \supset B$ if the formula *B or ~A* is true, and the identity *~A or ~B = ~(A and B)*), a Horn clause can be expressed as

  Head :- Body.

where *Head* is a positive literal, *Body* is a conjunction of negative literals (with the negation signs removed), and ":-" denotes that *Body $\supset$ Head*. *Head* is called the **clause head**, *Body* the **clause body**.

A clause with an empty body is called a **unit clause**, a clause with an empty head is called a **goal** or **query**, while other clauses are called **general clauses**.

A term containing no variables is said to be **ground**.

A ground literal is a **proposition**, in the sense of the propositional calculus. A ground clause is therefore a propositional formula.

A collection of clauses with the same head predicate (same principal functor and arity) is called a **procedure**. The procedure is called the **definition** of its head predicate.

A unary predicate whose definition consists of ground unit clauses is sometimes called a **type definition**. A definition is **recursive** if at least one of the clauses in its procedure is recursive.

A Prolog **program** is a collection of predicate definitions. Note that every clause in a program has exactly one positive literal, so that every clause has a non-empty head. A general clause in a Prolog program is sometimes called a **rule**.

It is important to note that a variable in a Prolog program has a scope limited to the clause in which it appears. Therefore variables with the same name appearing in different clauses are distinct. Most Prolog systems do not support the concept of a global variable.

The variable "_" is special. It is a shorthand notation for a variable name which occurs nowhere else in the clause. It is called the **anonymous variable**.

We will illustrate the definitions with the well-known *ancestor* example.

Example 2.1: *ancestor* program

  male(bob).
  male(jim).

female(thea).
female(edwina).
parent(thea, edwina).
parent( jim, thea).
married(bob, thea).

mother(Mother, Child) :-
    female(Mother), parent(Mother, Child).

ancestor(Older, Younger) :-
    parent(Older, Younger).
ancestor(Older, Younger) :-
    parent(Older, Intermediate),
    ancestor(Intermediate, Younger).

This example is a program consisting of definitions for the predicates *male/1*, *female/1*, *parent/2*, *married/2*, *mother/2* and *ancestor/2*. The definitions of *male/1*, *female/1*, *parent/2* and *married/2* are collections of ground unit clauses. The unary predicates *male/1* and *female/1* are type definitions. The definition of *ancestor/2* is recursive, while the definition of *mother/2* is not.

## 2.2   COMPUTING WITH A PROLOG PROGRAM

### 2.2.1   Logical view

A Prolog program is a static object. Formally, it is a set of axioms, or **theory**, in the Horn clause subset of the first-order predicate calculus. As a static object, it has much in common with a database. A database is turned into an information system by a computer program called a **database manager**, which permits a user to make queries on the database. The analogous computer program for Prolog is called a **Prolog interpreter**.

What a Prolog interpreter does is to attempt to prove theorems from the theory which is the conjunction of the clauses of the Prolog program. Let us call the program $P$ and the query, which is an atom, $Q$. A query is also called a **goal** (query is from the point of view of the user, while goal is from the point of view of the Prolog interpreter). Formally, the interpreter attempts to prove that the conjunction $P$ *and* $\sim Q$ is *false*.

Since the program $P$ is a conjunction of axioms, each of which is assumed to be true, then $P$ must also be true. Therefore, in order for the formula $P$ *and* $\sim Q$ to be *false*, we must have $\sim Q$ *false*, and therefore $Q$ *true*.

For example, suppose we have a query on the program of Example 2.1

male(bob)?                                                        (2.1)

If we call the conjunction of the clauses of Example 2.1 the program $A$, then the interpreter attempts to prove *false* (*disprove* or *refute*) the formula

A and ~male(bob)                                                          (2.2)

One of the axioms of $A$ is the clause *male(bob)*. We can make this explicit by expressing the program $A$ as

A = male(bob) and B                                                       (2.3)

where $B$ is the conjunction of the remaining clauses of Example 2.1. We can therefore express the formula (2.2) as

male(bob) and B and ~male(bob)                                            (2.4)

which must be *false*, since for any formula $F$, the conjunction $F$ *and* $~F$ is always *false*. We have therefore proved the query (2.1).

This may seem a roundabout way of doing things, and for propositional queries like (2.1), it is. However, the same procedure can be used for first-order queries, that is queries containing variables. For example, consider the query (in Example 2.1)

female(X)?                                                                (2.5)

By inspection of the program, we would accept as an answer

female(thea).                                                            (2.6)

or alternatively

female(edwina).                                                          (2.7)

Recall that, formally, a Prolog query is an atom all of whose variables are existentially qualified. (A query was defined above as a clause consisting entirely of negated universally quantified atoms, and we have the identity $\forall X ~p(X) = ~\exists X\, p(X)$.)

Formally, then, the Prolog interpreter attempts to prove query (2.5) by attempting to disprove the formula

A and $~\exists$ X female(X)                                             (2.8)

Now the program contains as axioms formulas (2.6) and (2.7). Therefore, the formula

$~\exists$ X female(X)                                                   (2.9)

must be false, since we can exhibit either formula (2.6) or (2.7) as counterexamples. We have therefore not only proved the formula

$\exists$ X female(X)                                                    (2.10)

but also identified two specific instances of X, namely

X = thea                                                                 (2.11)
X = edwina

These specific instances are called **answer substitutions**.

On the other hand, sometimes the interpreter may not be able to find a counterexample, and the query is disproved. For example, the query

married(edwina, X)?                                                      (2.12)

is *false*.

The task of a Prolog interpreter is therefore

- if the query is ground, produce the answer *yes* if it can prove the query, *no* if it cannot;

- if the query contains variables and if the interpreter produces the answer *yes*, also exhibit an answer substitution for each variable.

Note, by the way, that this behaviour is exactly that expected of a database manager when presented with similar queries. For this reason, a database manager will sometimes be referred to as an **inference engine**, as will sometimes a Prolog interpreter.

If an answer substitution can be found for a goal, the goal is said to be **satisfiable**. If there is a conjunction of subgoals, and mutually compatible answer substitutions can be found for all of them, then the conjunction of subgoals is said to be satisfiable.

So far, we have considered only queries which depend on procedures consisting only of unit clauses. We would also like to put forward queries which would require general clauses, such as those in the definitions of *mother* and *ancestor*.

Consider first the propositional query

mother(thea, edwina)?                                              (2.13)

As in the sequence (2.1)–(2.4), we can express the program $A$ as

$A$ = (mother(M, C) :- female(M), parent(M, C)) and             (2.14)
       female(thea) and parent(thea, edwina) and B

where $B$ is the remainder of the clauses in $A$. If we substitute the constant *thea* for the variable $M$, the constant *edwina* for the variable $C$; and make the conjunction of the negation of the query with the result, we obtain the formula

~mother(thea, edwina) and                                         (2.15)
(mother(thea, edwina) :-
        female(thea), parent(thea, edwina)) and
     female(thea) and parent(thea, edwina) and B

Applying the definition of implication, (2.15) becomes

~mother(thea, edwina) and                                         (2.16)
(mother(thea, edwina) or
        ~female(thea) or ~parent(thea, edwina)) and
     female(thea) and parent(thea, edwina) and B

Using the boolean algebra identity

(A or B) and ~B = A and ~B                                        (2.17)

formula (2.16) reduces to

~mother(thea, edwina) and                                         (2.18)
mother(thea, edwina) and
female(thea) and
parent(thea, edwina) and B

which is always *false*, for the same reason as (2.4). We have therefore established the truth of the formula (2.13), and the Prolog interpreter would answer *yes*. When the interpreter reports *yes*, the goal is said to *succeed*, otherwise the goal is said to *fail*.

A first procedural description of the behaviour of the Prolog interpreter is *Prolog Interpreter (First)*:

1   Attempt to find a clause in the program whose head can be made the same as the goal by substitutions for variables. If unsuccessful, report *no*.

2   If the clause is a unit clause, report *yes* and the substitutions made for any variables in the query.

3   Otherwise, repeat steps 1 and 2 for all the predicates in the clause body (called **subgoals**) with the substitution applied to their variables. Report *yes* if the interpreter reports *yes* for all subgoals. Report also the final substitutions for variables in the goal. If the interpreter reports *no* for any of the subgoals, report *no*.

In the example (2.13)–(2.18), the interpreter reports *yes*, but there are no variables in the goal, so that no substitutions are reported.

If we process the query

mother(thea, Child)?                                              (2.19)

Step 1 finds the clause defining *mother*, and finds that if it makes the substitution *Mother* = *thea*, the clause head is the same as the goal (2.19). The clause is not, however, a unit clause, so that step 2 does not apply and we must proceed with step 3, obtaining the two subgoals

female(thea), parent(thea, Child)                                 (2.20)

The first is a unit clause in the program, so the interpreter reports *yes* for this subgoal. The second can be made the same as a unit clause in the program by the substitution *Child* = *edwina*, so the interpreter reports *yes* for this subgoal also. All of the subgoals having succeeded permits the goal to succeed as well, with the substitution Child = edwina being reported for the variable present in the goal.

Step 3 of the Prolog interpreter procedure is called **expanding the goal**, or if the goal is a subgoal of a previous goal, **expanding the subgoal**.

The process of finding substitutions for variables so that a goal can match a clause head is called **unification**. The substitution with the fewest constants which makes the goal and the clause head the same is called the **most general unifier**, or **mgu** for short. The mgu is not the only possible substitution: for example in step 1 following (2.19), it would have been possible to substitute a constant for the variable *Child* as well as for the variable *Mother*. The substitution

Mother = thea                                                     (2.21)
Child = edwina

would lead to the subgoals (compare (2.20))

female(thea), parent(thea, edwina)                                (2.22) which would have succeeded since both subgoals are unit clauses in the program. However, an equally valid substitution would be

Mother = thea     (2.23)
Child = jim

which would produce the subgoals

female(thea), parent(thea, jim)     (2.24)

which fails because the second subgoal fails. Since at the time of unification the interpreter does not know which of the substitutions (2.21), (2.23) or other possible substitutions will lead to success, it follows the safest path of choosing the most general unifier.

Consider now the query

ancestor(thea, edwina)?     (2.25)

The Prolog Interpreter (First) procedure will report *yes*, in much the same way as for the query (2.13). However, for the query

ancestor(jim, edwina)?     (2.26)

we note that step 1 has a choice of clauses. If the first is chosen, the query will fail. If the second is chosen, the subgoals

parent(jim, I), ancestor(I, edwina)     (2.27)

will result. The first succeeds with the substitution $I = thea$, while if step 1 chooses the first clause of *ancestor* for the second subgoal, the further subgoal

parent(thea, edwina)     (2.28)

results, which will succeed.

The point is that the procedure *Prolog Interpreter (First)* must be modified to take into account that there may be several choices at step 1, and that there is not enough information available at that time to decide which to make. The algorithm must make one choice, then if that choice fails, make another; reporting failure upwards only if all choices lead to failure.

We are led to the concept of a **proof tree**. Its root is the original goal. We establish a set of branches leading from the root, one for each clause head which will unify with the goal. Each branch is labelled with the mgu of the goal with the associated clause head. If there are no clauses which will unify with the goal, a single, unlabelled, branch is created, leading to a node labelled *fail*. If there are branches, any associated with a unit clause are made to lead to a node labelled *succeed*. Figure 2.1 shows sample trees for these situations. The node *female(X)* on the left is called an *or-node*, because it has more than one successor to choose from.

In most cases a goal will be expanded by a clause with more than one subgoal. The arcs from the node associated with the clause head to the nodes associated with the subgoal are tied together. The node associated with the clause head is called an *and-node*. Figure 2.2 shows a proof tree of this kind. The node labelled *mother(Mother, Child)* is an *and*-node.

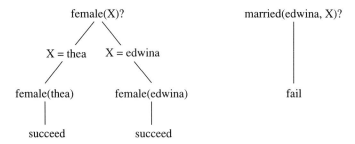

**Figure 2.1**   Simple proof trees.

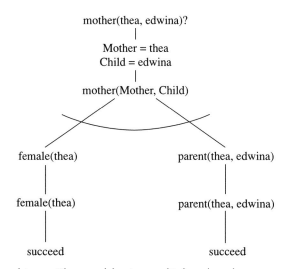

**Figure 2.2**   Proof tree with a goal having multiple subgoals.

Figure 2.3 shows a proof tree for a goal on the *ancestor* predicate. Note that the tree expands to the right without limit, reflecting the recursive clause in the predicate definition. Also note the arcs marked with thick lines. These arcs start with *succeed* nodes, and propagate up the tree. When an *and*-node is reached, the thick arc propagates upward only if all of the arcs leading to its subgoals have thick arcs. If at least one arc leading to the original goal at the root of the tree has a thick arc, then the goal succeeds. The portion of the tree whose arcs are thick designates the subgoals which have succeeded in order for the goal to succeed. This subtree may be called the **success subtree**.

A Prolog interpreter can be seen as a strategy searching the proof tree looking for success subtrees. The standard strategy used in Prolog implementations is a *depth-first* search, which traverses the proof tree from left to right, expanding the left-most subgoal until reaching either *succeed* or *fail*. If *succeed* is reached, the search returns to the nearest *and*-node and takes the next branch to the right. If *fail* is reached, the search returns to the nearest *or*-node, and takes the next branch to the right (this is called **backtracking**). The tree is laid out so that the branches in

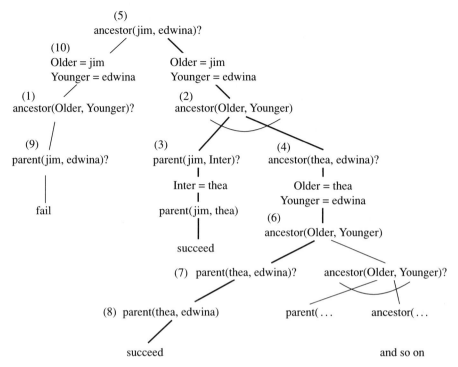

**Figure 2.3**  Proof tree for *ancestor.*

an *and*-node are left to right, as are the subgoals in the clause body, while the branches in an *or*-node are left to right, as the clauses appear in the program text. Examples of these appear in Figure 2.3.

Besides this theorem-proving style of query evaluation, Prolog interpreters generally have special predicates called **built-in predicates**, or **built-ins**. These can be syntactic shortcuts such as the *if-then-else* construct $p \rightarrow q; r$, which is interpreted as "if $p$ is true then the expression is true if $q$ is true. If $p$ is false, then the expression is true if $r$ is". Built-ins can also take semantic shortcuts, perform computations, or carry instructions to the interpreter to perform some special action. Built-ins are essential for the employment of Prolog for practical applications. For our purposes, however, most of the built-ins are inessential, so that those needed will be described at the relevant point.

Prolog programs can be used to construct and process complex data structures, such as lists. Lists are so common that there is a special syntax for list structures:

[] is the empty list

[a, b, c] is the list consisting of *a*, followed by *b*, followed by *c*

[H| T] is a list whose first element (called the *head*) is any substitution for the variable H. The remainder of the list (called the *tail*), which might be empty, is any substitution for the variable T.

The data structures represented in unit clauses are often trees or more general graphs. The *ancestor* example (Example 2.1) can be viewed as a directed acyclic graph, whose nodes are the populations of *male/1* and *female/1*, and whose arcs are the population of *parent/2*. The source of an arc is the *Older* argument, while the target is the *Younger* argument. The predicate *ancestor/2* is the transitive closure of the graph. This issue is discussed further in Chapter 3.

We sometimes want to know not only that one node is transitively connected to another, e.g. *ancestor(jim, edwina)*, but also what path the connection takes (in this case *[jim, thea, edwina]*). An adaptation of *ancestor/2* to this task is *anc_path (Older, Younger, Path)*, where *Path* will be bound to a list containing the path of relationships:

anc_path(Older, Younger, Path) :- a_p(Older, Younger, [Younger], Path).   (2.29)

1. a_p(Older, Younger, Path_so_far, [Older | Path_so_far]) :-
    parent(Older, Younger).
2. a_p(Older, Younger, Path_so_far, Path) :-
    parent(Intermediate, Younger),
    a_p(Older, Intermediate, [Intermediate | Path_so_far], Path).

anc_path(jim, edwina, Path)?

In the first execution (of clause 2), *Path_so_far = [edwina]*. In the second execution (of clause 1), *Path_so_far = [thea, edwina]*. Upon success, *Path = [jim, thea, edwina]*.

The transitive closure with path example (2.29) is a graph where there is only one path between any two nodes. If there are several paths, then the predicate will find all of them via backtracking. If the graph is cyclic, then backtracking can generate an indefinite number of solutions. Consider:

node(a).     node(b).     node(c).                     (2.30)
edge(a, b).  edge(b, c).  edge(c, a).

closure(Source, Target, Path) :- cl(Source, Target, [Target], Path).

1. cl(Source, Target, Path_so_far, [Source | Path_so_far]) :-
    edge(Source, Target).
2. cl(Source, Target, Path_so_far, Path) :-
    edge(Intermediate, Target),
    cl(Source, Intermediate, [Intermediate | Path_so_far], Path).

closure(a, c, Path)?

which will generate the series of solutions *Path = [a, b, c]*, *Path = [a, b, c, a, b, c]*, etc.

To correct this problem, clause 2 of (2.30) can be modified to check for cycles:

2. cl(Source, Target, Path_so_far, Path) :-              (2.31)
    edge(Intermediate, Target),
    not member(Intermediate, Path_so_far),
    cl(Source, Intermediate, [Intermediate | Path_so_far], Path).

The added clause *not member/2* expresses the predicate "the intermediate node has not been encountered yet". It uses a negation construct, which will be discussed below, and a predicate *member/2*, which is true if its first argument is an element in its second, which is a list. The definition of *member/2* is left to the reader.

### 2.2.2  Implementation view

It will be useful to know about some of the high-level data structures and operations used in implementing a Prolog interpreter. Examples refer to Figure 2.3.

A goal **calls** a procedure which **returns** if it succeeds and **backtracks** if it fails. A procedure consists of a number of clauses the heads of which are unified in turn with the goal. The set of clause heads comprises the branches of an *or*-node of the proof tree. An unsuccessful unification is a **fail** branch. An *or*-node is called a **choice point**. A pointer called the **alternate** keeps track of the first clause in the choice point which has not yet been tried (nil if none left at the current *or*-node). For example, when node (1) is the current node, node (2) is the alternate. When node (2) is the current node, the alternate is nil.

Unification consists of matching constants and **binding** variables. A variable is either **free** or **bound** to a constant (one free variable may be bound to another). **Bound** variables encountered in the process are dereferenced (all operations are performed on the ends of chains of bound variables). Data structures needed to support unification include a **variable-binding frame**, which keeps track of which variables are bound to what; and a series of **trail frames** which keep track of variables which are bound to constants or other variables occurring higher in the proof tree.

Both of these data structures are associated with each clause in the current potential **success subtree**. These and other structures are held in a frame on a stack-organized storage called the **environment stack**. The environment frame holds the state of the system. It includes an *alternate*, described above. As well, it includes a **continuation**, which is the next goal to be executed if the subgoal succeeds. The continuation is the next subgoal in the nearest higher *and*-node. When node (1) or (2) is being executed, the continuation is *nil*, while when node (3) is being executed, the continuation is node (4).

For convenience, the interpreter keeps a record of the **last choice point**, which is the alternate in the nearest *or*-node which has a branch not traversed (alternate not nil). The value of the last choice point at the time a clause is being executed is kept in the environment stack frame in a slot called the **backtrack point**. At node (1), the last choice point is node (5); at node (3), the last choice point is node (2), while at nodes (2) or (4), the last choice point is *nil*.

Working storage associated with processing the clause is organized in stack form, so the tops of the stacks used are also kept in the environment frame.

If a clause head unifies with the goal, its body, if any, becomes a new goal (or goal sequence). The leftmost subgoal is called and the *continuation* pointer is set to the next subgoal to the right if there is more than one subgoal. Otherwise the continuation remains pointing to the next subgoal in the nearest *and*-node containing a subgoal not yet expanded. If the current subgoal succeeds, the subgoal pointed to by the *continuation* is called. If the *continuation* is nil, the original goal must have succeeded. In the sequence of nodes (4), (6), (7), (8), the continuation is *nil*, since if that path succeeds, the goal (5) has succeeded.

If the current subgoal *fails*, then the environment associated with the *last choice point* is restored, and execution proceeds with the clause pointed to by the *alternate*. If the *last choice point* is nil, then there is no *success* subtree in the proof tree, and the original goal *fails*. The process of restoring the environment at the last choice point is called **backtracking**, and it involves undoing all the variable bindings made in traversing the proof tree below that node. Some of the variable bindings are stored in the part of the stack discarded when the environment is restored, but binding information for variables which occurred in the part of the current tree still active must be removed. The information kept in the *trail* is used to clear these bindings. When goal (9) fails, the bindings (10) must be undone when execution returns to the last choice point (5).

Variables are bound to terms. If a variable is bound to a term other than a variable, it is said to be **instantiated** to that term. The term may be another variable, a constant or a function. Arguments of a function may be variables, constants or other functions. When a variable is bound to a constant or function, the binding is a pointer to some constant text. In particular, any constant or function symbol in a term to which a variable is bound must appear somewhere in the program text. The program text is stored in data structures available to the Prolog interpreter.

Two basic strategies of implementation are commonly used: **structure-sharing** in which a variable binding is a pointer to a section of the program text as stored by the interpreter, and **copying**, where the text to which variables are bound is copied from the program stored in the interpreter to a **copy stack**. In copying, structures already on the copy stack are simply pointed to.

We summarize below the discussion of a Prolog interpreter:

1  *Start*: put the goal onto the empty goal stack.

2  *Choose subgoal*: Get the next goal for processing by popping the goal stack. If the stack is empty, then report *yes* and the substitutions made for any variables in the query. Otherwise, create a new choice point, and set *alternate* to the beginning of the program.

3  *Expand the goal*: starting from *alternate*, attempt to find a clause in the program whose head can be made the same as the goal by substitutions for variables. If unsuccessful, report *no* and backtrack (step 6). If successful, record the first clause not tried in *alternate*.

4  *Check for success*: if the clause is a unit clause, proceed to step 2.

5  *Save subgoals*: push the subgoals onto the goal stack from right to left. Proceed to step 2.

6  *Backtrack*: restore the state of execution of the last choice point. If there is no choice point, then report *no*. Otherwise, there is a choice point, so proceed to step 3.

An actual interpreter would be much more elaborate than this sketch, of course. In particular, the choice of subgoal and setting of the *alternate* pointer would be restricted to the definition of the procedure defining the goal's predicate. Furthermore, a Prolog program may have many possible solutions, and this interpreter produces only one. Practical interpreters often force failure after the goal so that all possible solutions are produced by backtracking.

## 2.3  NEGATED GOALS

So far, we have considered Prolog as a Horn clause system. This means that all goals must be positive. Such a program is called a **definite program**. Database systems, on the other hand, allow negative queries, and we would like Prolog to do something similar.

We can begin by considering a collection of **relational expression** built-ins which test numbers or character strings for equality, greater than, less than, etc. One of these is *not equals (!=)*. We could express the query "does *edwina* have any ancestors other than *thea*" by the query

ancestor(X, edwina), X != thea?                                             (2.32)

There is a stronger form of equality derived from the properties of Prolog which is implemented in the unit clause

equals(X, X).                                                               (2.33)

The goal

equals(X, Y)?                                                               (2.34)

succeeds if $X$ and $Y$ unify, i.e. a substitution exists which makes them the same. Examples of goals where *equals* succeeds are

equals(a, a)?                                                               (2.35)
equals(a, X)?
  X = a
equals(f(X, a), f(b, Y))?
  X = b
  Y = a

and examples where *equals* fails are

equals(a, b)?                                                               (2.36)
equals(f(X, a, Y), f(b, c, d))?

The predicate *equals* fails if it is impossible to find a substitution unifying its two arguments. It makes sense, therefore, to have a predicate *not_equals*, which is true if *equals* fails.

A simple generalization is to allow a goal which succeeds if the interpreter fails to find a solution. It is usual to implement this via a **modal operator** *not*. (A modal operator is a meta-predicate which expresses some property of the logical system in which the following formula is embedded, in this case failure to prove.) We augment the logic with the additional axiom

$$\text{not } F \supset \sim F \tag{2.37}$$

for a formula $F$.

We could therefore express the query "*bob* is not an ancestor of *edwina*" by

$$\text{not ancestor(bob, edwina)?} \tag{2.38}$$

Unfortunately, there are restrictions on the use of *not*. Consider the program

```
convicted(bob).                                              (2.39)
job_applicant(terry).
honest(X) :- not convicted(X).
mistrust(X) :- not honest(X).
reject_applicant(X) :- mistrust(X), job_applicant(X).
```

and we wish to get the list of job applicants which we will reject, using the query

$$\text{reject\_applicant(X)?} \tag{2.40}$$

To process the query (2.40), we first process the subgoal *mistrust(X)*, which succeeds if *honest(X)* fails. The subgoal *honest(X)* fails if *convicted(X)* succeeds, which it does with $X = bob$. The first subgoal therefore succeeds with $X$ still a free variable. The interpreter progresses to the second subgoal, which succeeds with $X = terry$, so the query (2.40) succeeds, with $X = terry$. We therefore conclude that we should reject Terry's application because Bob has a conviction.

The problem is that success of the goal *mistrust(X)*, with $X$ a free variable, is interpreted that *everyone* is mistrusted on the grounds that at least one person is not honest, which is not a valid logical conclusion, even though sometimes people behave that way.

If, however, the *reject_applicant* clause were altered to

$$\text{reject\_applicant(X) :- job\_applicant(X), mistrust(X).} \tag{2.41}$$

the first subgoal would succeed with $X = terry$, so the second would fail, since *honest(terry)* succeeds because *convicted(terry)* fails. We would not therefore reject Terry's application, which is the correct behaviour.

The precise conditions under which it is logically valid to use *not* are somewhat technical. It is common to restrict the use of *not* to predicates which are ground at the time of their execution, permitting for example (2.41) since the left-to-right execution will produce a binding for $X$ from *job_applicant* before *mistrust* is called. The same predicate in (2.39) would not be valid unless the variable $X$ in the query (2.40) is ground, so that *mistrust* is called with its argument bound.

We will call standard Prolog goals **positive subgoals**. Correspondingly, a **negative subgoal** is a goal preceded by *not*.

This type of negation is called **negation-as-failure**, since a goal is taken as false if it cannot be proven true. This is similar to the way negative queries are handled in database systems. Therefore, as in database systems, the question arises as to when it is semantically valid to use this kind of negation.

In a database system, it makes sense to make a negative query only if the database is assumed to contain all information relevant to the query. For example, a person may not be considered to be enrolled for a particular subject in a university unless the university database says so. If a query shows that a student's identifier is not in the database associated with a particular subject, then it is safe to assume that the student is not enrolled in that subject. On the other hand, the student record table may have an attribute containing the student's telephone number, if available. A query might show that a student has no telephone on record, but it would not be safe to conclude from that result that the student does not have a telephone.

The assumption that a database table contains all relevant information is called the **closed world assumption**. Whether the closed world assumption can be made is part of the information analysis from which the specification of the database is derived.

A similar assumption is relevant to Prolog. A negative query is semantically valid only if the closed world assumption has been made for the predicates relevant to answering the query. In our example (2.39), the closed world assumption holds for both the *convicted* predicate and for the *job_applicant* predicate. It may not hold for the *mistrust* predicate since there may be other potential reasons to mistrust someone.

Some applications of negation to the *ancestor* example are:

Person $X$ is the sister of a different person $Y$ if $X$ is a female and they have a parent in common:

```
sister(X, Y) :-    female(X),                              (2.42)
                   parent(Z, X), parent(Z, Y),
                   not equal(X, Y).
```

Person $X$ is childless if $X$ is married but has no children:

```
is_married(X) :- married(X, _).                            (2.43)
is_married(X) :- married(_, X).
has_children(X) :- parent(X, _).
childless(X) :- is_married(X), not has_children(X).
```

We have earlier defined a definite program to be a program all of whose goals are positive and each clause of which has a head predicate. A **normal** program may have negated goals, but each clause must still have a head predicate.

## 2.4   UPDATES

Prolog, as so far described, is a system for answering complex queries on a sort of database. It is a static system, since it has no means of changing the database. Database systems, on the other hand, are generally intended to model aspects of a changing world, so they accept updates to their tables. In most systems, one can add tuples to a relation, delete tuples from a relation, or modify existing tuples.

There is a conceptual difficulty with admitting updates to a Prolog program. Prolog is descended from a logical theorem-proving system, with a Prolog program conceptually a set of axioms. In standard logic, a set of axioms never changes. Not only that, if a logical theory is consistent, once a theorem is proved it always remains valid: no further theorem can be inconsistent with it. Logical systems with this property are called **monotonic**.

However, since Prolog is intended to be a practical programming language, and since many problems require programs to model systems with changing state, a number of features are generally available in Prolog systems to allow clauses to be updated. These and other features with no foundation in logic, which bend Prolog to practical purposes, are implemented using built-in predicates which are called **extralogical**.

A clause may be added to a procedure using the built-in *assert(X)*. The variable X is bound to a function. The function is added as a predicate to the Prolog database. Recall that functions and predicates are syntactically indistinguishable. Since a standard Prolog interpreter considers clauses in lexical order, there are frequently three built-ins related to *assert*:

asserta(X): adds X as the first clause in its procedure

assertz(X): adds X as the last clause in its procedure

assert(X): adds X to its procedure wherever the implementation finds most convenient.

Note that general clauses may be asserted as well as unit clauses, since the turnstile ":-" is considered to be a function (:-/2) , as is the conjunction connective "," (,/2). It is only necessary to construct such a function using the built-in which converts a list of characters to an atom.

A clause may be removed from a procedure using the built-in *retract/1*. The argument of *retract* has the form of a (positive) goal (recall again that predicates and functions are syntactically indistinguishable). The built-in unifies its argument with the head of a clause in the same way as a goal, then removes that clause from its procedure. The clause may be either a unit clause or a general clause. If no clause head unifies with its argument, then *retract* fails.

If there are several clauses which must be removed, they can all be removed by the program

retract(X), fail?                                                                                    (2.44)

using the built-in *fail*, which always fails. This is the same strategy as described earlier by which a Prolog interpreter finds all the answer substitutions which allow it to succeed for a goal.

Most implementations provide a built-in *retractall/1*, which performs the same function as (2.44).

Most Prolog systems do not provide direct support for modification of a clause: it is necessary to first *retract* the clause, binding it to the function which is *retract*'s argument. The program constructs a new function, possibly using part of the retracted function, then *asserts* it. For example, a count can be updated with the program

retract(count(N)), M is N + 1, assert(count(M)).                          (2.45)

Note: arithmetical computation is performed by the built-in *is*. In the term $X$ *is* $Y + Z$, the variable $X$ is instantiated to the sum of the terms to which $Y$ and $Z$ are bound. The latter terms must therefore be numerical constants of the appropriate type.

Here, the predicate *count/1* would have a single clause in its definition. The *retract* deletes that clause. The argument for *assert* is a similar clause, which is constructed with the variable $M$ bound to the value of the argument of the retracted clause incremented by 1. At the end of (2.45), there is again one clause in the definition of *count/1*, with an updated argument.

A Prolog system with *assert* and *retract* is no longer monotonic. Obviously the clauses in its procedures may change, but the theorems which are results of queries in clause bodies will also change. Monotonic logic is an area of much research, but is not well understood at present. The issue is treated in more depth in Chapter 12.

## 2.5   ALL SOLUTIONS

Database systems typically allow the user to obtain and work with the set of tuples which responds to a query. Prolog, as described so far, only allows individual solutions, each with its corresponding set of variable instantiations.

Since it is often convenient to reason about the set of solutions to a goal, most Prolog systems provide built-ins to compute them. We will discuss two: *bagof* and *all_solutions*.

First, recall the conventional way of getting a Prolog interpreter to find all the variable instantiations which satisfy a goal. This requires simply conjoining the goal with the built-in *fail*, which always fails. For example

ancestor(X, edwina), fail?                                                 (2.46)

in Example 2.1 will return the binding $X = thea$, then the binding $X = jim$, before responding *no*, since there are no more solutions to the *ancestor* goal.

Recall that the list of atoms *a*, *b* followed by *c* is *[a, b, c]*, that the notation *[H/T]* is a list function where the variable $H$ is bound to the first element of the list and the variable $T$ is bound to the remainder of the list, and that the empty list is designated *[]*.

The built-in *bagof* simply collects all these variable bindings into a list. The syntax is

bagof(<term>, <goal>, <list>)?                                            (2.47)

where <goal> is a goal, either simple or compound, and <term> is a term whose variables are drawn from those appearing in <goal>. The token <list> may be a variable which will be instantiated by the built-in to a list of terms, each of which is an instantiation of the variables in <term> from one solution to <goal>. It may also possibly be a constant list of such terms. If there are no solutions to <goal>, then <list> will be empty. For example, *bagof* applied to the goal in (2.46) would be

bagof(X, ancestor(X, edwina), L)?                    (2.48)

which succeeds with $L = [jim, thea]$.

An example where <list> is a constant is

bagof(X, ancestor(X, Y), [])?                    (2.49)

which succeeds for those persons who have no ancestors in the database *(Y = jim, Y = bob)* and fails for those persons who do *(Y = thea, Y = edwina)*. Note that these results are for cases in which $Y$ is bound to the indicated constant before the execution of *bagof*. If *bagof* is executed with $Y$ free, it will succeed with $Y = jim$ only, since the others fail and *bob* is not in the *parent* predicate.

If there are several solutions to a goal which have the same variable instantiations, then *bagof* will return a list with duplicate entries, since it simply collects these solutions into a list. For example

parent(jim, thea).                    (2.50)
parent(dorothy, thea).

bagof(X, parent(_, X), Children)?

will instantiate the variable *Children* to *[thea, thea]*.

Often the object of the query is to obtain the set of distinct solutions. This can be obtained by applying a simple program which removes duplicates from the result of *bagof*, but some implementations provide a built-in called *all_solutions*, with the same syntax as *bagof* (2.49).

In reality, *bagof* and *all_solutions* are not as simple as described here. First, there may be either an infinite number of solutions or the goal may go into an infinite loop in searching for a solution, so that the predicate will not terminate normally. Secondly, solutions may contain variables. While this is not a problem for *bagof*, it is not clear how to interpret the set of such solutions. For example

p(X).                    (2.51)
p(a).

all_solutions(Y, p(Y), L)?

Should $L$ be bound to *[X, a]*, or simply *[X]*, since $X$ and $a$ unify? It is probably best to restrict the use of *all_solutions* to situations where the result will always be ground. We return to this issue in Chapter 4.

Finally, we note that we can compute aggregations, such as the number of solutions, by processing the lists produced by *bagof* or *all_solutions*. For example, if we want to know the number of solutions to the query (2.48), we could use

bagof(X, ancestor(X, edwina), L), count(L, N)?                    (2.52)

count([], 0).
count([A|T], M) :- count(T, N), M is N + 1.

The issue of aggregation is treated in much more depth in Chapter 4.

## 2.6 DISCUSSION

From a database perspective, Prolog can be seen as a system which manages stored facts, with a similar function to databases, but which also manages derived facts and views. The correspondence between databases and Prolog is detailed in Chapter 3.

Database systems typically allow their users to update relations and to make queries, possibly through views. Not all views can be updated. Since systems implemented in Prolog can have very complex derivation rules, it makes sense to consider whether a given predicate can be updated by the user, in which case the predicate is called an **update type**. In the same way, not all predicates may be available to the user for making queries. Those which are available for queries are called **query types**. Predicates can be both update and query types, or sometimes neither (in which case they are called **intermediate types**). These issues are considered in more detail in Chapters 5 and 6.

We have dealt so far in this chapter with unit clauses and general clauses, both of which have one positive literal (the clause head). Clauses with no positive literals (goals or queries) have been treated as something external to the program. It is, however, common for an application to have a set of **integrity constraints**, which are implemented as a set of queries which must be satisfied for any valid instance of the system. In our formalism, these integrity constraints are clauses with no positive literal, which are stored and manipulated in much the same way as the other clauses. An integrity constraint is thus similar to a goal, in that a goal is a clause with no head predicate. A program with integrity constraints is not a normal program. Further consideration of integrity constraints is deferred until Chapter 11.

## 2.7 SUMMARY

We have presented in this chapter the main definitions about Prolog needed for the remainder of the book. These include

- the elements of Prolog;
- the basics of a Prolog interpreter and its implementation;
- negation and the closed world assumption;
- updating procedures;
- obtaining all solutions to a predicate.

## 2.8 FURTHER READING

The reader can find a much fuller exposition of Prolog as a programming language in Clocksin and Mellish (1987), Bratko (1986) or Sterling and Shapiro (1986). The classic formal treatment of Prolog is given in Lloyd (1987). A treatment oriented more towards deductive databases is given by Das (1992).

## 2.9   EXERCISES

Data consists of several extensional predicates:

male(Person) : true if Person is male.
female(Person) : true if Person is female.
parent(Parent, Child) : true if Parent is a parent of Child.
married(Husband, Wife) : true if Husband is married to Wife.
 Implicitly male(Husband), female(Wife).

2.1   Write a predicate *same_generation(Person1, Person2)*, which is true if Person1 and Person2 are the same number of generations away from some common ancestor. Note that a person is considered to be the same generation as him/herself.

2.2   Write a predicate *great_grandparent(Ancestor, Child)*, which is true if *Ancestor* is a great-grandparent of *Child*.

2.3   Write a predicate *ancestors(Child, List_of_female_ancestors)*, which is true if *List_of_ancestors* is a list containing only ancestors of *Child* in the direct female line.

2.4   Write a predicate *second_cousin(Person1, Person2)*, which is true if *Person1* and *Person2* share a great-grandparent but no nearer ancestors. Note that a person is NOT his/her own second cousin.

2.5   Write a predicate *same_sex_children(Woman)*, which is true if *Woman* has more than one child, and all of these children are the same sex.

2.6   Write a predicate *most_children(Parent, Number_of_children)*, which is true if *Parent* has at least as many children as any other parent, and *Number_of_children* is the number of children *Parent* has. (NOTE: this problem is a little trickier than the others.)

 **Hint**: if any problem requires more than 20 clauses, it is almost certainly wrong. My solutions have no more than 4 clauses for any of the problems.

2.7   Adapt the solution to Exercise 2.3 so that *List_of_female_ancestors* is bound to a list containing **all** ancestors of *Child* in the direct female line.

CHAPTER THREE

# Prolog and databases

There is a very close relationship between Prolog, as described in Chapter 2, and the relational algebra, with which the reader is assumed to be familiar.

## 3.1 PROLOG AND THE RELATIONAL ALGEBRA

We have seen that a Prolog program consists of a collection of clauses, which are classified as either unit clauses or general clauses. A database system consists of a schema and a number of relations, together with a query language based on the relational algebra. The query language supports at least the relational operations *select*, *project* and *join*, as well as the set-theoretic operation *union*. In this chapter, we examine the relationship between the two systems.

### 3.1.1 Relations

First of all, a Prolog procedure consisting of ground unit clauses is the same thing as a database relation. A clause in the procedure is equivalent to a tuple in the relation. A tuple consists of a set of attributes together with a value for each. A schema is essentially the relation name together with the attribute names, including a type for each.

A relation is frequently represented as a table with the attributes appearing as column headings and a row representing a tuple. A single tuple in this representation is simply a sequence of values, with the $i$th value being the value of the attribute appearing in the $i$th column heading. This tuple is represented as a unit clause by equating the relation name with the principal functor, and placing the value of the $i$th attribute in the $i$th argument position.

35

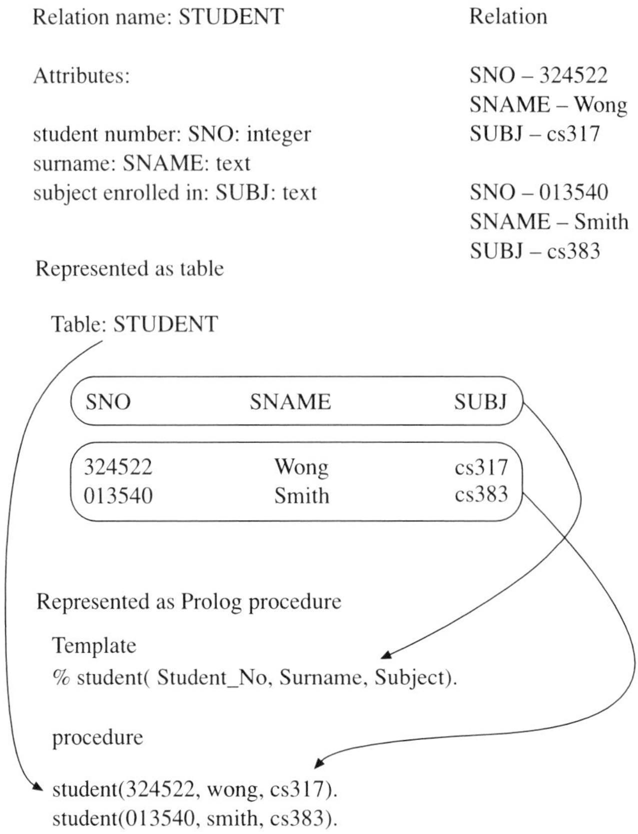

Relation name: STUDENT                          Relation

Attributes:                                     SNO – 324522
                                                SNAME – Wong
student number: SNO: integer                    SUBJ – cs317
surname: SNAME: text
subject enrolled in: SUBJ: text                 SNO – 013540
                                                SNAME – Smith
Represented as table                            SUBJ – cs383

Table: STUDENT

| SNO | SNAME | SUBJ |
| --- | --- | --- |
| 324522 | Wong | cs317 |
| 013540 | Smith | cs383 |

Represented as Prolog procedure

Template
% student( Student_No, Surname, Subject).

procedure

student(324522, wong, cs317).
student(013540, smith, cs383).

**Figure 3.1**   Correspondence between a relation and a Prolog procedure.

There is in Prolog no explicit representation of the schema. It is, however, common to document the procedure with a **template**, consisting of a clause with the principal functor of the procedure, having as arguments variables whose names are suggestive of the attributes. Figure 3.1 contains an example of this correspondence. It shows a relation named *student*, its representation as a table, and its representation as a Prolog procedure. Note that the "%" appearing in the template is a common identifier for a comment in Prolog, indicating that the template is part of the documentation, not of the procedure.

### 3.1.2   Select

A relational selection is represented as a Prolog query or goal, The selection

$$\sigma_{SNO=013540}(STUDENT) \tag{3.1}$$

in SQL

SELECT * FROM STUDENT WHERE SNO = 013540                    (3.2)

has as its value the relation consisting of the single tuple

<SNO=013540, SNAME=Smith, SUBJ=cs383>                       (3.3)

The corresponding Prolog query would be

student(013540, Surname, Subject)?                          (3.4)

where the selection criterion from (3.1) is expressed by the first argument position of the goal being instantiated to the constant *013540*. More complex selection
criteria are implemented by relational expression built-ins in Prolog. For example,
if we wanted all students whose surname came after "V" in alphabetical order, we
would have the SQL query

SELECT * FROM STUDENT WHERE SNAME > "V"                     (3.5)

and the corresponding goal

student(013540, Surname, Subject),                          (3.6)
Surname > "V" ?

The Prolog interpreter would instantiate the variables to

Surname = wong                                              (3.7)
Subject = cs317

This example brings up an important difference between Prolog and the relational
algebra: Prolog's inference engine operates **tuple-at-a-time**, computing bindings of
the query variables to terms occurring in a single clause of the procedure; while a
database manager, the relational algebra's equivalent of an inference engine, identifies the subset of the relation which satisfies the selection conditions: it operates
**set-at-a-time**.

To get a Prolog system to compute the equivalent of the relational algebra *select*
operation, we need to use the *all_solutions* built-in. In this example

all_solutions(                                              (3.8)
    student(Student#, Surname, Subject),
    student(013540, Surname, Subject),
    Students)?

would instantiate the variable *Students* to a list of terms of the form *student(Student#,
Surname, Subject)*, which corresponds exactly to the solution to the relational *select*
(3.1).

### 3.1.3   Project

The relational operation *project* is performed in Prolog by choice of the variables
of interest. For example, the projection which computes the set of subjects in which
the students in the STUDENT table have enrolled is

$\pi_{\text{SUBJ}}(\text{STUDENT})$                                                                      (3.9)

in SQL

SELECT SUBJ FROM STUDENT                                                        (3.10)

which for our example table would be {cs317, cs383}.

   The corresponding Prolog goal which would have these values as solutions would
be

subjects(Subject) :- student(_, _, Subject).                                        (3.11)
subjects(Subject)?

As before, the solution to the relational operation (3.9) must be accumulated using
the *all_solutions* built-in

all_solutions(                                                                          (3.12)
     Subject,
     subjects(Subject),
     Subjects)?

The variable *Subjects* is instantiated to the list *[cs317, cs383]*.

### 3.1.4  Join

The relational algebra *join* operation is represented in Prolog using conjunction of
goals. In the common *natural join*, the join condition is specified by shared variables. For example, suppose in addition to the *STUDENT* relation of Figure 3.1, we
have an additional *SUBJECT* relation whose attributes are *subject code* (*SUBJ*) and
*subject title* (*TITLE*). We wish to join the two relations

STUDENT $\underset{\text{SUBJ = SUBJ}}{\bowtie}$ SUBJECT                                                  (3.13)

in SQL

SELECT * FROM STUDENT, SUBJECT                                              (3.14)
     WHERE STUDENT.SUBJ = SUBJECT.SUBJ

   If the *SUBJECT* relation were represented by the procedure

subject(Subject_Code, Title)                                                         (3.15)

then the individual solutions to the join (3.13) would be expressed in Prolog as

student(Student_No, Surname, Code),                                           (3.16)
subject(Code, Title)?

where the variable *Code* expresses the natural join condition. As in the examples
(3.8) and (3.12), the whole relation must be collected using the *all-solutions* built-
in, which we will leave as an exercise for the reader.

### 3.1.5    Combinations

In a typical join query, the user is interested in a subset of the attributes. A join is therefore typically combined with a projection. In query (3.13), we might be interested only in student surname and subject title, so the query would be

$$\pi_{\text{SNAME, TITLE}} \text{ STUDENT} \underset{\text{SUBJ = SUBJ}}{\bowtie} \text{SUBJECT} \qquad (3.17)$$

in SQL

```
SELECT STUDENT.SNAME SUBJECT.TITLE                       (3.18)
   FROM STUDENT, SUBJECT
   WHERE STUDENT.SUBJ = SUBJECT.SUBJ
```

The corresponding Prolog goal (3.16) would be modified into a clause with subgoals

```
taking(Surname, Title) :-                                (3.19)
   student(Student_No, Surname, Code),
   subject(Code, Title).
```

with the query goal

```
taking(Surname, Title)?                                  (3.20)
```

The Prolog clause (3.19) can also be considered to be the definition of a *view*, corresponding to the relational algebra view definition

$$\text{TAKING} = \pi_{\text{SNAME, TITLE}} \text{ STUDENT} \underset{\text{SUBJ = SUBJ}}{\bowtie} \text{SUBJECT} \qquad (3.21)$$

in SQL

```
CREATE VIEW TAKING(SNAME, TITLE)                         (3.22)
SELECT STUDENT.SNAME SUBJECT.TITLE
   FROM STUDENT, SUBJECT
   WHERE STUDENT.SUBJ = SUBJECT.SUBJ
```

The union of two relations in the relational algebra is expressed in Prolog by the use of several clauses to define a procedure. For example, if we wanted the union of the surname and subject title for students who are enrolled in subject *cs317* or who have student number beginning with "0", we would define the procedure *want*

```
want(Surname, Title) :-                                  (3.23)
   student(Student_No, Surname, cs317),
   subject(cs317, Title).
want(Surname, Title) :-
   student(Student_No, Surname, Code),
   Student_No < "100000",
   subject(Code, Title).
```

Finally, it is often convenient to think of relations as defined in terms of *domains* and *roles* rather than attributes of elementary types. Domains are expressed in Prolog as predicates, defined by extension. The defining predicate of a domain can be a predicate used for some other purpose, or can be a unary type predicate as in the *person* predicate used in the *ancestor* examples in Chapter 2. These definitions in the relational system would be tables with a single column. For example, we could define a view *classmate* which had two roles, both with the domain STUDENT:

    classmate(Student_1, Student_2) :-                              (3.24)
        student(Student_1, _, Subject),
        student(Student_2, _, Subject),
        Student_1 ≠ Student_2.

### 3.1.6   Prolog and relational algebra in a nutshell

We have so far in this chapter indicated the syntactical relationships between databases and Prolog. At the level of representation:

■  any relation can be expressed as a procedure consisting of ground unit clauses;

■  any procedure consisting of ground unit clauses can be expressed as a relation;

■  any view can be expressed as a procedure consisting of general clauses.

At the level of inference, Prolog has a tuple-at-a-time solution strategy, while the relational algebra is implemented using database managers with a set-at-a-time solution strategy. Prolog needs the *all_solutions* built-in to compute the set of tuples which are answers to a relational query.

Prolog with *all_solutions* therefore includes the relational algebra. On the other hand, there are constructs in Prolog which cannot be expressed in the relational algebra:

■  unit clauses containing variables or functions;

■  procedures with recursion, either direct or indirect.

Chapter 4 considers in more detail the logical integration of Prolog with database. The remainder of this chapter looks at the integration of database technology with Prolog implementation technology. The aim is to have a practical environment allowing large procedures which persist between invocations of a program, which can be updated, and which can be shared among several users.

### 3.2   PERSISTENT PROLOG IMPLEMENTATION

Having established that there is a close formal relationship between Prolog and the relational algebra, the question arises as to how to build a piece of software which has the expressability of Prolog but the persistent data store capability of a relational database.

At first glance, it would appear that a solution might be to take a good Prolog and a good database manager and couple them together. Upon investigation, however, it turns out that the problem is not so easy. The basis of the problem is that a Prolog interpreter is designed around efficient tuple-at-a-time reasoning, while a database is designed around efficient set-at-a-time reasoning. This mismatch, sometimes called **impedance mismatch**, leads to severe difficulties in obtaining a good persistent Prolog.

From the point of view of a Prolog interpreter, the problem is that the database manager generates a set of solutions all at once. If the Prolog system accepts the entire set, then it has the problem of storing what could be a large number of possibly irrelevant tuples – irrelevant since it is common for only a few alternatives in a procedure to be satisfiable at the same time as the other subgoals in its clause body.

If the database manager retains the set of results, it can release them one at a time to the Prolog system using the cursor mechanism used in embedded database applications. However, a database manager is typically equipped with only a few (say 8) cursors, while a recursive Prolog procedure can easily generate a very large number of calls which are simultaneously active. Furthermore, a Prolog program can generate updates on database predicates while they are being queried. This means that the database must keep track of the tuples which responded to a query in the state as they were at that time. If any change is made after the query is initiated, it is not visible to that query. Another way of stating this requirement is that the database must initiate a transaction when the database goal is initiated, and this transaction endures until the Prolog exhausts all its alternatives, possibly by a cut. (A **cut** is a Prolog built-in which tells the interpreter to ignore all further alternatives to the current goal.)

On the other hand, a database manager is designed to perform query optimization. It takes a complex query all at once, performs analysis on it and its system catalogs, and decides an execution strategy which requires close to a minimum computation cost. A straightforward coupling of a Prolog interpreter to a database will only issue simple, selection-type queries on the database manager. All the joins are performed by the Prolog interpreter. As we have already noted, this can result in a large number of unnecessary tuples in the Prolog system. Furthermore, the query optimization facilities in the database manager are not used, possibly resulting in greatly excessive execution costs.

Some implementations have altered the Prolog interpreter to delay execution of queries on database predicates so as to accumulate as large a join as possible, then issuing them as a single complex query. This can require a complex and subtle modification to the Prolog system.

Most databases are designed to store simple atomic data values, while Prolog systems are designed to store and manipulate complex structures. A database manager requires some subtle modification to be able to store arbitrary structures while retaining the indexing and other capabilities upon which its query execution strategy is based.

Practical database systems support transactions (with a commit/rollback protocol), whereby a series of updates can be guaranteed to be applied either simultaneously or not at all. The tuple-at-a-time nature of Prolog reasoning makes it difficult to support transactions, since a goal may remain active for a long period of time as its various alternatives are tried. Database systems also generally support multiple user access, with a concurrency control mechanism based on the transaction. To support concurrency control, a transaction first locks the resources it needs, performs its calculations and updates, then either commits or rolls back and releases its resources. Again, the diffuse nature of Prolog, with long-lasting goals and tuple-at-a-time reasoning, makes it difficult to determine in advance what resources are likely to be needed and also may require resources for an unpredictable length of time. Most Prolog systems therefore do not support either transactions or multiple access, and it is difficult to integrate them with database systems which do have these features.

The most common approach to integrating databases with logic programming, as we will see in Chapter 4, is to augment a database manager with a restricted subset of Prolog which preserves set-at-a-time reasoning. This admittedly partial solution has required substantial research into optimization techniques, some of the results of which are contained in Chapters 8 to 12. This solution, based on set-at-a-time reasoning, also makes it practicable to support transactions and concurrency control, since these features can be inherited from database technology.

## 3.3  RELATIONAL REPRESENTATION OF COMPLEX DATA TYPES

A relational database system is based on a class of operators which take relations as inputs and produce relations as outputs. A relation is a complex data object. A single relation may consist of many millions of individual data items with specified relationships between them. Think of the relation which stores information about a bank's customers. Each customer may be described by dozens of attributes, and there may be millions of customers.

A relation may be a complex data structure, but information systems applications often require data structures which are even more complex. Consider a system involving students, subjects and enrolments as shown in Figure 3.2. An instance of *enrolment* requires an instance of both *student* and *subject*. The purpose of recording instances of either *student* or *subject* is to support possible instances of *enrolment*. The population of this data structure can be seen to be essentially a collection of instances of one complex type of object in the universe of discourse.

A data structure represented in a conceptual modelling language can also be represented equivalently as a system of relations and constraints, the most important of which from the present point of view is the foreign key constraint.

The ERA model of Figure 3.2 is represented in the relational model as a set of relations:

(3.25)

student(ID#, Sname, Course).
subject(ID#, Title).
enrolment(StudentID#, SubjectID#, Grade).

The relation *enrolment* has two foreign key constraints: *enrolment.StudentID# = student.ID#* and *enrolment.SubjectID# = subject.ID#*.

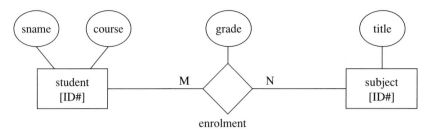

**Figure 3.2**  Sample complex data structure.

It is possible to construct a great variety of data structures by this method. There are, however, some special kinds of data structures which have useful properties. It is useful for a system designer to be able to recognize these special data structures, so as to take advantage of standard representations and queries which exploit their special properties.

### 3.3.1  Hierarchical data structures

One useful data structure is the hierarchy. A familiar example is shown in Figure 3.3. Each customer possibly has several invoices, and each invoice consists of possibly several line-items. As with the previous example, this structure is represented in a relational system by three relations: customer, invoice and line-item. The hierarchy is represented by two foreign key constraints: the identifier for an instance of *customer* must be stored with an instance of *invoice*, and the identifier for an instance of *invoice* must be stored with an instance of *line-item*. The dashed relationship between *line-item* and *customer* is a derived relationship which will be discussed below.

This system is again a single complex type of object in the universe of discourse. An instance of *line-item* makes sense only if there is an instance of *invoice*, and an instance of invoice makes sense only if there is an instance of *customer* which has

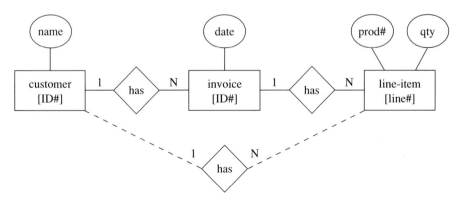

**Figure 3.3**  Sample hierarchical data structure.

made that purchase. Instances of *customer* exist only to support potential instances of *invoice*, and an instance of *invoice* cannot exist without an instance of *line-item* (indicated by the mandatory constraint).

The rules of ERA allow us to construct derived fact types. The derived fact type in Figure 3.3 is possible because the entity types *customer* and *line-item* each participate in a fact type with *invoice*. This derived fact type is the join of the two *has* fact types, with the join role *invoice* projected out. Constraints can also be derived. The uniqueness constraint on the *line-item* role of the derived fact type is derived from the uniqueness constraints on the two *has* fact types. The mandatory constraint on the same role is derived in a similar way. Recall that the uniqueness constraint identifies the role as the domain of a functional association, so that the uniqueness constraint on the derived fact type comes from the derivation being by functional composition.

Derivation of fact types in this way may or may not make sense in the universe of discourse. In the case of Figure 3.3, the derived relationship has a sensible interpretation: the set of line-items associated with all invoices for a particular customer. The user of the system might like to compute this derived fact type, which can be represented using a view, say

> customer-has-line-item(CustID#, Line#) :-                    (3.26)
>     customer-has-invoice(CustID#, InvID#),
>     invoice-has-line-item(InvID#, Line#).

A similar derivation could be made from the two fact types in Figure 3.2 having *enrolment* as a role. This derived fact type is essentially the same as the *enrolment* entity type, so that the derived fact type would be redundant in that universe of discourse. A user in the system of Figure 3.2 would not be likely to request the described derivation.

We have established so far that complex data structures can be described using conceptual modelling tools, and that these complex data structures can be represented as collections of relations linked together by foreign key constraints. Furthermore, the relationships described in the conceptual model can be augmented by derivations made possible by the rules of the conceptual modelling language used. Derived relationships may or may not be useful in the universe of discourse. If a derived relationship is useful, it can be represented by a view definition in the relational implementation.

One of the properties of conceptual modelling tools such as NIAM or entity-relationship modelling is that a reasonably good relational implementation of an application can be automatically computed from its description in the modelling language. It is also possible to automatically compute the view definitions of useful derived relationships. However, the CASE tool implementing the modelling method does not know which derived relationships to implement unless instructed by the user. A large conceptual model may have very many possible derived relationships, only a few of which are useful.

One way for the user to instruct the CASE tool as to which derived relationships might be useful is via the names given to the fact types. One often finds fact types given generic names (the two named fact types in Figure 3.3 are both *has*). We might be able to recognize generic names which tell us whether derived relationships are useful. The name *has* is probably not strong enough to make this inference. For example, the unnamed fact types of Figure 3.2 having a role *enrolment* could easily have been named *has*.

There are generic terms which do have implications for structure. Consider that the fact types of Figure 3.3 might, instead of *has*, be named *names-a-set-of*. This name would not make semantic sense without a functional association from a member of the set to its name. If the two base relationships had this name, then the same name could be inferred for the derived relationship, on the basis that an instance of *customer* names a set of instances of *line-item* which is the union of the sets of instances of *line-item* named by each of the set of invoice instances in the set of instances of *invoice* named by the instance of *customer*. (This is a re-statement of the derivation rules in the diagram of Figure 3.3.) Names which have semantic implications can be used to derive other names and their semantic implications.

Note that in this example, the domains of the three relationships are different. This limits the derived relationships to derivations which can be accomplished by a fixed number of joins – essentially the derivations which can be accomplished using the relational algebra. We have seen in the present chapter that a relational algebra expression can be represented as an expression in Prolog. Prolog permits recursive relationships. Anticipating Chapter 4, we would like to be able to have recursive joins in our query language. The remainder of the present chapter describes some complex data structures for which recursive derived fact types are not only possible, but essential.

### 3.3.2   Homogeneous relationships

Sometimes in information systems relationships (typically binary) are found in which all domains are the same. Several of these have been encountered in Chapter 2. The *parent* relationship is shown in Figure 3.4. The relational representation of this relationship is the predicate *parent(Older, Younger)*, both of whose arguments are from the domain *person*. This type of relationship is called a **homogeneous** relationship.

A homogeneous relationship offers more possibilities for derived relationships than a heterogeneous system, since there can be an indefinite number of compositions. Our predicate *parent* supports

parent(Older, Intermediate), parent(Intermediate, Younger)                     (3.27)

parent(Older, Intermediate-1),                                                  (3.28)
    parent(Intermediate-1, Intermediate-2),
    parent(Intermediate-2, Younger)
etc.

The semantics of the relationship name *parent* are not preserved under these compositions. The compositions do, however, make semantic sense: projections from them are given names:

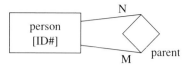

**Figure 3.4** The *parent* relationship.

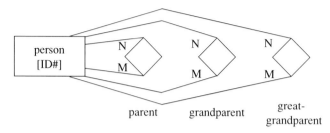

**Figure 3.5** Derived relationships from *parent*.

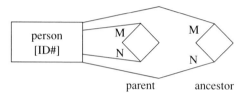

**Figure 3.6** The *ancestor* relationship.

grandparent(Older, Younger) :-                              (3.29)
    parent(Older, Intermediate), parent(Intermediate, Younger)

great-grandparent(Older, Younger) :-                        (3.30)
    parent(Older, Intermediate-1),
    parent(Intermediate-1, Intermediate-2),
    parent(Intermediate-2, Younger)
etc.

forming the structure shown in Figure 3.5.

Some relationship names do persist under composition. Following the *parent* example, we have seen in Chapter 2 the use of the *ancestor* relationship, which is transitive:

ancestor(Older, Younger) :-                                   (3.31)
    ancestor(Older, Intermediate),
    ancestor(Intermediate, Younger).

The predicate *ancestor* is derived from the predicate *parent* by the clause

ancestor(Older, Younger) :- parent(Older, Younger)             (3.32)

These clauses (3.31) and (3.32) are combined in the usual definition of *ancestor* seen in Chapter 2, and illustrated in Figure 3.6

ancestor(Older, Younger) :- parent(Older, Younger)                    (3.33)
ancestor(Older, Younger) :-
   parent(Older, Intermediate),
   ancestor(Intermediate, Younger).

### 3.3.3   Transitive data structures and graphs

Any data structure equivalent to that of Figure 3.6 and (3.33) is equivalent to a
directed graph and its transitive closure. By equivalent to, we mean that there is an
entity type substituted for the *person* type, and two homogeneous binary predicates,
one whose name is substituted for *parent* and the other substituted for *ancestor*. The
prototypical such predicate substitutes *arc* for *parent*, and *derived-arc* for *ancestor*.
In this way a graph data structure can be represented in a relational database, and
its transitive closure can be represented as recursive joins using Prolog. Any type
can serve as a node type, and hence the domain of the homogeneous relationship.
An arc has a direction. Its source is its first argument, and its target its second.

   There are many special forms of graphs. The special forms can be specified using
a combination of integrity constraints on the conceptual model (analog of Figure
3.6) and by additional predicates. We will consider a few generally useful cases:
chain, tree, directed acyclic graph, directed graph and undirected graph.

*Chain*

A **chain** is a graph in which each node is connected by an arc to at most one other,
and which has no cycles, as in Figure 3.7. The chain condition is enforced by the
uniqueness constraints on the *arc* relationship. Notice that the *derived* relationship
is many-to-many even though the *arc* relationship is one-to-one.

   A graph is cyclic if there is a derived arc from any node to itself. A Prolog
representation of this condition is

   cyclic :- derived-arc(X, X).                                   (3.34)

so that the criterion for a chain is both the uniqueness constraints of Figure 3.7
and the lack of solutions to the predicate (3.34). A concrete example of a problem
modelled as a chain is a sequence of messages, where each message may be in
reply to at most one other message. The nodes are of type *message*, the edges are

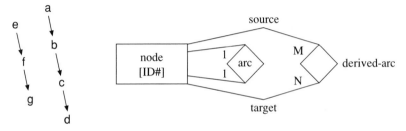

**Figure 3.7**  A chain object type, with two chain objects.

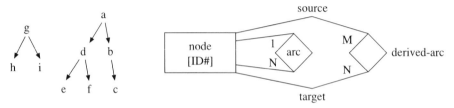

**Figure 3.8**  A tree object type, with two tree objects.

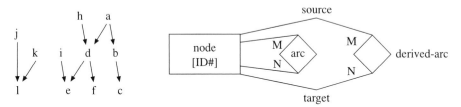

**Figure 3.9**  Directed acyclic graph object type, with two DAGs.

named *reply-to(MessageID#, Reply-to-messageID#)*, and the closure, say, *linked-to(MessageA, MessageB)*, where *MessageA* is a reply to *MessageB*, either directly or indirectly. Note that the population of the fact type can be several distinct chains, as illustrated in Figure 3.7.

## Tree

A **tree** is a graph in which every node is the target of an arc from at most one source, and which is not cyclic, as in Figure 3.8 where predicate (3.34) has no solutions. As before, the *derived-arc* relationship is many-to-many.

A familiar example of a tree in the computing field is a directory structure, where the nodes are of type *directory*, an arc is a subdirectory relationship, and a derived arc is an access path. Note again that a population of a tree fact type may contain several distinct trees.

## Directed acyclic graph

A **directed acyclic graph (DAG)** is a graph for which there are no solutions to predicate (3.34), as illustrated in Figure 3.9.

The *ancestor* predicate with which we started is a typical example of a DAG. Note that it is possible for the population to include several distinct DAGs. Note also that there is no requirement for a DAG to be connected, so a single DAG may have several disconnected components.

## Directed graph

A graph with no other constraints is called a **directed graph**, as shown in Figure 3.10.

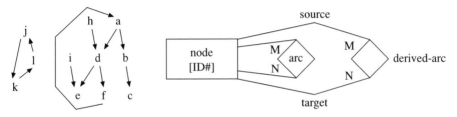

**Figure 3.10**  Directed graph object type, with two instances.

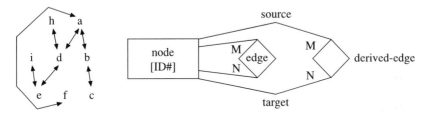

**Figure 3.11**  Undirected graph.

A computing example of a directed graph is where the nodes are procedures and the derived-arcs are call relationships (source predicate calls target predicate). The graph is cyclic if the procedures can be recursive. A more outward-looking example is where the nodes are street intersections and the derived-arcs are blocks in a one-way street network. Note that, like the DAG, a directed graph type may have several instances, and an instance may consist of several disconnected components.

*Undirected graph*

Figure 3.11 illustrates an **undirected graph**. An undirected graph is a graph where for each arc there is another arc with source and target reversed. The combination of an arc between two nodes and its reverse is often called an **edge**.

The edge of an undirected graph can be derived from the underlying *arc*

edge(A, B) :- arc(A, B).                                              (3.35)
edge(A, B) :- arc(B, A).

and this derived predicate can be used to construct the criterion predicate for undirected graphs

undirected :- not(arc(A, B), not edge(A, B)).                        (3.36)

in other words, that there is an edge between any two nodes between which there is an arc.

A two-way street network, where the nodes are street intersections and the edges are blocks, is an example of an undirected graph. Another example is an electric circuit, where the nodes are circuit elements and the edges are conductive paths.

### 3.3.4  Elementary graph functions

Graphs are a very important and widely used data structure. There is a well-developed theory of graphs, with many important conceptual constructs supported by good algorithms. This material is beyond the scope of the present work. However, some elementary graph functions are often useful in deductive database applications. One of these is the concept of **cycle**, which was defined in (3.34).

Two useful concepts in directed graphs are source and sink. A **source** is a node which is the source of arcs but the target of none, while a **sink** is a node which is the target of arcs but the source of none. They are defined

source(A) :- arc(A, _), not arc(_, A).                                        (3.37)

sink(A) :- arc(_, A), not arc(A, _).                                          (3.38)

In a chain, there is only one source and sink, both of which are referred to as **anchors** (*a* and *d* of Figure 3.7 are anchors of one chain, while *e* and *g* are anchors of the other). In a tree, there is one source (the **root**) and possibly many sinks (the **leaves**). In Figure 3.8, node *a* is a root, while nodes *c*, *e* and *f* are leaves. Similarly, node *g* is a root, and nodes *h* and *i* are leaves. A DAG also has possibly many sources. In Figure 3.9, *a*, *h* and *i* are sources, while *c*, *e* and *f* are sinks of one graph, while nodes *j* and *k* are sources of the other, whose only sink is node *l*. The concepts apply to general graphs (nodes *h* and *i* of Figure 3.10 are sources, *c* and *e* are sinks), but not to undirected graphs, since every node in an undirected graph is part of a cycle.

The first special case considered above, the chain, is not commonly found as an independent data type, but is very often constructed in the course of processing more complex graphs. A path from one node to another is a chain. We have seen in Chapter 2 that it is often convenient to represent a path as a list of nodes. Furthermore, in most applications a given node can appear only once in a path. If the path represents a cycle, generally at most one node appears twice. The following predicates illustrate how a path is formed in the various special cases of graph which we have considered.

In the acyclic cases (chain, tree, DAG), where (3.34) has no solutions, one definition of *path* is (3.39). The path is initialized in the goal, such as (3.40).

path(A, B, PathSoFar, [A | PathSoFar]) :- arc(A, B).                          (3.39)
path(A, B, PathSoFar, Path) :-
    arc(A, I),
    path(I, B, [A | PathSoFar], Path).

path(A, B, [], Path)?                                                         (3.40)

In the cyclic cases, the predicate must test the constructed path to avoid cycles, so (3.39) is modified to something like (3.41)

path(A, B, PathSoFar, [A | PathSoFar]) :- arc(A, B).                      (3.41)
path(A, B, PathSoFar, Path) :-
    arc(A, I),
    not member(I, PathSoFar),
    path(I, B, [A | PathSoFar], Path).

where the predicate *member* is true if *I* is a member of the list *PathSoFar*.

It will be instructive for the reader to apply the *path* predicate to the examples of Figures 3.7–3.10.

One of these special graph structures, the tree, is an example of a (homogeneous) hierarchical data structure. As in the example of Figure 3.3, if we start with a node instance *R* which is the root of a (sub)tree, then *R* can be interpreted as the name of a set of nodes which are the target of arcs whose source is *R*. (In a tree, these nodes are often called *children* of *R*.)

children(R, C) :- arc(R, C).                                             (3.42)

The children of the children are a set of nodes two steps removed from *R*. The children of those nodes are a set of nodes three steps removed from *R*, etc. A predicate which identifies the nodes *N* steps removed from *R* is given in (3.43). Note that the node *R* is considered to be 0 steps removed. (3.43) is defined for $N \geq 0$.

nodes-removed-level(R, R, 0).                                            (3.43)
nodes-removed-level(R, C, N) :-
    N > 0,
    M is N − 1,
    arc(R, I),
    nodes-removed-level(I, C, M).

In the example in Figure 3.8, if $R = a$, then the solutions of (3.43) for $N = 0$ are $\{a\}$, for $N = 1$, $\{d, b\}$, and for $N = 2$, $\{c, e, f\}$.

### 3.3.5   Identifying graph data structures in conceptual models

We have established that applications often require complex data structures, and that conceptual models in modelling languages like NIAM or entity-relationship modelling provide good descriptions of these complex data structures. We have also established that it is possible to have reserved generic names for fact types which can be used to infer that derived fact types are useful. Finally, we have established that homogeneous fact types can be used to model graph data structures.

Graph data structures need both arcs and derived arcs. It would be convenient if the modelling language allowed us to indicate which homogeneous fact types were intended to model graph structures, and to name both the arc and derived-arc. For example, Figure 3.12 is a representation of Figure 3.6, where the fact type is annotated with → to indicate that it models a graph data structure. The role at the shaft of the arrow is the source of the arc, and the role at the head of the arrow is the target of the arc. Two names are given. The first (*parent*) is the name of the arc fact type, and the second (*ancestor*) is the name of the derived-arc fact type. The

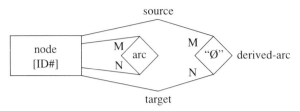

**Figure 3.12**    Alternative representation of Figure 3.6, using graph annotations.

further annotation Ø indicates that the graph is acyclic. This annotation shows in a compact way that the *parent* relation is a collection of directed acyclic graphs, whose transitive closure view is named *ancestor*. Adding the uniqueness constraints of Figure 3.7 would make the graphs acyclic chains, while adding the uniqueness constraints of Figure 3.8 would make the graphs trees.


## 3.4   SUMMARY

This chapter has described the relationship between the relational algebra/SQL and Prolog, and has considered the design problems involved in implementing a shared persistent Prolog environment. Finally, a database-oriented Prolog representation is given for several special cases of data structures, including graph data structures, together with some elementary predicates for processing them.


## 3.5   FURTHER READING

A much more extensive discussion of the relationship between logic programming and databases is contained in Ullman (1988), Ceri *et al.* (1990) and Li (1984). The material on the implementation of a database-like Prolog system is taken largely from Colomb (1990). There are many good texts about graphs.


## 3.6   EXERCISES

Consider the relational data schema below, with the attribute names defined in the following data dictionary. The schema describes a universe of discourse relating to a University department.

Department(deptname, heademp#, extgrant, intgrant, fax# OP)

Academic(emp#, empname, deptname, status, ext#, chair OP)

Award(emp#, degree, uni, yr)

Phone(ext#, room)

Department: attributes of a University department
  deptname: name of department, e.g. Computer Science
  heademp#: employee number (*emp#* from *Academic*) of the Head of Department
  extgrant: dollar value of external grants awarded to department last financial year
  intgrant: dollar value of internal grants awarded to department last financial year
  fax#: telephone number of departmental fax machine

Academic: attributes of an individual University academic staff member
  emp#: employee number
  empname: name of staff member
  deptname: department which employs the staff member (from *Department*)
  status: one of Lecturer, Senior Lecturer, Associate Professor, Professor
  ext#: telephone extension on the University PABX (from *Phone*)
  chair: if status = Professor, the name of the Chair the professor occupies (e.g.
    Professor of Information Systems, Professor of Software Engineering)

Award: attributes of an academic's professional qualifications
  emp#: employee number (from *Academic*)
  degree: degree awarded (e.g. B.E., Ph.D., M.Sc.)
  uni: university which awarded the degree
  yr: year in which the degree was awarded

Phone: attributes of the telephones used by academics
  ext#: telephone extension on the University PABX
  room: room number in which the phone is located

3.1   Translate the following from SQL to Prolog

  (a)   create view Occupies(emp#, room) = select emp#, room
                                    from Academic, Phone
                                    where Academic.ext# = Phone.ext#

  (b)   select    Academic.emp#, empname, degree
        from      Department, Academic, Award
        where     Department.deptname = Academic.deptname
        and       Academic.emp# = Award.emp#
        and       empname not = "Cantor"
        and       fax# is not null
        and       yr between 1965 and 1985

  (c)   select    deptname, empname, degree
        from      Academic, Award
        where     Academic.emp# = Award.emp#
        and       status = "Professor"
        and       uni = "UQ"
        union
        select    deptname, empname, "nil"
        from              Academic

```
where   status = "Professor"
and     emp# not in
           (select emp# from Award where uni = "UQ")
```

3.2    Translate the following from Prolog to SQL

    (a)   telephone_directory(Emp#, Empname, Deptname, Ext#, Room) :-
            academic(Emp#, Empname, Deptname, _, Ext#, _),
            phone(Ext#, Room).

    (b)   share_office(Emp#) :-
            academic(Emp#, _, _, _, Ext#, _),
            academic(Emp#_2, _, _, _, Ext#_2, _),
            phone(Ext#, Room),
            phone(Ext#_2, Room),
            Emp# != Emp#_2

        academics_sharing_offices(List_of_academics) :-
            all_solutions[Emp#, share_office(Emp#), List_of_academics).

3.3    Apply the *path* predicate (3.39) to the example in Figure 3.9, starting with node *h*. Show all solutions.

3.4    Apply the *path* predicate (3.39) to the example in Figure 3.10, starting with node *h*. What happens when you attempt to compute all solutions?

3.5    Apply the *path* predicate (3.41) to the example in Figure 3.10, starting with node *h*. Show all solutions.

3.6    Consider the following application model, which is based on the way manufacturing organizations manage their inventories.

    Manufacturer M makes products that require assembly of parts. An assembly (e.g. automobile) may be made up of several subassemblies (e.g. chassis, body, engine, carburettor) and parts (e.g. bolts). Each subassembly is made up of further subassemblies and parts. The lowest-level subassemblies are made entirely of parts. A bill of materials keeps track of how many of each lower-level subassembly and part is required to build each (sub)assembly. A unit (product, part or subassembly) has an indentification number and a description. It is not possible for a unit to be directly or indirectly a component of itself.

    Describe the data structures needed for this application in a conceptual model, using the methods of this chapter. If a graph structure is suitable, name the most specific relevant structures considered in the text, and include it in the conceptual model using the conventions of Figure 3.12.

# Datalog and bottom-up evaluation

This chapter describes a subset of Prolog which forms a natural extension to the relational algebra.

## 4.1 DATALOG

### 4.1.1 Motivation and definition

We have seen some of the difficulties in integrating Prolog with databases. Not only are the difficulties practical, there are also substantial theoretical issues. Horn clause logic, upon which Prolog is based, is a subset of the first-order predicate calculus, but one which preserves much of its power. Horn clause logic also inherits some of the theoretical problems of predicate calculus.

One of these difficulties is **non-termination**. Although it is possible to build automatic theorem provers for the first-order predicate calculus, and indeed there are many quite useful theorem provers, if a formula is true there are algorithms which will find a proof in a finite number of steps; but if there is no proof no algorithm will terminate on all formulas. In addition, there may be an infinite number of solutions. For these reasons, it is not in general possible to do set-at-a-time reasoning in Prolog. Even if, in fact, there are a finite number of solutions, one cannot guarantee that the theorem-proving algorithm has found them all after any finite time.

A relational database, on the other hand, is decidable and finite, with set-at-a-time reasoning the preferred method of inference. Its main theoretical deficiency is lack of computational power due to absence of recursion. What is needed is a subset of logic weaker than Horn clause logic but stronger than relational database theory, which preserves finiteness and therefore set-at-a-time reasoning.

Such a subset has been developed: it is called **datalog**. It is Prolog with the restrictions:

- unit clauses are always ground;

- function symbols are not allowed;

- it is negation-free.

In practice, most deductive database implementations permit carefully circumscribed relaxations of these restrictions, particularly negation, as we will discuss later. An additional technical property required to support the restriction that unit clauses be ground is that any variable which appears in the clause head also appears in the clause body (a clause with this property is called **safe**).

The unit clauses are a relational database. The subset of unit clauses of a datalog program is called its **extensional database**, or **EDB**. The other clauses are called its **intensional database**, or **IDB**. The IDB contains all the views, derived facts and integrity constraints of relational databases, but also permits recursion. Datalog is therefore strictly more powerful than relational databases. A datalog program, possibly with some carefully defined extensions, is frequently called a **deductive database**, or **ddb**.

The IDB is analogous to the set of views in a relational database. One of the important characteristics of views is that to a user, a view is indistinguishable from a table, at least for queries. A table is represented as its set of tuples. It therefore makes sense to characterize the IDB as a set of tuples.

## 4.1.2   Naive algorithm for bottom-up evaluation

Calculation of the set-of-tuples representation of an IDB is done using a technique called **bottom-up evaluation**. The simplest implementation of bottom-up evaluation is called the **naive algorithm**, which is based on the way in which views are computed in relational databases. A view is defined by a relational algebra expression. The view is materialized starting from the database tuples and performing the selections, joins and projections in some appropriate order. We can consider this computation as an operation $T$ starting from one set of tuples (which we will call a database) and yielding another. If we denote the population of all views by $V$, we have

$$T : EDB \rightarrow V$$

If we then combine the EDB with the view population, we have the database $EDB \cup V$. We can, if we like, apply $T$ to $EDB \cup V$, but we will still obtain $V$, since views in the relational theory cannot be recursive.

We saw in the last chapter that a clause in Prolog can be seen as a relational algebra expression, where the clause head determines the attributes onto which the result is projected. The object of the evaluation algorithm is to find sets of tuples for each relation corresponding to a clause head in the IDB. Initially, all the IDB relations are empty. We have only the EDB relations. If we consider the IDB as a set of view definitions, then we can apply the $T$ operator. In this case, however, the views may be recursive, so that if we apply $T$ to the database $EDB \cup V$, we can obtain some additional tuples, since the IDB may contain joins involving relations defined in the IDB. We formalize this situation by considering a series of applications of $T$:

$$M_0 = EDB$$
$$M_1 = M_0 \cup T(M_0)$$
$$M_2 = M_1 \cup T(M_1)$$

and so on

For example, consider a variation of the *ancestor* database seen in Chapter 2, which performs transitive closure on a directed acyclic graph, without taking account of paths, as in Example 4.1.

Example 4.1

EDB:

| | |
|---|---|
| person(bill). | parent(bill, peter). |
| person(mary). | parent(bill, paul). |
| person(peter). | parent(mary, peter). |
| person(paul). | parent(mary, paul). |
| person(john). | parent(paul, john). |
| person(sue). | parent(paul, sue). |
| person(alice). | parent(sue, alice). |
| person(eva). | parent(sue, eva). |

IDB:

A1:    ancestor(Older, Younger) :- parent(Older, Younger).
A2:    ancestor(Older, Younger) :- parent(Older, Middle),
                                    ancestor(Middle, Younger).

We have

$M_0 =$

| | |
|---|---|
| person(bill). | parent(bill, peter). |
| person(mary). | parent(bill, paul). |
| person(peter). | parent(mary, peter). |
| person(paul). | parent(mary, paul). |
| person(john). | parent(paul, john). |
| person(sue). | parent(paul, sue). |
| person(alice). | parent(sue, alice). |
| person(eva). | parent(sue, eva). |

$T(M_0) =$

ancestor(bill, peter).
ancestor(bill, paul).
ancestor(mary, peter).
ancestor(mary, paul).

    ancestor(paul, john).
    ancestor(paul, sue).
    ancestor(sue, alice).
    ancestor(sue, eva).

$M_1 = M_0 \cup T(M_0)$
$T(M_1) =$

    ancestor(bill, john).
    ancestor(bill, sue).
    ancestor(mary, john).
    ancestor(mary, sue).
    ancestor(paul, alice).
    ancestor(paul, eva).
    plus the tuples in $T(M_0)$

$M_2 = M_1 \cup T(M_1)$
$T(M_2) =$

    ancestor(bill, alice).
    ancestor(bill, eva).
    ancestor(mary, alice).
    ancestor(mary, eva).
    plus the tuples in $T(M_1)$

$M_3 = M_2 \cup T(M_2)$
$T(M_3)$ is only the tuples in $T(M_2)$
$M_4 = M_3 \cup T(M_3) = M_3$

Notice that in the example we eventually reach a point where $T$ does not add any tuples to the database. The database in the sequence where $T$ does not add any new tuples is called the **fixed point** of the operator $T$. (Naturally, this depends on the initial EDB and on the IDB.) The successive $M_i$ are called **partial materializations** of the view. The fixed point can be considered as the infinitely-repeated application of the $T$ operator, denoted $T{\uparrow}\omega$.

A very important property of datalog is that the operator $T$ has a fixed point for any EDB and any IDB. This is because datalog has been carefully defined to remove any sources of infinity. The EDB and IDB are both finite. Since there are no function symbols, there is no way of creating any new attribute values, so that there are only a finite number of possible tuples in the relations defined by the IDB.

That is to say that given any EDB and IDB, the sequence of databases $M_0$, $M_1$, $M_2, \ldots$, defined by successive application of the $T$ operator, will always contain an index $i$ such that $M_j = M_i$ for $j > i$ and $M_j$ is a strict subset of $M_i$ for $j < i$. We call this database $M_i$ the *perfect model* of program $P = EDB \cup IDB$, and will designate it by $M$. The perfect model has the useful property that if we view $P$ as a Prolog program, every tuple in it will give the answer *yes* if presented as a query goal. Not only that, any ground query goal which would give the answer *yes* is a tuple in the perfect model. This property can be verified for our *ancestor* example (Example 4.1), whose perfect model is

| person(bill). | parent(bill, peter). | ancestor(bill, peter). |
|---|---|---|
| person(mary). | parent(bill, paul). | ancestor(bill, paul). |
| person(peter). | parent(mary, peter). | ancestor(mary, peter). |
| person(paul). | parent(mary, paul). | ancestor(mary, paul). |
| person(john). | parent(paul, john). | ancestor(paul, john). |
| person(sue). | parent(paul, sue). | ancestor(paul, sue). |
| person(alice). | parent(sue, alice). | ancestor(sue, alice). |
| person(eva). | parent(sue, eva). | ancestor(sue, eva). |

| | |
|---|---|
| ancestor(bill, john). | ancestor(bill, alice). |
| ancestor(bill, sue). | ancestor(bill, eva). |
| ancestor(mary, john). | ancestor(mary, alice). |
| ancestor(mary, sue). | ancestor(mary, eva). |
| ancestor(paul, alice). | |
| ancestor(paul, eva). | |

The fact that a perfect model exists is important because it confirms that we can think about datalog programs in the same sort of way as we think about databases: as sets of tuples. It thus confirms our hopes that datalog, although more powerful than database theory, is still similar enough so that most of what we know about database theory will carry over. Note that the requirement that all datalog clauses be *safe* ensures that the perfect model is ground.

### 4.1.3   Propositional systems

The reader will recall from their study of logic that the propositional calculus is a subset of the first-order predicate calculus. A propositional system has no variables, so that all clauses are ground; consequently there is no quantification. This means that there is no method of grouping unit clauses or of analysing the internal structure of a ground formula. A proposition is therefore generally regarded as a sentence which can either be true or false. Because any internal structure of a sentence is invisible to the propositional calculus, a generic sentence is frequently represented as a single character, e.g. $p$, $q$.

A propositional IDB is a collection of formulas such as

$$p :\text{- } q, r, s. \tag{4.1}$$
$$p :\text{- } t.$$

A propositional EDB is simply a collection of proposition symbols. For example (4.2) could be an EDB corresponding to the IDB (4.1)

$$r. \tag{4.2}$$
$$t.$$

The perfect model for the DDB (4.1) + (4.2) is

$$r. \tag{4.3}$$
$$t.$$
$$p.$$

This example illustrates that an EDB predicate in a propositional system can have at most one tuple. The propositional calculus is usually formulated so that each **elementary proposition** (unit clause) has a truth value, either *true* or *false*. The propositional DDB models this structure, using negation as failure, by

presence of tuple = truth value *true*                    (4.4)
absence of tuple = truth value *false*

A propositional EDB can therefore be seen as an assignment of truth values to the elementary propositions. Computation of the perfect model can be seen as the assignment of truth values to the propositions which are defined in the IDB. These propositions are the consequents of IDB clauses. The perfect model computation is equivalent to propagating the truth values of the EDB propositions through the IDB rules. A query is the determination of the truth value of a proposition.

Propositional systems are therefore much easier to work with than first-order systems, but are less expressive. Their practical importance comes from the fact that most expert systems encountered in practice are essentially propositional Horn clause systems. They are also important from a theoretical point of view, since there are a number of issues which do not depend upon variables and quantification, notably stratification, described below.

### 4.1.4  Bottom-up versus top-down

From a practical point of view, the existence of a valid bottom-up evaluation scheme presents different ways of processing queries. A deductive database is a Prolog program, so that the standard top-down, depth-first search method will solve a query. As we saw in Chapter 2, the depth-first search method is space-efficient: it takes only one stack frame per level of recursion; and in some common special cases may take only one stack frame for an entire query evaluation. The method is also quite general: it works for full Prolog as well as the restricted datalog. It is probably the method of choice if a single solution is desired for a query.

On the other hand, depth-first search has some disadvantages, some of which are especially serious in a datalog program. First, the order of subgoals matters in depth-first search. For example, if the IDB in the *ancestor* example (Example 4.1) were altered to that given in Example 4.2, a query like *ancestor(alice, bill)?* would never terminate. (Note that the query has no solutions.)

Example 4.2
　　A1′    ancestor(Older, Younger) :- parent(Older, Younger).
　　A2′    ancestor(Older, Younger) :- ancestor(Older, Intermediate),
　　　　　　　　　　　　　　　　　　　　　　　　parent(Intermediate, Younger).

Rule *A1′* would fail, and rule *A2′* would generate the subgoal *ancestor(alice, Intermediate)?* Rule *A1′* would fail on the subgoal, then rule *A2′* would generate again the subgoal *ancestor(alice, Intermediate_1)?* and so on. In databases, the order of terms in a join is irrelevant. This means that if depth-first search is used to evaluate goals, some IDBs which would make sense from a database viewpoint will not work properly.

Secondly, the top-down approach makes use of the powerful method of unification to create the variable bindings from which the solution is built. The joins on which the bottom-up method is based require only **matching**, the ability to tell whether two constants are the same. Matching is a much less expensive operation than unification, so that the elementary operation on which bottom-up evaluation is based is computationally simpler than that for top-down.

Thirdly, joins in bottom-up are evaluated all at once, while in top-down the joins are evaluated one solution at a time. Evaluation all at once presents opportunities for using the join optimization technology developed in the database world. This faster computation of joins is especially valuable if the set of solutions to a query is desired, which is characteristic of database applications.

We would therefore like to be able to use bottom-up evaluation as a method of processing queries. Unfortunately, the algorithm we have is not very practical (which is why it is called the **naive algorithm**). In particular, each application of the $T$ operator repeats all the computation of the previous application. Not only that, the termination condition requires testing the equality of two possibly very large sets of tuples.

The simplicity which makes the naive algorithm valuable for proving the desirable properties of the perfect model makes it a poor basis for constructing a practical deductive database system.

## 4.2 SEMI-NAIVE BOTTOM-UP ALGORITHM

A little thought will reveal that the naive algorithm can be greatly improved by removing redundant computation. We want to evaluate IDB rules only if there is a chance that they will generate new tuples.

First, we note that an IDB rule can generate tuples in the first application of $T$ to the EDB only if all of its subgoals are EDB relations. No rule with a subgoal defined entirely in the IDB can generate any tuples since all the IDB relations are empty at this stage. (Note that, as we will see in Chapter 8, it is sometimes reasonable to have procedures defined partly in the EDB and partly in the IDB.)

Secondly, no rule all of whose subgoals are defined entirely in the EDB can generate any new tuples after the first application of $T$.

Generally, no rule in the $i+1$st application of $T$ can generate any new tuples unless one of its subgoals is an IDB relation which had new tuples generated in the $i$th application of $T$.

More formally, if we have the sequence EDB $= M_0, M_1, \ldots, M_n = M$, we can identify the new tuples at each stage as $\Delta_1, \Delta_2, \ldots, \Delta_n$, where

$\Delta_1 = M_1$ difference $M_0$
$\Delta_2 = M_2$ difference $M_1$
$\ldots$
$\Delta_n = M_n$ difference $M_{n-1}$

When we apply $T$ to $M_0$, we only consider the rules in IDB all of whose subgoals are defined in EDB. When we apply $T$ to $M_i$, $i > 0$, we only consider the rules in IDB at least one of whose subgoals is a relation which has tuples in $\Delta_i$. A rule which generates new tuples in a particular application of $T$ is said to **fire** on that application.

The calculation of $\Delta_i$ is reminiscent of the calculation of derivatives using the product rule in the differential calculus. The first step is to compute a superset of new tuples, which we will designate $\Delta'$. If a clause $h$ has only one IDB subgoal $p$, and a conjunction of EDB subgoals $e$, then the new tuples of $h$ are

$\Delta'h$ :- $\Delta p$, e.

If $h$ has several IDB subgoals $p_1, p_2, \ldots, p_n$, then the new tuples of $h$ are

$\Delta'h$ :- $\Delta p_1, p_2, \ldots, p_n$, e.
$\Delta'h$ :- $p_1, \Delta p_2, \ldots, p_n$, e.
. . .
$\Delta'h$ :- $p_1, p_2, \ldots, \Delta p_n$, e.

At each stage, only the clauses of $\Delta'h$ for which $\Delta p_i$ is non-empty need be evaluated. Further, the other subgoals have all their relevant tuples already computed in the accumulating perfect model, so can be treated similarly to EDB predicates. Finally, it is possible that $\Delta'h$ contains some tuples which were already computed, so that we must remove them:

$\Delta_i h = \Delta'h$ difference $M_{i-1}$

To summarize, we have

$\Delta_1 = T(M_0)$
$M_1 = \Delta_1 \cup M_0$
$\Delta_2 = \Delta T(M_1)$
$M_2 = \Delta_2 \cup M_1$
etc.

The algorithm terminates at step $n$ when $\Delta_n$ is empty.

This modified algorithm, called the **semi-naive algorithm**, produces the same result as the naive algorithm.

We show in Example 4.3 the results of the semi-naive algorithm applied to the program of Example 4.1. $\Delta_1$ is produced entirely by rule $A1$, which has only EDB relations in its subgoals. All the rest are produced entirely by rule $A2$.

Example 4.3

IDB:

    A1:    ancestor(Older, Younger) :- parent(Older, Younger).
    A2:    ancestor(Older, Younger) :- parent(Older, Middle),
                                     ancestor(Middle, Younger).

$\Delta_1 =$

    ancestor(bill, peter).
    ancestor(bill, paul).
    ancestor(mary, peter).
    ancestor(mary, paul).
    ancestor(paul, john).
    ancestor(paul, sue).
    ancestor(sue, alice).
    ancestor(sue, eva).

$\Delta_2 =$

    ancestor(bill, john).
    ancestor(bill, sue).
    ancestor(mary, john).
    ancestor(mary, sue).
    ancestor(paul, alice).
    ancestor(paul, eva).

$\Delta_3 =$

    ancestor(bill, alice).
    ancestor(bill, eva).
    ancestor(mary, alice).
    ancestor(mary, eva).

$\Delta_4$ is empty, so the semi-naive algorithm terminates.

Example 4.4 shows that when there is more than one IDB subgoal in an IDB rule, one rule can generate more than one contribution to $\Delta$. Generally, there can be a contribution to $\Delta$ from an IDB rule for each IDB subgoal in that rule.

Example 4.4: IDB rule

The rule is true if two people are allied by marriage, i.e. they have descendants who are married to each other. (The predicate *is-married* is an example of an undirected graph.)

    allied(Person_1, Person_2) :-
    is_married(Spouse_1, Spouse_2),
       ancestor(Person_1, Spouse_1),
       ancestor(Person_2, Spouse_2).
    is_married(Spouse_1, Spouse_2) :-
       married(Spouse_1, Spouse_2).
    is_married(Spouse_1, Spouse_2) :-
       married(Spouse_2, Spouse_1).

Assume that *married* is an EDB relation, and that *ancestor* is as defined in Example 4.3. If $M_i(ancestor)$ is the $i$th materialization of *ancestor* (the entire *ancestor* relation as computed at the end of the $i$th application of $T$), and $\Delta_i(ancestor)$ are the tuples for the *ancestor* relation computed during the $i$th application of $T$, then the new tuples in the $i+1$st application of $T$ for the *allied* relation are

$\Delta_{i+1}$ (allied) =
    allied(Person_1, Person_2) :-
        is_married(Spouse_1, Spouse_2),
        $\Delta_i$(ancestor(Person_1, Spouse_1)),
        $M_i$(ancestor(Person_2, Spouse_2)).
$\cup$
    allied(Person_1, Person_2) :-
        is_married(Spouse_1, Spouse_2),
        $M_i$(ancestor(Person_1, Spouse_1)),
        $\Delta_i$(ancestor(Person_2, Spouse_2)).

The main point of Example 4.4 is that a step of the semi-naive algorithm generates new tuples for an IDB rule only if the previous step generated new tuples for at least one of its subgoals. Therefore we must consider new tuples generated for each of its subgoals in turn.

We conclude that the semi-naive algorithm is a practical method for computing the perfect model of a deductive database program. Unfortunately, for practical systems the perfect model is often extremely large and the user is only concerned with a small part of it. In Chapter 8 we look at ways to transform rules so that the semi-naive algorithm can form the basis for a deductive database system useful in practice.

### 4.3   NEGATION AND STRATIFICATION

The definition of datalog given at the beginning of this chapter excluded negation. Negation is an important feature of databases, and its inclusion in datalog is necessary for it to be a superset of database theory. The problem with negation is that the naive algorithm is not entirely satisfactory for queries with negative subgoals. (Consequently, neither is the semi-naive algorithm, which gives the same result.)

Example 4.5
    EDB
       a.
    IDB
       R1:   p :- not q.
       R2:   q :- a.

If we evaluate rule *R1* before rule *R2* we obtain the model $\{p, q, a\}$, since when we evaluate *R1* there are no tuples in the relation $q$. On the other hand, if we evaluate *R2* first we obtain the model $\{q, a\}$, since *R2* places a tuple in $q$ before *R1* is evaluated. (Recall that the model $\{p, q, a\}$ is interpreted as "the propositions $p$, $q$ and $a$ are all true", and that the model $\{q, a\}$ is interpreted as "the propositions $q$ and $a$ are both true, but the proposition $p$ is false".)

Intuitively, it seems unreasonable to evaluate *R1* first, since we are not giving the rest of the program the chance to put tuples into relation $q$ (determine the truth or falsity of proposition $q$). In the depth-first top-down evaluation, the interpreter would exhaust all means of proving $q$ before allowing $p$ to succeed. We can express this preference for a reasonable order of execution as

Rule: *Compute negatives before using.* Evaluate all rules producing instances of a relation before any rule having that relation negated in its body.

Unfortunately, it is not possible to follow this rule for all IDBs. Consider the program given in Example 4.6.

Example 4.6

R1:  p :- not q.
R2:  q :- not p.

On the other hand, we can prove that if it is possible to apply the *"Compute negatives before using"* rule at all, any sequence of execution which follows the rule gives the same result. If it is possible to follow the rule, we say that the program is **stratified**. In a datalog program with stratified negation, the model computed using the above rule is the perfect model.

There is a simple algorithm for determining whether an IDB is stratified. It uses a graph whose nodes are the rules of the IDB. There is an arc from a source rule to a target rule if the source rule is part of the definition of a predicate which is a subgoal in the target rule. Each arc is labelled *positive* if the subgoal in the target rule is positive and *negative* if the subgoal in the target rule is negative. This graph is called the **dependency graph** of the IDB.

**Stratification theorem**: A program is stratified if its dependency graph has no cycles with a negative arc.

Figure 4.1 illustrates several dependency graphs. Programs $A$ and $D$ are stratified while programs $B$ and $C$ are not. In program $A$, R2 is evaluated before R1. In program $D$, either both $p$ and $q$ are true or both $p$ and $q$ are false. If some other rule allows us to put a tuple in one or the other, then program $D$ says that they both should have a tuple. On the other hand, in programs $B$ and $C$ we cannot decide whether to evaluate R1 or R2 first, since in either case the results are different if we start with R1 than if we start from R2.

It is of course possible to have non-stratified first-order programs as well as propositional programs. We will use an example from a hypothetical federated database system.

Example 4.7

Let us assume that there are three sites, A, B and C. Site A is responsible for sales, and maintains a subtype structure on the organization's customers, which includes a predicate identifying *standard-customers* and returns the discount allowed for each such customer. Site A has a view definition

standard-customer(C#, Discount) :-
    customer(C#, Discount),
    not special-discount(C#, Special-type, Special-Discount).

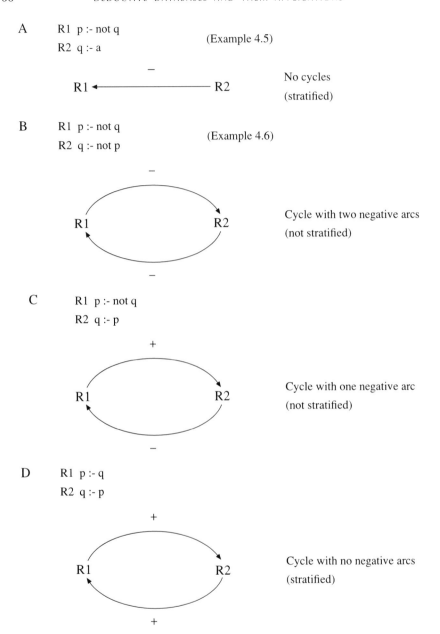

**Figure 4.1** Sample dependency graphs.

The export schema for site A includes only the view, not its definition.

Site B supports a sales analysis department, one of whose tasks is to identify "good" customers, who might be candidates for favoured treatment. Site B has a view

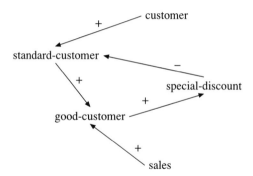

**Figure 4.2** Dependency diagram for federated database (Example 4.7).

good-customer(C#, Revenue) :-
   standard-customer(C#, Discount),
   sales(C#, Revenue),
   good-customer-revenue-threshold(T),
   Revenue ≥ T.

Again, only the view is exported.

Finally, site C supports the marketing department. One of the tasks of the marketing department is to offer special discounts to customers under certain conditions. One of its views is

special-discount(C#, good-customer, Disc) :-
   good-customer(C#, Revenue),
   good-enough-threshold(T),
   Revenue ≥ T,
   good-customer-discount-rate(Disc).

As usual, only the view is exported.

In the federated database, the views of Example 4.7 interact. The dependency diagram is given in Figure 4.2.

There is a cycle in the diagram: *standard-customer → good-customer → special-discount → standard-customer*, and the arc *special-discount → standard-customer* is negative. Our example is not stratified. Looking at it carefully, you can see that if a customer does not have any special discounts, but generates enough revenue, they will be given a special discount, which will result in their not being eligible for a special discount.

Looking at the situation even more carefully, you can see that the difficulty does not affect every customer. Customers whose revenue is not high enough will be represented in *standard-customer* and possibly *good-customer*, but not in *special-discount*. The concept of stratification is a little stronger than necessary.

In fact, it is possible for a program not to be stratified but to be satisfactorily computable. Notice that at site C, all tuples put into *special-discount* give the attribute *Special-type* the value *good-customer*. Suppose that the view at site A were modified to exclude the special discounts of type *good-customer*. If this were done, then

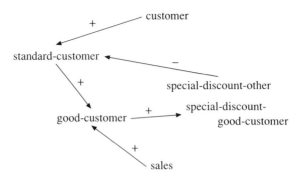

**Figure 4.3**  Program of Figure 4.2 modified so as to be stratified.

no customer tuple would ever encounter the entire cycle of Figure 4.2. Site C would only consider a customer for a special discount of type *good-customer* if they did not already have such a discount, and the granting of such a discount would not prevent site A from classifying the customer as a standard customer.

The concept of stratification is therefore a sufficient condition for a program to have a well-defined model, but is not necessary. More stringent conditions have been proposed, but they tend to suffer from computational difficulties. However, it is often possible to modify a program with a well-defined model, but which is unstratified, to obtain a stratified version. For example, if the different types of the predicate *special-discount* were given different names, then the cycle in Figure 4.2 would disappear, as in Figure 4.3. There is now no cycle, so that the modified program is stratified.

Because the definition of stratification is easily verified and covers most of the applications appearing in practice, deductive database theory is generally restricted to stratified programs.

A **stratification** of a program $P$ is a partition of its IDB into sets of rules $P_1$, $P_2, \ldots, P_n$ with no negative arcs between them in the dependency graph. Moreover, if $i < j$, no negative subgoal in $P_i$ is defined in $P_j$. Any stratified program has at least one stratification. For example, the stratified programs in Figure 4.1 have the stratifications:

A: stratum 1 contains R2, stratum 2 contains R1.

D: there is one stratum, containing both R1 and R2.

The stratified program in Figure 4.3 has the stratification:

Stratum 1: customer, special-discount-other

Stratum 2: standard-customer, good-customer, special-discount-good-customer

We modify the naive and semi-naive algorithms to compute the perfect model first for $P_1$, then for $P_2$, and so on. The perfect model for $P$ is the union of the perfect models for the partitions. Any stratification of $P$ produces the same perfect model for $P$. This modification of the naive algorithm is the formal equivalent of the "*Compute negatives before using*" rule, and will be assumed in the following.

## 4.4 AGGREGATION

Database systems typically allow **aggregation functions** in their query languages. For example SQL provides COUNT, SUM, MAX, MIN and AVERAGE, as well as GROUP BY. Since aggregation is closely related to the set of solutions of a predicate, it is reasonable to base the syntax for aggregation functions on the syntax for a set of solutions. Recall that for datalog the set of solutions for a predicate is finite and computable.

In Chapter 2 we presented the following syntax for the *set of solutions* built-in:

$$\text{solutions}(f(X),\ p(X,\ Y),\ L) \tag{4.5}$$

where $X$ and $Y$ are disjoint sets of variables. The product is a list (bound to $L$) of $f(X)$ for each distinct $X$ which is a solution to $p(X, Y)$.

In datalog, we do not need a special facility for *set of solutions*, since the computational model of datalog is view definition, which is the materialization of the set of tuples defined by the view. Every predicate in datalog computes the set of solutions. However, aggregation generally results in a scalar value. A workable syntax for aggregation is

$$\text{aggregate}(V = \text{aggregate\_function}(X),\ p(X,\ Y)) \tag{4.6}$$

where $X$ is a single variable, $Y$ is a set of variables not containing $X$, and *aggregate_function* is the name of the aggregation function. The variable $V$ is bound to the value of the aggregation function applied to the instantiation of the variable $X$ over each distinct instantiation of $X$ and $Y$ which is a solution to $p$. An exception is the function *count* which has no arguments, and which binds to $V$ the total number of distinct solutions to the predicate $p$. This syntax is exactly equivalent to the corresponding syntax in SQL, taking into account the relationship between SQL and Prolog developed in Chapter 3.

*Group_by*, on the other hand, produces a set of tuples. A syntax for *group_by* is

$$\text{group\_by}(Z,\ V = \text{aggregate\_function}(X),\ p(X,\ Y,\ Z)) \tag{4.7}$$

where $Z$ is the collection of variables on which to group, and $X$ and $Y$ are as for *aggregate*. For each distinct combination of values of the *group-by* variables, $V$ is bound to the value of the aggregate function for $p(X, Y, Z)$ where the variables in $Z$ are restricted to that combination of values. Again, this syntax corresponds exactly to GROUP BY in SQL.

Example 4.8

Assume the predicate *sale(Customer, Date, Amount)*, which records sales of amount *Amount* in dollars to customer *Customer* on date *Date*.

| Customer | Date | Amount |
|---|---|---|
| 1 | 3/5 | $100 |
| 2 | 4/6 | $150 |
| 3 | 4/6 | $100 |

aggregate(V = count, sale(_, _, _)) binds V to 3.
aggregate(V = sum(Amount), sale(_, _, Amount)) binds V to 350.
aggregate(V = sum(Amount), sale(_, 4/6, Amount)) binds V to 250.
group_by(Date, V = sum(Amount), sale(_, Date, Amount)) produces the tuples
    <3/5, 100>, <4/6, 250>.
group_by(Amount, V = count, sale(_, _, Amount)) produces the tuples
    <100, 2>, <150, 1>.

Recursion can introduce problems in computing aggregations analogous to the problems with negation, which resulted in the introduction of the concept of stratification.

Example 4.9

Consider another hypothetical federated database situation, where site A is the sales analysis department and site B is the marketing department. The sales analysis department has the task of determining the profitability of a customer, which it does using the predicate

    profit(C#, Profit) :-
        aggregate(Profit = sum(Revenue), revenue(C#, Product, Revenue)).

where

    revenue(C#, Product, Revenue) :-
        sales(C#, Product, Number),
        list-price(Product, List-Price),
        discount(C#, Product, Disc),
        cost(Product, Cost),
        Revenue is Number * (List-Price * (100 − Disc)/100 − Cost).

The predicate *discount* implies that a customer has a possibly different discount rate for each product.

    The marketing department has the task of determining the discounts to be offered to each customer for each product, using the predicate

    discount(C#, Product, Disc) :-
        profit(C#, Profit),
        discount-threshold(T),
        Profit ≥ T ⇒ standard-discount(P, Disc);
            Disc is 0.

so that a customer is offered a standard discount on each product only if their profitability is greater than a given amount.

The problem with Example 4.9 is that the profit is calculated using an aggregation which requires knowing the profit. We can adapt the dependency diagram to show this phenomenon, as in Figure 4.4. If we adopt the annotation *a* to an arc if the source predicate appears in an aggregation in the target predicate, we see that there is a cycle in the dependency diagram which includes an aggregation arc: *discount* → *revenue* → *profit* → *discount*.

    We say that a program is *aggregation stratified* if its dependency diagram has no cycles involving aggregation.

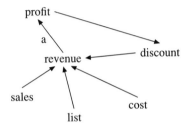

**Figure 4.4** Dependency diagram cycle involving aggregation.

If a program is aggregation stratified, the aggregation can in principle be evaluated after the perfect model has been computed, even if the predicate being aggregated is recursive. For example:

$$\text{aggregation}(\text{NChildren} = \text{count}, \text{ancestor}(\text{Parent}, \text{Child})) \tag{4.8}$$

if *Parent* is bound in the query, computes the number of children of that parent.

As with (negation) stratification, the definition of aggregation stratification is somewhat stronger than necessary. Consider Example 4.10.

Example 4.10

This is from a bill of materials application. The EDB includes the predicates

% true if a unit is atomic (has no parts)
part(ID#)

% true if a unit is not atomic
assembly(ID#)

% a part is obtained from a supplier at a cost
supplies(PartID#, Supplier, Cost)

% assembly ID# is made up of Qty of the immediate component identified by
   CompID#. This relation defines arcs in a directed acyclic graph.
made-up-of(ID#, CompID#, Qty)

% assembly ID# costs CA currency units to assemble, irrespective of the cost of
   its components.
cost-to-assemble(ID#, CA)

The IDB consists of two predicates:

% the cost to manufacture one of unit ID#. If the unit is a part, then the cost of
   that part from its supplier, otherwise, the cost of each component of the
   assembly plus the cost of making the assembly.
cost-to-mfg(ID#, Cost) :- part(ID#), supplies(ID#, Supplier, Cost).
cost-to-mfg(ID#, Cost) :-
   assembly(ID#),
   aggregate(ComponentCost = sum(CostCont),
      cost-contribution(ID#, _, CostCont)),
   cost-to-assemble(ID#, CA),
   Cost is ComponentCost + CA.

% the cost of a component of an assembly.

```
cost-contribution(ID#, CostCont) :-
    made-up-of(ID#, CompID#, Qty),
    cost-to-mfg(CompID#, CompCost),
    CostCont is CompCost * Qty.
```

This straightforward formulation of the problem builds up the cost of an assembly from the bottom up. The cost to manufacture a part (*cost-to-mfg*) is its purchase cost, while the cost to manufacture a subassembly is the cost of its parts plus the cost to assemble it. Naturally, the cost of a subassembly (*cost-contribution*) depends on the cost to manufacture each of its parts. Even though the aggregation is well defined, this formulation is not aggregation stratified (the loop *cost-contribution* → *cost-to-mfg* → *cost-contribution* involves aggregation).

In some cases, it is possible to reformulate the problem as an aggregation-stratified program. For the *cost-to-mfg* example (Example 4.10), we note that we do not actually need to know the component costs of a subassembly to know how many times its assembly cost contributes to the cost of the product. We can use a transitive closure predicate to calculate how many of each part and subassembly are required to make one unit of a product. Each part contributes its cost, and each subassembly contributes its cost to assemble. A suitable transitive closure predicate might be

```
all_components(WholeID#, [PartID#], PartID#, Qty) :-          (4.9)
    made-up-of(WholeID#, PartID#, Qty).
all_components(WholeID#, [SubID# | Path], PartID#, Qty) :-
    made-up-of(WholeID#, SubID#, QW),
    all_components(SubID#, Path, PartID#, QP),
    Qty is QW * QP.
```

where *Qty* units of component *PartID#* are needed to make one unit of *WholeID#* via the derivation path *Path*. We need the derivation path because it is quite possible for the same part to contribute to a product via several different subassemblies. Consider how many components of an aircraft contain rivets, for example. Without the derivation path, the semi-naive algorithm would remove duplicates, so that if the same part were needed in the same quantity from two different paths, only one tuple would be computed.

Given this definition of *all_components*, the predicate *cost-to-mfg* can be reformulated as in Example 4.11.

Example 4.11

```
cost-to-mfg-a(ID#, Cost) :-
    aggregation(CompCost = sum(PartCost),
        cost-contribution-a(ID#, PartID#, PartCost)),
    cost-to-assemble(ID#, CA),
    Cost is CA + CompCost.
```

cost-contribution-a(ID#, PartID#, Cost) :-
  all_components(ID#, Path, PartID#, Qty),
  part(PartID#),
  supplies(PartID#, Supplier, UnitCost),
  Cost is UnitCost * Qty.

cost-contribution-a(ID#, PartID#, Cost) :-
  all_components(ID#, Path, PartID#, Qty),
  assembly(PartID#),
  cost-to-assemble(PartID#, CA),
  Cost is CA * Qty.

This second formulation is aggregation stratified.

We will assume in the following that if a deductive database supports aggregation that all programs are *aggregation stratified*.

## 4.5 TOP-DOWN REVISITED

So far, we have seen that datalog with stratified negation is a reasonable extension of relational database technology into Horn clause logic. The extension is reasonable because it gives us a system more powerful than relational database technology; but which is finite and preserves the ability to think of the program in terms of the set of tuples defined by any relation, whether the relation is stored (EDB) or derived, perhaps recursively, with integrity constraints (IDB).

In our comparison of top-down with bottom-up execution of a deductive database query, we noted that the bottom-up approach was superior when the entire perfect model is required. Later (Chapter 8) we will see that the semi-naive algorithm is a basis for effective computation of most queries where the set of responses is required. On the other hand, we noted that top-down computation is superior in some circumstances, especially when a single tuple is required.

We have an algorithm for top-down computation: the depth-first search inference engine of Prolog. However, we have noted that this algorithm is somewhat deficient, in that, unlike relational database theory, it is sensitive to the order of subgoals in the IDB. The wrong order can produce an infinite loop, even though the solution exists and is finite. When top-down computation is appropriate, we would like an algorithm which gives the same result as the bottom-up algorithm.

Such an algorithm is a **queue-based Prolog interpreter**, which proceeds by **breadth-first search**.

Recall the description in Chapter 2 of the Prolog inference engine. At step *Choose_subgoal*, the interpreter chooses a subgoal to expand by passing control to the first subgoal in the current clause. This choice was described as constituting *depth-first search*, since the interpreter always proceeds deeper into the proof tree until it comes to a leaf node in the form of a unit clause.

This depth-first strategy is responsible for the possibility that the interpreter will get into an infinite loop in situations such as Example 4.2. This sort of behaviour is tolerated in Prolog because there are other sources of infinity: some goals have an infinite number of solutions, while others can proceed indefinitely without finding a solution. Both of these are consequences of the semi-decidability of Horn clause logic, and so are fundamental. The simplicity and space-efficiency of depth-first search is therefore sufficiently beneficial that some additional possibility of falling into an infinite loop is tolerated.

We have seen earlier in this chapter that in datalog there is no fundamental source of infinity, so that the infinite loops introduced by depth-first search are a more serious disadvantage.

Fortunately, there are other ways to choose subgoals. It is possible to think of all the subgoals which have been reached but not yet expanded as being held in a data structure by the interpreter. It makes no logical difference which subgoal is chosen for expansion at the *Choose_subgoal* step: all the subgoals must succeed for the goal to succeed. In the standard depth-first search strategy, the data structure has the form of a stack (the **goal stack**). When a clause body is entered, the subgoals are pushed onto the goal stack from right to left. The action of the *Choose_subgoal* step is to pop the goal stack.

Another strategy is to hold the goals in a queue (the **goal queue**). When a clause body is entered, the subgoals are queued from left to right. The *Choose_subgoal* step is now to dequeue the first goal from the goal queue. This strategy is **breadth-first**, since all the goals in a clause body are expanded before any of the subgoals arising from any of them. This strategy will never loop in a datalog program, and will find all and only the solutions in the perfect model on backtracking.

We will look at the breadth-first execution of Example 4.2, which looped indefinitely using depth-first search.

Example 4.12

IDB:

    A1′   ancestor(Older, Younger) :- parent(Older, Younger).
    A2′   ancestor(Older, Younger) :- ancestor(Older, Intermediate),
                                     parent(Intermediate, Younger).

EDB as in Example 4.1.

Given the query *ancestor(alice, bill)?* As in Example 4.2, rule *A1′* fails, since *parent(alice, bill)* is not in the EDB. Rule *A2′* generates the two subgoals

    ancestor(alice, Intermediate),
    parent(Intermediate, bill).

which are queued. Since the goal queue was empty, the first choice is to expand *ancestor(alice, Intermediate)?* Since there is no tuple in the *parent* relation with first argument *alice*, this subgoal is also expanded using rule *A2′*, making the goal queue now

    parent(Intermediate, bill).
    ancestor(alice, Intermediate_1).
    parent(Intermediate_1, Intermediate).

The goal *parent(Intermediate, bill)?* is dequeued next. This subgoal fails, since there is no tuple in the *parent* relation with *bill* as its second argument. Since *parent(Intermediate, bill)?* is one of the top-level subgoals of the query goal *ancestor(alice, bill)?*, the query goal fails, as it should.

We can see that the breadth-first search terminates while the depth-first search does not, since the recursive subgoal *ancestor(Older, Intermediate)* in clause *A2′* is expanded only if the EDB predicate *parent(Intermediate, Younger)* succeeds.

The actual operation of a queue-based interpreter is of course more complex than this. For example, mechanisms are needed for managing alternatives and for discarding the remaining subgoals in a conjunction if one of the conjuncts fails. Nevertheless, the main cost of the breadth-first interpreter is additional storage. The depth-first algorithm needs to maintain only as many choice points as required to get to the deepest leaf of the proof tree. Since the breadth-first algorithm expands all branches of the proof tree one step at a time, it needs to store many more choice points. Also, a variable-binding frame and copy stack is needed for each clause body which is open, and there are many more open clause bodies.

Whether this additional storage cost is practical depends greatly on the computing equipment available and on the problems to be solved in a particular application being attempted. Notwithstanding practical considerations, we will assume in the following that a top-down evaluation of a query is done using the breadth-first interpreter algorithm.

Even with the breadth-first top-down interpreter, there is a difference in behaviour between top-down tuple-at-a-time evaluation of a program and bottom-up set-at-a-time evaluation. The difference occurs in predicates involving cyclic data structures. If the *parent* relation defines a cyclic graph, then the top-down tuple-at-a-time evaluation will generate an infinite number of solutions. (More exactly, the set of solutions is finite, but it will generate some of them an infinite number of times.) This is because there are an infinite number of derivation paths in a cycle. The bottom-up set-at-a-time evaluation looks only at the solutions, and will terminate when no new solutions are generated. This is generally an issue with tuple-at-a-time evaluation strategies.

## 4.6 THE ARTIFICIAL INTELLIGENCE PERSPECTIVE: PRODUCTION RULES

We have so far looked at deductive databases as a generalization of the relational database tool of the database community, and as a specialization of the Prolog tool of the logic programming community. Besides these two, a similar technology called **production rules** is in use in the artificial intelligence community. They appear in a variety of guises in many systems and platforms, but most of the instances are variations on the **OPS-5** programming language.

For historical reasons, the syntax of OPS-5 is very different from both SQL and datalog. To avoid confusing the present reader, we will use an artificial syntax closely related to datalog. Anyone who pursues the expert systems literature should expect to encounter a wide variety of syntaxes expressing similar concepts.

Data in an OPS-5 program is held in what is called **working memory**. The element of data, called appropriately a **working memory element** or **wme**, is essentially a collection of EDB tuples. For our purposes, we can take a wme element to be the same as a database tuple.

The computation in an OPS-5 program is specified in a set of production rules. A **production rule** has a left-hand side (LHS) and a right-hand side (RHS). The left-hand side is a conjunction of conditions on wmes, rather like a datalog clause body. A production rule is said to be **capable to fire** if there exists a set of wmes which can simultaneously satisfy all the conditions in its LHS. This is exactly the situation in which a datalog rule can fire during bottom-up evaluation. If a rule is capable to fire, all of its variables are instantiated to ground values, and one of the possible sets of wmes satisfying its conditions is selected. This set is called the **instantiation** of the LHS.

The right-hand side of a production rule specifies one or more actions. One possible action is to add a new wme (*make*). The new wme can be of any class, and can have any attributes. A value is either a constant in the text of the RHS or the instantiation of a variable which has appeared in the LHS. No variables can appear in the RHS which have not already appeared in the LHS. *Make* is essentially the same as creating a tuple for the head predicate in a datalog IDB rule during bottom-up evaluation.

The other possible actions are deletion (*remove*) or modification (*modify*) of one of the wmes in the rule's instantiation. *Modify* is implemented as *remove* followed by *make*. The processing is tuple-at-a-time, so that there may be additional sets of wmes which satisfy the constraints in the left-hand side. The action is exactly that produced by the *retract* built-in in Prolog, which has no counterpart in datalog. The datalog example (Example 4.1) is re-expressed in a production rule form in Example 4.13.

Example 4.13

Initial wmes

|                |                      |
|----------------|----------------------|
| person(bill).  | parent(bill, peter). |
| person(mary).  | parent(bill, paul).  |
| person(peter). | parent(mary, peter). |
| person(paul).  | parent(mary, paul).  |
| person(john).  | parent(paul, john).  |
| person(sue).   | parent(paul, sue).   |
| person(alice). | parent(sue, alice).  |
| person(eva).   | parent(sue, eva).    |

Rules

A1:  parent(Older, Younger) $\Rightarrow$ make ancestor(Older, Younger).
A2:  parent(Older, Middle) & ancestor(Middle, Younger) $\Rightarrow$
        make ancestor(Older, Younger).

A very common special case of an expert system is a classification-type system, which uses propositional reasoning. These systems generally monitor a situation and assign it to a class. Examples are diagnostic systems, which monitor a set of symptoms and assign a diagnosis, systems which determine eligibility for social security benefits, and systems which determine credit-worthiness in financial institutions. These sorts of systems are discussed in more detail in Chapter 10. They are rarely non-monotonic.

The more general first-order expert systems mainly construct a solution of some kind given a set of data input. Examples are systems which construct a computer system configuration given an order for the main components, systems which construct a pest management strategy given the state of a crop and the presence of a pattern of pests, and systems which assist a student to construct a feasible and suitable program of study within a collection of subject offerings and degree rules.

The production rules, like the IDB in datalog, form a static description of the program. The static description is turned into action by an inference engine, in the same way that one of the datalog inference engines (top-down depth-first or breadth-first; bottom-up naive or semi-naive) is needed to process a query in a deductive database. Recall that we have considered that the top-down strategies are tuple-at-a-time, and the bottom-up strategies are set-at-a-time.

In OPS-5, the inference engine operates according to a bottom-up tuple-at-a-time procedure called the **recognize/act cycle**, which has three steps:

1   Find all rules whose left-hand side can be satisfied, selecting for each such rule a particular instantiation. This set of rules is called the **conflict set**.

2   Select one of the rules (with its instantiation) to fire. The process by which this selection is made is called **conflict resolution**.

3   Perform the actions specified by the right-hand side of the selected rule with its instantiation.

Once a rule has been selected and its actions performed, a new conflict set is computed and the process repeats. The OPS-5 interpreter terminates when the conflict set is empty.

Production rule inference engines differ mainly in their conflict resolution strategy. Many systems allow the programmer to choose a strategy. A typical strategy performs the selection through a number of nested criteria. For example:

■   *most specific*: Choose the rule with the most conditions in its left-hand side.

■   *most recent*: If there is more than one rule with maximum specificity, then choose the rule with the most recently created wme in its instantiation. To implement this criterion, each wme must have attached to it a time-stamp of some kind. Also, when one set of wmes is being selected to be the instantiation for this firing of the rule, the most recent wmes must be selected.

■   *arbitrary*: If there is still more than one rule in the conflict set, then choose one arbitrarily, for example by the order of its appearance in the program text (lexical order).

Once a rule is fired, the associated instantiation is marked so that it cannot cause that rule to fire again. This is called **refractoriness**.

We illustrate the recognize/act cycle from Example 4.13. With the initial set of wmes, there are several instantiations of rule *A1*, but no instantiations of rule *A2*. The conflict set consists therefore only of *A1*, so an instantiation for *A1* is selected. The only criterion which applies is *arbitrary*, so the lexically first is chosen: *Older = bill, Younger = peter*. The RHS of *A1* inserts the wme *ancestor(bill, peter)*. There are now instantiations for each of the conjuncts in the LHS of *A2*, but no combination of them which satisfies the conjunct. The conflict set still contains only *A1*. This situation continues, with wmes *ancestor(bill, paul), ancestor(mary, peter), ancestor(mary, paul)* and *ancestor(paul, john)* inserted.

At this point, besides *A1*, the LHS of rule *A2* is satisfied, with *Older = bill, Middle = paul, Younger = john*; and also with *Older = mary, Middle = paul, Younger = john*. Since *A2* is more specific than *A1*, *A2* is selected. The most recent instantiation is that with *Older = mary*, so the wme *ancestor(mary, john)* is inserted, then *ancestor(bill, john)*. Neither of these new wmes generate any instantiations for *A2*, so *A1* continues, generating *ancestor(paul, sue)*. *A2* then generates *ancestor(mary, sue)*, then *ancestor(bill, sue)* before its instantiations are exhausted.

Rule *A1* now generates *ancestor(sue, alice)*, so that rule *A2* can generate successively *ancestor(paul, alice), ancestor(mary, alice)*, and *ancestor(bill, alice)*. Finally rule *A1* generates *ancestor(sue, eva)*, and *A2* generates *ancestor(paul, eva), ancestor(mary, eva)*, then *ancestor(bill, eva)*. At this point, neither rule has any instantiations, so the conflict set is empty and the cycle terminates.

The resulting set of *ancestor* wmes is the same as that generated by datalog from Example 4.1. Notice how the sequence of generation is determined by the conflict resolution strategy.

From a database or logic programming perspective it might seem strange that production rule systems place such importance on conflict resolution. Other than the obvious fact that tuple-at-a-time processing must be done one tuple at a time on a serial computer, it doesn't make any difference to the final result in either database, datalog or pure Prolog which rule is selected to fire at any time, since the entire equivalent of the conflict set will eventually fire; and if the system is stratified, any sequence of firing gives the same result.

Conflict resolution is important in OPS-5 because it is possible for a rule action to remove wmes, therefore remove instantiations from rules, and therefore to remove rules from the conflict set without their having fired. Rules whose action removes instantiations from rules in the conflict set are called **non-monotonic rules**. (Non-monotonicity is discussed in more detail in Chapter 12.) The programming model for OPS-5 thus allows operations which the deductive database programming model does not.

The important thing for our purpose is that the programming model for OPS-5 includes everything which the deductive database model does. In other words, it is possible to use OPS-5 and other production rule systems as platforms on which to implement deductive databases, so long as the problem is of a suitable size, and a bottom-up, tuple-at-a-time computation rule is sufficient. (Note that the problem of generation of the same solution an infinite number of times occurs with this computation rule, since it is tuple-at-a-time.)

Computation of the conflict set is the most expensive part of the recognize/act cycle. The problem is essentially the same as evaluating a datalog program tuple-at-a-time, and the formulation above is similar to the naive algorithm. Practical systems incorporate a number of optimizations for computation of the conflict set, which are very similar in philosophy to the semi-naive algorithm.

Expert-system style problems are often capable of solution by deductive database techniques. They typically do not require a large EDB. Even if they do, it is often the case that they need to make queries on large databases, but have relatively few tuples in the perfect model other than the EDB. It is not difficult generally to access databases from production rule systems. SIRATAC, mentioned in Chapter 1, is an example of an expert system which can be implemented as a deductive database. Some of its rules have conditions which are queries on a relational database.

Of course, since production rule systems offer non-monotonic facilities, such facilities are often used in the formulation of expert systems solutions. Production rule systems often do not support aggregation, so one very common use of non-monotonicity is to compute aggregations. Most of the non-monotonicity in the SIRATAC system is used for this purpose.

Other uses of non-monotonicity are to switch between generation of a potential solution and testing the solution in a generate-and-test paradigm, and to switch between processes when some event occurs. Non-monotonicity in production rule systems is revisited in Chapter 12.

## 4.7   ACTIVE DATABASES

Active database technology is a blend of deductive database technology and production rules. Active databases are built around the concept of *trigger*. In standard SQL databases, the programmer can specify a program to be executed whenever one of the EDB predicates is updated in a particular way. For example, suppose an organization has two distinct information systems containing information about its employees: one supporting the personnel department and the other the telephone directory in the PABX. It is essential that every employee whose telephone number is in the PABX system also appears as a current employee in the personnel system. The personnel system therefore has a trigger, activated when an employee is deleted from the personnel system, which sends a message to the PABX system requesting the PABX system to delete the employee's telephone number from its directory.

The activation of a trigger is analogous to the detection of a ready-to-fire condition in the left-hand side of a production rule, and the program run is analogous to the production rule's right-hand side. The machinery of production rule systems is not very useful in SQL-92 database systems, since the rules for triggers (updates on base tables only) are so restrictive that it would be unusual for more than one trigger to be active at one time, and the conditions under which a trigger is activated are easy to compute.

In active databases, the antecedent of a trigger can be expressed in terms of changes in the population of views, instead of simply updates to base tables. For example, in the bill of materials application described in Examples 4.10 and 4.11, an active rule could send a message to the marketing department whenever a change in either the cost of a part or a cost of assembly changes the manufacturing cost of a product by a nominated percentage.

It is possible for there to be a large number of such rules, in the same way that an expert system often has many rules. The problems of implementation of active databases therefore include the problem of implementing a recognize/act cycle. In addition, there is potentially a large amount of computation needed to propagate a change to a base table sufficiently to detect a change in the population of a possibly recursively defined view.

Active databases, therefore, are related to deductive databases both in their rule structure and in the processes to detect changes in populations of views. The latter problem is closely related to the maintenance of integrity constraints, developed in Chapter 11.

### 4.8   STRUCTURE

Datalog was developed as a decidable subset of Prolog suitable for extending database systems by recursive views. The need for decidability is the reason for the exclusion of function symbols. This can, however, be a serious limitation.

For example, we saw in Chapters 2 and 3 that a common use of recursive views is to perform operations on graphs, notably transitive closure. Example 4.14 illustrates this situation. We saw further that one often needs not only the pairs of nodes transitively connected but also the path by which they are connected. Two Prolog procedures were given in Chapter 3, one for directed acyclic graphs and the other for general directed graphs. The first, in Example 4.14 below for acyclic graphs, poses difficulties for bottom-up evaluation. The first tuple in *cl* is generated by clause 1, and has a free variable *Path_so_far* in the structure bound to *Path*. It would take a very sophisticated evaluation strategy to compute this predicate correctly in datalog.

Example 4.14

closure(Source, Target, Path) :- cl(Source, Target, [Target], Path).

1. cl(Source, Target, Path_so_far, [Source | Path_so_far]) :- edge(Source, Target).
2. cl(Source, Target, Path_so_far, Path) :-
      edge(Intermediate, Target),
      cl(Source, Intermediate, [Intermediate | Path_so_far], Path).

closure(a, c, Path)?

An alternative formulation of this predicate suitable for a bottom-up evaluation strategy is given in Example 4.15. Here, the path is built up from ground structures starting with the edges by the execution of clause 1, and successively longer chains by the successive executions of clause 2. Note that the datalog predicate in Example 4.15 generates a perfect model giving all possible paths. A query such as *closure (a, c, Path)?* will select those paths from the perfect model with source *a* and target *c*.

Example 4.15

```
closure(Source, Target, [Source]) :- edge(Source, Target).
closure(Source, Target, [Source | Path_so_far]) :-
    edge(Source, Intermediate),
    closure(Intermediate, Target, Path_so_far).
```

The predicate in Example 4.15 clearly offers no theoretical problem: the potential issues are computational. First, the implementation must be able to store the structures in a persistent medium. The second issue is one of computational efficiency, since the test whether an iteration of the semi-naive algorithm has produced new tuples must test the list *Path* in addition to the atomic attributes *Source* and *Target*.

If the graph contains cycles, we showed in Chapters 2 and 3 that the preceding procedure would not terminate. A revised procedure was introduced which adds the subgoal *not member/2* to the second clause of *closure* in Example 4.16. The effect of this new subgoal is to prevent a node from occurring more than once in *Path*. The difficulty introduced is that *member/2* is not usefully regarded as an IDB predicate. Its function is to perform a test on two bound variables. The deductive database must therefore have the facility to define predicates which are neither EDB nor IDB. If this facility is available, then the issue reverts to computational efficiency.

Example 4.16

```
closure(Source, Target, [Source]) :- edge(Source, Target).
closure(Source, Target, [Source | Path_so_far]) :-
    edge(Source, Intermediate),
    not member (Source, Path_so_far),
    closure(Intermediate, Target, Path_so_far).
```

A different problem with structure occurs in the hierarchical search of a tree-data structure, as described in Chapter 3. The approach described in Chapter 3, repeated here for convenience, involves a computational built-in to increment a level counter.

Example 4.17

```
nodes-removed-level(R, R, 0).
nodes-removed-level(R, C, N) :-
    N>0,
    M is N-1,
    arc(R, I),
    nodes-removed-level(I, C, M).
```

This formulation of the problem is predicated upon a top-down evaluation strategy, since the computation of $M$, the lower-level number, depends on $N$, the higher-level number. A more natural formulation assuming a bottom-up evaluation strategy is

```
nodes-removed-level(R, R, 0).
nodes-removed-level(R, C, N) :-
    N is M+1,
    arc(R, I),
    nodes-removed-level(I, C, M).
```

It is possible in principle for the deductive database to automatically reformulate at least this specific example so that it could be executed properly using either strategy, but the problem for arbitrary computational predicates is extremely difficult.

We conclude that there is no reason in principle not to allow predicates with function symbols in deductive databases, so long as they are known to terminate for bottom-up evaluation and they are computationally practicable. However, in pure datalog the same formulation of the IDB will serve both in bottom-up and top-down evaluation; whereas if structures are added the design of the IDB predicates must take the evaluation strategy into account.

### 4.9   SUMMARY

This chapter has developed the definition of datalog, a subset of first-order predicate calculus suitable as an extension of the relational algebra to systems requiring recursive views. We have examined theoretical and computational issues. Theoretical issues include the notions of perfect model, stratification for systems involving negated subgoals, aggregation functions and the use of function symbols. Computational issues include the semi-naive algorithm for practical computation of the perfect model, the breadth-first or queue-based Prolog interpreter, the use of production rule systems to implement deductive database applications, and active databases.

### 4.10   FURTHER READING

The material on datalog is taken mainly from Ullman (1988, 1989), and is also largely contained in Ceri *et al.* (1990). An introduction to this material may be found in Elmasri and Navathe (1994). A good introduction to OPS-5 is Brownston *et al.* (1985). The syntax of aggregation is loosely based on the *Aditi* system, developed at the University of Melbourne, Victoria, Australia.

### 4.11   EXERCISES

Consider the following EDB:

|  |  |  |
|---|---|---|
| parent(jim, jimmy). | parent(christine, jake). | parent(christine, adam). |
| parent(heather, christine). | parent(jimmy, jake). | |

and the *ancestor* IDB:

    ancestor(Older, Younger) :- parent(Older, Younger).
    ancestor(Older, Younger) :- parent(Older, Middle),
        ancestor(Middle, Younger).

4.1   Compute the perfect model of the ancestor relation given this EDB.

4.2   Add the rules

   unrelated(P1, P2) :- person(P1), person(P2), not related(P1, P2).
   person(P) :- parent(P, _).
   person(P) :- parent(_, P).
   related(P, P) :- person(P).
   related(P1, P2) :- ancestor(P2, P1).
   related(P1, P2) :- ancestor(P1, P2).
   related(P1, P2) :- ancestor(A1, P1), ancestor(A2, P2), related(A1, A2).

to the IDB. Consider the program $P$ = EDB ∪ IDB.

(a)   Stratify the program $P$ making use of the dependency graph.
(b)   Compute the perfect model for $P$.
(c)   Compute an interpretation for $P$ by executing the strata in reverse order. Discuss the difference.

4.3   Add the rule

   num-relations(P, N) :- aggregation(N = count, related(P, _)).

(a)   Is the program aggregation stratified? Make use of the dependency graph.
(b)   Evaluate *num-relations* where $P = jim$.

4.4   Construct the dependency graphs for Examples 4.10 and 4.11. Discuss the difference with respect to aggregation stratification.

4.5   Compute and comment on the bottom-up evaluation of

   successor(s(0), 0).
   successor(s(s(X)), s(X)) :- successor(s(X), X).

## CHAPTER FIVE

# Knowledge design

In this chapter, we look at adapting proven tools used in designing database systems to the problem of designing deductive database systems: both advanced information systems and expert systems.

### 5.1 DATA, INFORMATION AND KNOWLEDGE

The readers of this text are assumed to be familiar with conventional database technology, and also with modelling techniques enabling them to apply database technology to the design of information systems. The material in this and the following chapters is independent of the particular information modelling technique employed, but we will use examples drawn from the variety known as **entity-relationship modelling** (ERA). This text so far has concentrated on the technology of deductive databases, so that the reader should have a clear idea of how deductive database technology relates to and differs from conventional relational database technology. We now turn our attention to design methods to assist in applying deductive database technology to the design both of information systems and also to a large class of knowledge-based systems, including expert systems.

As noted in Chapter 1, a deductive database can be seen as an extension of relational database theory to include a number of aspects which are part of an information system but not generally integrated with the database schemas:

- view definitions;
- integrity constraints;
- derived facts.

In addition, deductive database technology allows recursively defined views.

Deductive database technology also provides a framework for investigation of the properties of updates, although there is much more research needed before a sound treatment of the problem is available. Chapter 12 covers some aspects of updates.

Recall from Chapter 3 that a relation is a predicate definition, a simple query is a goal, and a complex query (which is the same thing as a view definition) is a Horn clause. Most of the commonly encountered integrity constraints can also be expressed as Horn clauses, as will be seen in Chapter 11. Most of the commonly occurring rules for deriving facts can also be expressed as Horn clauses. This chapter and the closely related Chapters 6 and 7 concentrate mainly on view definitions and definitions of derivation rules: those parts of the deductive database which are expressed as general Horn clauses.

### 5.1.1  Functional associations

A fundamental notion in database theory and in information analysis is that of **functional association**: set A is functionally associated with set B if there is a correspondence between members of A and members of B such that a member of A corresponds to exactly one member of B. There may be many functional associations between two sets: each correspondence is given a name. A functional association is said to **map** members of A into members of B.

A familiar example is that a relation can be considered as a set of mappings between the key domain(s) and the non-key attribute domains. This kind of functional association, where the correspondence between the two sets is stored in a table, will be called an **implicit** functional association: for example in an order-entry application the correspondence between a part number and its selling price.

Another familiar example is a computation rule, where the member of set B corresponding to a particular member of set A can be determined by a mathematical formula, or some other computation rule, and need not be stored. This kind of functional association will be called an **explicit** functional association: for example if the relationship between selling price and cost price for a product is determined by a markup rate:

$$\text{selling\_price(Cost\_price)} = \text{Cost\_price} \times 1.25 \tag{5.1}$$

The predicate definition relating cost price to selling price can be expressed as a Horn clause:

$$\text{cost/sell(Cost\_price, Sell\_price) :- Sell\_price is Cost\_price * 1.25.} \tag{5.2}$$

as can the predicate definition relating an order for parts to its total price:

$$\begin{aligned}
&\text{order/cost(Order\#, Cost) :-} \tag{5.3}\\
&\quad\text{aggregate(sum(Price),}\\
&\qquad\text{(order/item(Order\#, Item\#),}\\
&\qquad\quad\text{item/cost(Item\#, Cost\_price),}\\
&\qquad\quad\text{cost/sell(Cost\_price, Price)),}\\
&\qquad\text{Cost).}
\end{aligned}$$

which is an aggregation based on a join.

Explicit functional association given by (5.3)

| order/cost | | order/item | | item/cost | |
|---|---|---|---|---|---|
| 1 | 100 | 1 | 123 | 123 | 55 |
| | | 1 | 345 | 345 | 45 |
| 2 | 72 | 2 | 992 | 992 | 72 |

Implicit functional association given by tables

**Figure 5.1** Derived fact may be seen as either explicit or implicit functional association.

The functional associations represented in (5.2) and (5.3) are both explicit functional associations. It is worth noting, however, that the clause in (5.3) is a view definition. Its perfect model is a set of tuples for the *order/cost* relation. There is an implicit functional association between the space of possible populations of the two body predicates *item/cost* and *order/item* and the tuple space for the head predicate, which contains the perfect model. Recall that a join between two relations is a subset of their Cartesian product. This relationship is illustrated in Figure 5.1. Note that the functional association is between the entire population of the body predicates and the entire perfect model. Crudely, a given database state functionally determines the population of a given view.

We now have the vocabulary to define what we will refer to as data, information and knowledge.

**Data** will refer to the collection of indivisible objects which are stored in the information system. From the point of view of logic, data is the set of constants of Chapter 2. From the point of view of ERA modelling, data is the set of members of the value sets for the attributes.

**Information** will refer to the implicit functional associations between items of data. These are the unit clauses of logic or the relations of database technology. The definitions of information predicates (EDB) will be taken as equivalent to database schemas.

**Knowledge** will refer to the explicit functional associations involving data and information. These are the Horn clauses of logic, or the view definitions and derivation rules (IDB) of database technology. Note that the head predicate of a Horn clause predicate definition is also a database schema, due to the perfect model semantics, as illustrated in Figure 5.1. The predicate *order/cost* can be seen as either a relation or as a derivation rule.

### 5.1.2 Classifying objects

Our task is to build an information system. This system is intended to be used by a person or organization as a tool in their activities. As such, it will make reference to aspects of objects in the person's or organization's environment. The information system is built from data, information and knowledge. The first problem,

### The Object Classification Problem

Is a particular object data, information or knowledge?

*The interest rate on savings accounts is 5%*

**Data**

interest_rate_on_savings_accounts:% = 5

**Information**

account_type/interest_rate:%("savings", 5)

**Knowledge**

account/interest_rate (X, 5) :-
    account/account_type(X, "savings").

account/interest(A, I):-
    account/account_type(A, "savings"),
    account/mean_balance(A, B),
    I is B * (5/100).

**Information**

account/account_type("1234", "savings").
account/mean_balance("1234", 200).
account/interest("1234", 10).

account/interest_rate("1234", 5).
account/interest_rate("4567", 5).

**Figure 5.2** The object classification problem.

therefore, is how to classify the objects: is a particular object data, information or knowledge?

We emphasize that the object classification problem is a design problem, not a problem of scientific discovery. An object is not intrinsically data, information or knowledge. The design question is rather "How is it most useful for the purpose of constructing the information system we have in mind to classify this object?". Figure 5.2 shows how a simple object can plausibly be classified as data, information in three different ways, and as knowledge in two different ways. The representation as data is simply a labelled constant. The first information representation assumes that there are several account types, each with an interest rate. The first representation as knowledge is very similar. In both cases, the value "5" is functionally dependent on the string "savings". The second representation as knowledge computes the interest rate from the mean balance. The second representation as information represents the interest rate implicitly: it can be computed from the balance and interest. Finally, the last representation as information removes the intermediate *account_type*, making the interest rate directly dependent on the account code. Choice between these different ways of classifying the object is based on the role the object plays in the information system, whether it is a specific instance of a more general concept, how often it changes, what sorts of changes can be expected, etc.

### 5.1.3   Goal dependency

An important aspect of the representation of knowledge is the use to which the knowledge is to be put. In particular, information and knowledge express functional associations: how are these functional associations to be used? For example, consider the relationship between interest rate, balance of account and interest payment given by the mathematical expression

$$\text{interest} = \text{balance} \times \text{rate} \tag{5.4}$$

Mathematically, knowledge of any two of these variables is sufficient to determine the third.

The representation of relationship (5.4) depends on the computational properties of the knowledge representation scheme used. For example, suppose (5.4) were to be used for two purposes: given *balance* and *rate*, determine *interest*; and given *interest* and *balance*, determine *rate*. In the knowledge representation scheme used in Pascal program statements, relationship (5.4) would be expressed as

$$\text{interest} := \text{balance} * \text{rate}; \tag{5.5}$$
$$\text{rate} := \text{interest} / \text{balance};$$

Given representation (5.5), we are unable to use (5.4) to determine *balance* given *interest* and *rate*. In order for this representation to be acceptable, the application's requirements must be limited to the computations available.

This property of knowledge representation schemes is called **goal dependency**: an expression is goal dependent if it has distinct inputs and outputs. Relationship (5.4) can be expressed in a good implementation of Prolog in a non-goal dependent form:

$$\text{Interest is Balance * Rate.} \tag{5.6}$$

since the Prolog interpreter can instantiate any of the variables given instantiations for the other two.

Database relations and Prolog predicates are not in principle goal dependent. The relationship between account type and interest rate given by the table

$$\text{account\_type/interest\_rate(A\_type, Rate)} \tag{5.7}$$

can be used to determine the interest rate for a particular type of account or all the accounts which have a particular interest rate. Indeed, (5.7) can be used to verify that a particular account type has a particular interest rate, or to list all the account types with their interest rates. Similarly, the predicate defined by (5.8) can be used in four possible ways:

```
account/interest_payment(Account#, Interest) :-                              (5.8)
    account/account_type(Account#, A_type),
    account_type/interest_rate(A_type, Rate),
    account/balance(Account#, Balance),
    Interest is Balance * Rate.
```

In practice, however, it is often useful to introduce goal dependencies. For example, if we wished to use (5.7) only to find the interest rate for a given account type, we might introduce an index on the attribute *account_type*. In (5.8), if we wished to only use the predicate for computing the interest payable for a given account, we might stipulate that the first argument *Account#* will always be bound but that the second *Interest* will always be free, then use the magic sets transformation as described in Chapter 8 to get a faster implementation of the knowledge represented.

We have been considering goal dependency between the attributes of a relation or a predicate. This kind of goal dependency relating to functional dependencies is called **information goal dependency**. There is another kind of goal dependency called **knowledge-goal dependency** which relates to the expression of the relationships in the bodies of the clauses used to define the predicates. If (5.8) is an expression in Prolog, it is knowledge-goal dependent, since the computation must proceed from the predicates in the clause body to the clause head. We cannot compute the body clauses given instantiations of the head variables. For example, the predicate *account_type/interest_rate* is not defined by clause (5.8). If we wished to derive tuples from that predicate, we would need the additional predicate definition:

```
account_type/interest_rate(A_type, Rate):-                                   (5.9)
    account/interest_payment(Account#, Interest),
    account/account_type(Account#, A_type),
    account/balance(Account#, Balance),
    Interest is Balance * Rate.
```

Representations in Prolog and its derivatives are always knowledge-goal dependent, since the Horn clauses used allow expression only of *if* relationships between predicates. Expression in a stronger form of logic using *if and only if* relationships would not be knowledge-goal dependent. However, the theorem provers available for these stronger forms of logic are typically much slower in execution than good Prolog or datalog systems. The additional generality of knowledge representation gained is typically not worth the penalty in execution speed. The issue of knowledge-goal dependency is raised again in Chapter 11, in the context of integrity constraints.

When representing knowledge, we must take into account how it is to be used.

### 5.1.4 Update/query types

An important aspect of the information system we build is the identification of those things in it which the user is able to see and those things in it which a user is able to change. From the user's point of view, this is the essence of the information system. Many systems have several classes of user, with different privileges. For a given class of user, we call those types of object in the information system the user can see **query types**, and those types of object the user can change **update types**. We have encountered these terms in Chapter 2, and have seen that objects can be query types, update types, both or neither. The last are called **intermediate types**, and are artifacts of the implementation.

The **scope** of an update type is

- data if change to labels;
- information if change to tuples;
- knowledge if change to clauses.

An example of data as update type is the global search and replace common in word processing systems. In information systems, data is rarely in the scope of the update types.

The main purpose of database systems is to record changes in the universe of discourse, so that most EDB predicates are in the scope of update types. Not all, however. Information about the structure of the universe in which the information system is used is often recorded as information which the user is not allowed to change: for example the table of valid account types. Introduction of a new account type would probably require new applications software, so would be done only by the programming staff, not by the user.

Knowledge in information systems is generally business rules, for example the details of how interest is calculated for different types of accounts or when a customer is eligible for a certain kind of discount, so is historically not in the scope of the update types, since a change is a change to business practice which may have wide ramifications in the information system. One of the benefits of the specification of information systems as deductive databases is that the scope of the update types can often be extended.

The knowledge in expert systems is often updated by a particular class of user, so is an update type for that class of user. In particular, the University Calendar deductive database found in the exercises for this chapter has the IDB subject prerequisite rules in the update types for the academic management class of user, but not for the student class. On the other hand, the EDB predicate containing the subjects in which a student is enrolled is an update type for the student (generally via a University administrative clerk) but not for the academic staff.

The **form** of a query type is

- data if the user wants values of certain labels;
- information if the user wants certain tuples;
- knowledge if the user wants certain rules.

An example of data as a query form is that the user might want to know the different account type codes, say during data entry. This example would be a query type but not an update type.

As with update types, the purpose of most database systems is to allow the user to keep track of the state of the universe of discourse, so that most EDB predicates are query types. Not all, however. Implementation-specific information is often held in the database for convenience. For example, many fourth generation languages store programs in database tables. These tables are neither query nor update types for the user. In particular, the magic predicates of Chapter 8 are update types but not query types.

Knowledge is often the form of a query type. The user may wish to query business rules. Expert systems often have an explanation facility, which is essentially a query on the knowledge base. In the University Calendar example, both students and academics need query access to the subject prerequisite structure and to the course rules, all of which are stored as knowledge.

> When representing knowledge, we must consider who can access it and who can update it.

## 5.2  MODELLING KNOWLEDGE

There are many tools used by systems analysts to assist them in the construction of database-oriented information systems. These tools include Entity-Relationship-Attribute (ERA) analysis, and Binary-Relationship analysis in many forms. A major component of a knowledge-based system or deductive database is a relational database. Further, knowledge consists of relationships between information and between information and data. One would therefore expect that these information design tools would be applicable in part to the construction of knowledge-based systems.

Modelling tools generally involve two aspects: data structures, which are a bridge between the natural language descriptions of the universe of discourse and the formal representations in the ultimate implementation; and a graphical representation of the data structures, which is intended to facilitate understanding of the model both by the domain expert and by the systems analyst or knowledge engineer. Typically some of the detail of the data structure is represented in graphical form and some is represented in more or less formal textual languages.

We have suggested that Horn clause logic is a convenient way of representing knowledge. It is not the only way. Although we will assume Horn clause knowledge representation, the material is generally applicable to, for example, production rules.

## 5.2.1  Information modelling

From the point of view of Horn clause logic, the data consists of a set of labels (the constants) and the information consists of a set of predicates whose definitions consist entirely of unit clauses (the EDB). The knowledge consists of a set of predicate definitions which include general clauses: clauses with subgoals in their bodies (the IDB). Modelling of knowledge will start from the result of data and information analysis: the populations of labels and the EDB database schemas.

The method of knowledge modelling described is independent of any method of information modelling: we are concerned only with the product of the information analysis. However, we will have occasion to exhibit information modelling. When we do so, we will use the notation of ERA modelling, including its enhancement to represent subtypes.

The entity types, value sets of attributes, and subtype relationships are the product of data analysis, while the associations between entities and attributes, the relationships and constraints are the product of information analysis.

### 5.2.2 Knowledge diagrams

What remains to model is the knowledge: the IDB predicate definitions and the integrity constraints. We focus on the IDB predicate definitions, and begin by recalling that the predicate being defined (**head predicate**) looks to the user exactly like an EDB predicate. It therefore makes sense to include these predicates in the information analysis, noting that they are derived types.

The derivation rules are left. In most information analysis methods, derivation rules are represented textually: as statements in natural language, statements in SQL, mathematical formulas, etc. In the exposition of the information modelling techniques, derivation rules play a very minor part: the examples presented will typically have only a few derivation rules in a diagram with many entities. In practice, the derivation rules are not modelled at all: they are recorded in the specification and translated directly into code.

The purpose of knowledge-based systems or deductive databases is explicitly to represent derivation rules in a form compatible with the representation of information structures. We would therefore expect that a knowledge design method would incorporate mechanisms to help the domain expert and the systems analyst/knowledge engineer to visualize a large set of derivation rules, and to keep track of a large number of relationships between predicates.

The detail of the knowledge is represented as Horn clauses. There appears to be no particular advantage in representing the detail in a graphical language. However, the process of knowledge acquisition can require many interviews with domain experts and will generally require much revision before it can be regarded as satisfactory. There is an advantage in a graphical model which represents the knowledge coarsely: it gives an overview and allows annotations which can guide the knowledge acquisition process.

The granularity of the knowledge diagram will be the **clause group** (the set of clauses defining an IDB predicate). In modelling a clause group, we wish to keep track of which predicates are used to define the head predicate, without particular concern for the nature of the relationship. We use a graphical language, as illustrated in Figure 5.3. The predicates are represented as small solid circles, with their

Clause group

```
spare_part/sale_price(S, P) :-
        spare_part/cost_price(S, C),
        C < 20, P is C * 1.3.
spare_part/sale_price(S, P) :-
        spare_part/cost_price(S, C),
        C >= 20, P is C * 1.25.
```

Modelled as

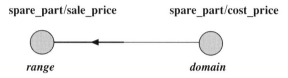

**Figure 5.3**  Modelling knowledge.

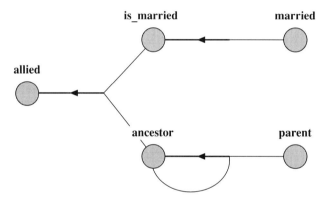

**Figure 5.4**  Further example of knowledge model.

names in close proximity. The head predicate (the range of the functional association) is indicated by a thick line with an intermediate arrowhead. The domain predicates are associated with the head predicates by thin lines terminating at the base
of the thick arrow. The resulting picture is intended to give an indication of a flow
of tuples from the domain predicates to the head predicate: the perfect model relationship. Since computational predicates are neither EDB nor IDB, they are indicated by a clear circle (see Figure 5.6). These knowledge diagrams are exactly the
dependency diagrams of Chapter 4 expressed in a richer notation.

There can be several body or domain predicates, and the head predicate may
appear in the body as a recursive subgoal. Figure 5.4 contains a model of the knowledge in Examples 4.1 and 4.4.

The models illustrated are complete. The IDB predicates are those to which a
thick arrow points. The EDB predicates have no arrow pointing to them. In addition,
the relationships shown are **categorical**: the head predicate is completely defined

in terms of the body predicates shown (possibly in more than one clause, and possibly not all body predicates appear in the same clause). In addition, the definition of each predicate is **unique**. Recall from Chapter 4 that the materialization of the view defined by an IDB predicate is computed as a series of partial materializations. Each partial materialization is computed from the previous one by the $T$ operator. A predicate definition is unique if during one iteration of the $T$ operator a particular set of tuples in the current partial materialization instantiating one of the clause bodies will generate at most one additional tuple in the next partial materialization. In other words, each instantiation of the body predicates of all clauses defining an IDB predicate is functionally associated with a single tuple in the perfect model. This condition is stronger than the population-to-population functional association defined by the perfect model, and noted earlier in this chapter.

During the course of knowledge acquisition, it is often the case that the knowledge gathered so far is not complete. Some examples of incompleteness are:

- IDB predicate noted but not yet defined;

- non-categorical definition (clause bodies so far do not define all possibilities). (Note that if only the first clause of the example predicate had been supplied, the predicate would be undefined for cost price less than 20);

- non-unique (defines possibilities in more than one way. If the first clause of the example predicate had the relation $C \leq 20$, then both clauses of the example predicate would apply if the cost price is 20).

We have noted that the knowledge diagram is essentially the same thing as the dependency graph described in section 4.3. It would therefore make sense to annotate the knowledge diagram to indicate dependence of the head predicate on a predicate appearing in a negative subgoal. In this way the knowledge diagram will indicate whether the knowledge base is stratified. Similarly, it makes sense to annotate the knowledge diagram to indicate the dependence of the head predicate on a predicate appearing in an aggregation, so that it is easy to see whether the system is aggregation stratified. We will adopt the convention of a single I for negation, and a double II for aggregation. The knowledge diagram for the non-stratified example from Figure 4.2 is shown in Figure 5.5.

The Horn clause representation of the knowledge of Example 4.7 is repeated here for convenience:

    standard-customer(C#, Discount) :-
       customer(C#, Discount),
       not special-discount(C#, Special-type, Special-Discount).

    good-customer(C#, Revenue) :-
       standard-customer(C#, Discount),
       sales(C#, Revenue),
       good-customer-revenue-threshold(T),
       Revenue ≥ T.

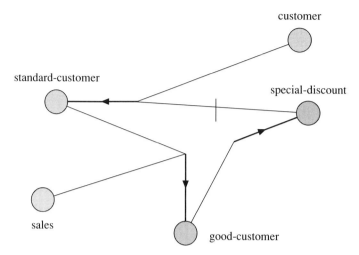

**Figure 5.5**  Knowledge diagram for non-stratified Example 4.7 from Figure 4.2.

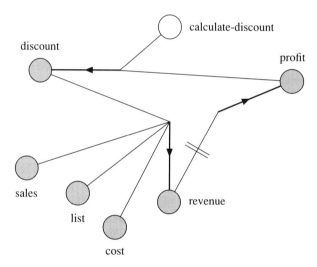

**Figure 5.6**  Knowledge diagram for non-aggregation-stratified Example 4.9 from Figure 4.4.

special-discount(C#, good-customer, Disc) :-
    good-customer(C#, Revenue),
    good-enough-threshold(T),
    Revenue ≥ T,
    good-customer-discount-rate(Disc).

The non-aggregation-stratified example of Figure 4.4 is shown in Figure 5.6. Note the computational predicate *calculate-discount*.

The Horn clause representation of the knowledge in Example 4.9 is repeated here for convenience. Note that the computational predicate *calculate-discount* has been introduced, its contents having been removed from the predicate *discount*.

profit(C#, Profit) :-
    aggregate(Profit = sum(Revenue), revenue(C#, Product, Revenue)).

revenue(C#, Product, Revenue) :-
    sales(C#, Product, Number),
    list-price(Product, List-Price),
    discount(C#, Product, Disc),
    cost(Product, Cost),
    Revenue is Number * (List-Price * (100 − Disc)/100 − Cost).

discount(C#, Product, Disc) :-
    profit(C#, Profit),
    calculate-discount(Profit, Disc).

calculate-discount(Profit, Disc) :-
    discount-threshold(T),
    Profit ≥ T ⇒ standard-discount(P, Disc);
        Disc is 0.

## 5.3 DESIGNING A KNOWLEDGE BASE

A knowledge-based system in general incorporates a database system. Some aspects of knowledge bases are formalizations of things appearing in database applications, so that the knowledge-specific portion of the knowledge-based system includes some things which appear also in database systems, notably constraints. We have seen that a knowledge-based system contains data, information and knowledge, and that the problem of design of a knowledge base is seen as the problem of classifying aspects of the application model as data, information or knowledge. Data is represented as labels in populations, information as tuples in relations, while knowledge is represented as Horn clauses.

The specifications for a system are derived from a natural language description of the system's context and requirement. The resulting knowledge model is a statement in the first-order predicate calculus, whose principal interpretation is in the natural language description, i.e. the meaning of the symbols and formulas in the knowledge model is determined by referring to the natural language description. There is a large difference in structure and degree of formality between the natural language description and the knowledge model. It is convenient to bridge that gap with a semi-formal set of natural language statements called the **application model**. This concept is familiar in conceptual modelling of information systems, and in particular is central to the NIAM method and its relatives. The application model is either produced explicitly from the natural language description by the systems analyst in the process of creating the conceptual model, or is perhaps more commonly generated from the conceptual model to make the model more easily understood by the domain experts.

Statements in the application model are assertions restricted to the following types of sentences:

■   an individual exists and is of a type

>   Clyde is an elephant.
>   X is a bird.

■   two or more objects exist in a relationship

>   Sylvester and Tweety are antagonists
>   The Broncos and X played in the final.

■   a population exists

>   There are students.

■   a relationship exists

>   Lecturers are assigned to classes.

■   an association exists between relationships

>   Selling price is determined by cost price and markup factor.

■   quantified statements

>   All classes have lecturers assigned.

Some facts are **particular facts**, in that they make specific statements about specific objects: for example *bob is assigned to lecture cs317*. Some facts are **general facts**, in that they describe relationships between populations, for example *lecturers are assigned to classes*. The distinction is similar to the distinction in ERA modelling between entity or relationship types (general fact), and population of instances (particular facts).

Statements in the application model must, as well as being assertions of the nominated kinds, satisfy a number of *individual requirements*:

■   *Uniqueness of wording.* Each use of the same word refers to the same object in the system's environment. Each instance of a given object in the system's environment is referred to by the same word.

■   *Type identification.* Every atomic object is identified as a label or a population. Every label is identified as a member of a population (type).

■   *Atomic requirement.* A statement contains at most one functional association.

For example, the statement:

>   "#234 is a spare part number; these are the part numbers which lie between #100 and #999"

should be decomposed into four statements:

"#234 is a spare part"
"Spare part numbers are less than 1000"
"Spare part numbers are greater than 99"
"All spare part numbers are part numbers"

The reader is assumed to be familiar with the creation of application models of this sort, and used to extracting from them data and information models.

We focus in deductive database technology on representation of knowledge in the form of Horn clauses. Application model statements which become represented as knowledge typically are complex sentences describing associations between relationships, containing phrases such as "is determined by", "if", "if ... then". For example:

An applicant can be admitted for the degree of Bachelor of Science if that student has attained a grade of high achievement in Senior English and Senior Mathematics, and has an overall QTAC score of 900 or greater.

might be translated into Horn clause form as

```
eligible_for(bs, Applicant) :-
    secondary_result(Applicant, senior_english, SER),
        SER ≥ high_achievement,
    secondary_result(Applicant, senior_math, SMR),
        SMR ≥ high_achievement,
    qtac_score(Applicant, S), S ≥ 900.
```

Another example is:

A person is eligible for entrance to the electoral roll if that person is a citizen of Australia, is at least 18 years of age, and is not judged to be legally insane or is not serving a prison sentence in respect of a felony.

which might be translated into Horn clause form as:

```
potential_voter(Person) :-
    citizen_of_australia(Person),
    age(Person, Age), Age ≥ 18,
    not legally_insane(Person),
    not imprisoned_for_felony(Person).
```

These statements are considered to be atomic in the sense of the individual requirements.

Note that the *potential_voter* example is essentially propositional. The four body predicates are essentially properties of *Person*. In a propositional expert system shell, the knowledge might appear as

potential_voter :-
   citizen_of_australia,
   age $\geq$ 18,
   not legally_insane,
   not imprisoned_for_felony.

where the propositions in the clause body are set *true* or *false* by, for example, interviewing the user.

An important class of knowledge which is considered in more detail in Chapter 11 is constraints. Constraints can apply to:

- data: e.g. size, type and range of label;

- information: e.g. subtype, foreign key and inter-value constraints;

- knowledge: e.g.
    selling price must depend on buying price
    certain variables must be bound (an expression of information-goal dependency)
    if a rule is changed, all cases which were previously correctly classified are still so

Statements containing phrases like *all ... must*, or *no ... may* are generally profitably classified as constraints. Constraints on data and information are generally represented as Horn clauses that define views which must remain empty. A convenient way to do this is for the deductive database system to have a reserved predicate name, say *bad*, and for the constraints to be expressed as clauses in its definition. If after an update the deductive database system finds that the predicate *bad* is true, it will reject the update. Integrity constraints appear in the example of section 5.4. They are covered in much more detail in Chapter 11.

Constraints on data and information can generally be represented as first-order logic statements, but constraints on knowledge generally cannot. However, as we will see in Chapter 6, the IDB of a deductive database can be stored in the repository supporting a CASE tool, which is essentially a relational database. The knowledge constraints become in many cases first-order statements about the representation of the IDB in the repository.

It is useful to identify examples of the standard complex data structures outlined in Chapter 3. It is generally much easier to adapt a standard predicate to a specific situation than to develop a complex search predicate from scratch. Besides the generic complex structures given in this text, an organization may have additional standardized structures in its software library.

## 5.4  HIERARCHICAL THESAURUS EXAMPLE

This section contains an extended example, which may help the reader integrate the various aspects of the method. The domain of the example is the field of indexing documents for information retrieval, and describes a **hierarchical thesaurus**. The application model is divided into sections, and each 'sentence' in each section is numbered. This identification system will help relate the knowledge design constructs back to the application model.

### 5.4.1   Application model

1   [1]A document is indexed by possibly several index terms. Index terms are related to each other in a number of ways. [2]An important relationship is *broader term/ narrower term*. [3]A broader term than a given term, when used in a search, will always retrieve documents indexed by the given term, and possibly others. [4]A narrower term than a given term will, when used in a search, retrieve only some of the documents indexed by the given term. [5]In addition to the general broader/ narrower term, there are a number of specific classes of broader term/narrower term relationships which have specific additional properties. [6]In particular, if a term is the name of a set of objects, then the name of a superset is a broader term, and the name of a subset is a narrower term (*is-a*). [7]Also, if a term is the name of a set of objects, the name of one of its members is a narrower term (*instance-of*). [8]Conversely, the name of a set of objects is a broader term than the name of one of its members (*set-of*). [9]Finally, if a term names an object, then the name of an ingredient for the object is a narrower term (*ingredient-of*), and the converse relationship is a broader term.

2   [1]Besides the broader term/narrower term relationship, there are terms which are *related to* a given term in such a way that documents retrieved by the related term are sometimes relevant to a search using the given term, but not in a systematic way (*related terms*). [2]As for broader term/narrower term, there are a number of specific classes of related term relationships which have specific properties: [3]in particular, a term which names a source for the object named by the given term (*source-of*); [4]and a term which names an object similar to the given object (*similar-to*).

3   [1]No term can be a broader term than itself, either directly or indirectly. [2]No term can be a related term to a term which is broader or narrower than itself, either directly or indirectly.

4   [1]We would like to be able to make the following queries on this system:

   ■ [2]Find all objects having *is-a* relationships either directly or indirectly (*subtype-of*);

   ■ [3]If an object has narrower terms of class *ingredient*, find all sources for all ingredients, noting that some *source-of* relationships are associated with supertypes (*source-of-ingredient*);

   ■ [4]Find all set objects having at least one instance having an ingredient which is similar to a given term (*possible-use-for*). For example *possible-use-for(leek, Use)?*

## 5.4.2  Sample population

Term  prepared food
  Broader term  nil
  Narrower term
    *is-a*  soup
        cake
        bread
  Related term  meal

Term  soup
  Broader term
    *is-a*  prepared food
  Narrower term
    *instance-of*  onion soup

Term  dairy food
  Broader term
    *is-a*  food product
  Narrower term
    *instance-of*  butter
  Related term
    *source-of*  dairy

Term  vegetable
  Broader term
    *is-a*  food product
  Narrower term
    *instance-of*  onion
  Related term  leek
    *source-of*  greengrocer

Term  onion soup
  Broader term
    *instance-of*  soup
  Narrower term
    *ingredient-of*  onion
        butter
        water

Term  onion
  Broader term
    *instance-of*  vegetable
    *ingredient-of*  onion soup
  Related term
    *similar-to*  leek

Term  butter
  Broader term
    *instance-of*  dairy food
    *ingredient-of*  onion soup

Term  food product
  Broader term: nil
  Narrower term
    *is-a*  vegetable
        dairy food
  Related term
    *source-of*  supermarket

Term  leek
  Broader term
    *instance-of*  vegetable
  Related term
    *similar-to*  onion

The data structures involved here are interlocking graphs. The nodes are terms. One set of arcs, forming a directed acyclic graph, is provided by the *broader term* relationships. The other set, forming an undirected graph, is provided by the *related term* relationships. The types of broader and related terms select subgraphs. Note in particular that the *is-a* broader term forms a transitive subgraph of the *broader term* directed acyclic graph.

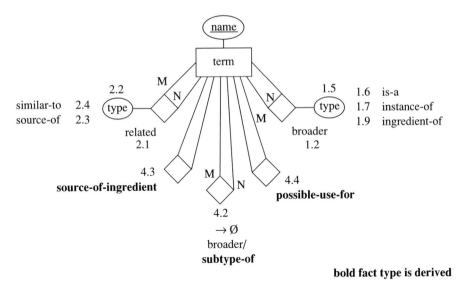

**Figure 5.7** Data/information model for hierarchical thesaurus example.

### 5.4.3 Data/information model

An information model for the above example is shown in Figure 5.7, using the ERA method. Each construct in the data/information model is labelled with the sentence in the application model from which it is derived. Note that the derived relationships *source-of-ingredient*, *possible-use-for*, and *subtype-of* appear in the information model. Note also that the derived relationship *subtype-of* is indicated to be a transitive directed acyclic graph whose arc type is *broader*, using the notation of Chapter 3.

### 5.4.4 EDB definition

broader(Broader, Narrower)

related(Term1, Term2)

typed-broader(Broader, Narrower, Type)

typed-related(Term1, Term2, Type)

This EDB definition has a predicate for each base type in the data/information model. Other formulations of the EDB are possible. For example, if an additional label "unspecified" is added to both entity types *broader type* and *related type*, then the predicates *broader* and *related* could be collapsed into *typed-broader* and *typed-related*, respectively. This design choice can be considered as an implementation decision. The information and knowledge model are part of the specification of the system, and a major goal of the specification of the system is a clear understanding of its behaviour, both to ensure its correctness and to determine its suitability for the user's purpose. For this reason, it is probably better to develop the knowledge model from a sub-optimal table design which is closely related to the representation of the information in the information modelling method chosen. When the system is eventually implemented, a more efficient table design can be chosen and the knowledge design adapted.

### 5.4.5    Knowledge model

A knowledge diagram for this example is given in Figure 5.8. As with Figure 5.7, the update types and query types are annotated with the number of the sentence in the application model from which they are derived. Note the two predicates

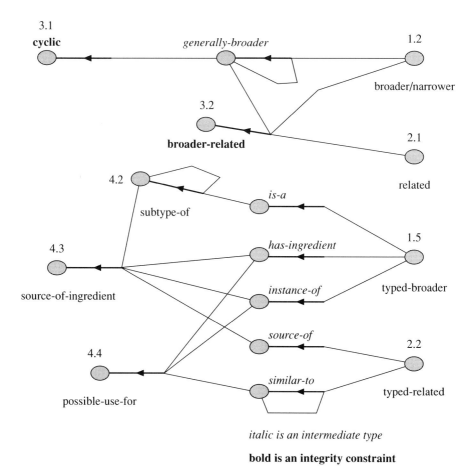

*italic is an intermediate type*

**bold is an integrity constraint**

**Figure 5.8**  Knowledge model for hierarchical thesaurus example.

*broader-related* and *cyclic*, which implement the two integrity constraints from paragraph 3 of the application model. These do not appear in the information model, since they generate no tuples in the perfect model. There are a number of other predicates in the knowledge model which do not appear in the information model: *generally-broader, is-a, has-ingredient, instance-of, source-of* and *similar-to*. These predicates are intermediate types introduced to simplify or clarify the expression of the knowledge. Intermediate types have no annotation, since by definition they do not appear in the application model, being instead artifacts of the design. (These intermediate types may be used for improving the quality of the knowledge representation, as described in Chapter 7.) It is not necessary to show all such predicates on the knowledge diagram (or any for that matter). In this instance they appear on the diagram since they have some meaning in the application domain, and they make the knowledge diagram clearer. Most of these are used in more than one predicate definition.

### 5.4.6   Horn clause representation of knowledge

Integrity constraints

% Example of closure of directed acyclic graph, path not important

generally-broader(T1, T2) :- broader(T1, T2).
generally-broader(T1, T2) :- broader(T1, T), generally-broader(T, T2).

cyclic :- generally-broader(T, T).

broader-related :- generally-broader(B, N), related(N, B).
broader-related :- generally-broader(B, N), related(B, N).

Other IDB

is-a(Superset, Subset) :- typed-broader(Superset, Subset, is-a)

has-ingredient(Total, Ingredient) :-
    typed-broader(Total, Ingredient, ingredient-of).

instance-of(Set, Instance) :- typed-broader(Set, Instance, instance-of).

source-of(Item, Source) :- typed-related(Item, Source, source-of)

similar(Item1, Item2) :- typed-related(Item1, Item2, similar-to).[1, 2]

similar(Item1, Item2) :- typed-related(Item2, Item1, similar-to).

% Example of closure of undirected graph, path not important

similar-to(Item1, Item2) :- similar(Item1, Item2).
similar-to(Item1, Item2) :- similar(Item1, I), similar-to(I, Item2).

---

[1] The predicate *similar* has two clauses, since there is no constraint that if one term has a related term of type *similar-to*, the second term has the first term as a related term.

% Example of closure of directed acyclic graph, path not important

subtype-of(Supertype, Subtype) :- is-a(Supertype, Subtype).
subtype-of(Supertype, Subtype) :-
    is-a(Supertype, Term), subtype-of(Term, Subtype).

source-of-ingredient(Total, Source) :-
    has-ingredient(Total, Ingredient),
    source-of(Ingredient, Source).
source-of-ingredient(Total, Source) :-
    has-ingredient(Total, Ingredient),
    one-of(Ingredient, Set),
    source-of(Set, Source).

% Example of hierarchical data structure based on a tree

one-of(Ingredient, Set) :- instance-of(Set, Ingredient).[2]
one-of(Ingredient, Superset) :-
    instance-of(Set, Ingredient),
    subtype-of(Superset, Set).

possible-use-for(Term, Use) :-
    similar-to(Term, Term1),
    has-ingredient(Total, Term1),
    instance-of(Use, Total).

This extended example has demonstrated the flow of the problem solution through the several tools recommended in this chapter. Starting with the application model, we first construct an information model incorporating both the base predicates and the derived predicates. Having now all the predicates which are either query types or update types, we construct a knowledge diagram which shows the relationships between them. In addition, we name predicates defining the integrity constraints from the application model, and show how these predicates relate to the query and update types. In addition, we may define some intermediate predicates which may help to simplify the diagram or make it clearer. Finally, we show the EDB predicate schemas and the detailed representation of the knowledge as IDB predicates. We may introduce some additional intermediate types at this stage, which we may not wish to show on the knowledge diagram. Note that the knowledge model contains three close analogs of the *ancestor* predicate (*subtype-of*, *generally-broader* and *similar-to*).

### 5.5  OTHER FORMS OF KNOWLEDGE: PRODUCTION RULES

The knowledge design and diagramming techniques advocated in this chapter have been specific to datalog. They can, however, be adapted to other forms of knowledge

---

[2] The intermediate predicate does not appear on the knowledge diagram. It is introduced to simplify the expression of the knowledge, but is not used in any other predicate definitions. It was therefore omitted from the knowledge diagram.

representation, in particular to production rules. Since this text does not contain a thorough development of the production rule formalism and mechanisms, we do not develop the knowledge design techniques in much detail, but simply sketch the adaptations which might be required.

First, the building block of datalog knowledge representation (an atom) is essentially a database schema. This is why we advocate the use of a standard information analysis method. The analogous part of the production rule mechanism is the working memory element (wme), which can also be represented as a database schema. Therefore an information analysis method would also be useful in a production rule environment.

Secondly, the knowledge diagram shows the relationships between clause heads and the subgoals and computational predicates in the clause bodies. A similar technique could show the relationships between the conditions of the left-hand side and the actions in the right-hand side. The diagramming language would have to be altered, since there can be several actions in the right-hand side, but this would not affect its spirit.

Thirdly, the annotations on the knowledge diagram would be somewhat different, depending on the capability of the production rule system intended as the implementation platform. Production rule systems generally support negation in the left-hand side, so the | annotation would remain, but most do not support aggregation. On the other hand, the action can delete (or update) a wme as well as add one. A || annotation on the action would be useful to assist in detection of the production rule equivalent of non-stratification.

## 5.6 SUMMARY

One of the main themes of this text is that there is a very close relationship between information systems and expert systems, which is made apparent by the deductive database formalism. An information system is traditionally built by carefully modelling the data then leaving the processing, including the business rules, to the programmers. An expert system is traditionally built as a model of the rules, leaving the definition of the terms involved implicit.

We have attempted to show in this chapter that knowledge is based on data and information, and therefore knowledge can be modelled by extensions of techniques used for modelling information and data. In particular, knowledge can be acquired by an extension to the commonly-used systematic methods for developing a specification for an information system.

We therefore not only have a uniform language for representing both information systems and expert systems, but a uniform set of conceptual tools to assist in their construction.

## 5.7 FURTHER READING

The material in this chapter is drawn largely from Debenham (1989). ERA modelling is described, for example, in Elmasri and Navathe (1994). Object-role modelling or NIAM is described, for example, by Halpin (1994). Advanced information modelling from the entity-relationship perspective is described, for example, by Batini *et al.* (1992).

## 5.8  EXERCISES

5.1   Simple expert system: Given below is a simple propositional expert system. Select the data and information using an appropriate information analysis technique, then model the knowledge.

Example 10.1 (from Chapter 10 pp. 181–182): Barbecue planner expert system

rain_forecast → call_off

bob → all_foods

mary → vegetarian_fish

jim → meat

vegetarian_fish & not meat → lentil_burgers

meat & not vegetarian_fish → steak

meat & vegetarian_fish → fish

all_foods → hot_dogs

The update types, with their intended interpretations, are

*rain_forecast* – the weather forecast is rain

*bob* – Bob has accepted an invitation to the barbecue

*mary* – Mary has accepted an invitation to the barbecue

*jim* – Jim has accepted an invitation to the barbecue

The query types, with their intended interpretations, are

*call_off* – the barbecue is to be called off

*lentil_burgers* – lentil burgers will be served

*steak* – steak will be served

*fish* – fish will be served

*hot_dogs* – hot dogs will be served

The intermediate types, with their intended interpretations, are

*vegetarian_fish* – someone has been invited who is a vegetarian but will tolerate fish

*meat* – someone has been invited who prefers meat but will tolerate fish

*all_foods* – someone has been invited who has no strong food preferences

The perfect model is intended to contain at most one of the query types other than *call_off*: in other words, the person planning the barbecue is expecting to serve only one type of food.

5.2   Commercial example: The following is a fragment of a specification of an information system which includes some knowledge. Your task is to select the data and information using an appropriate information analysis technique, then to model the knowledge. You should select the portions of the specification which contain the knowledge, and turn them into an application model satisfying the individual requirements. Use the application model to construct a model of the knowledge using the diagrams indicated, then translate the knowledge into clauses using the relations and data labels identified in your preliminary information analysis.

**Specification**: The fragment is part of the process of preparation of invoices by a costume jewellery wholesaler, CJW Pty Ltd (CJW). CJW is able to enforce retail price maintenance, so all outlets retail the product at the same price. We want to be able to produce an invoice for a particular customer who has ordered a number of items of a single product. The invoice will include the retail price, wholesale price, sales tax and cost. Cost is the total of wholesale price and sales tax.

Wholesale price and sales tax are determined in two different ways. For boutique customers, wholesale price is the list price of the product less a discount depending on the class of customer. Sales tax is a percentage of the wholesale price depending on the class of the product. For department stores, the order is placed at retail price. The wholesale price is computed by first getting a cost which is a discount from the retail price, depending on the class of the customer. The wholesale price and sales tax are then computed such that the cost is the total of the wholesale price and sales tax as for the boutique customers.

A printed invoice would include

Customer number, product number, quantity ordered, retail price per unit, discount rate, total wholesale price, total sales tax and total cost.

If a boutique, the invoice would also include list price per unit. Total wholesale price is computed from the list price times the quantity less the discount.

If a department store, total wholesale price is computed from the retail price times the quantity less the discount less provision for sales tax, as described above.

5.3   Data structures: Draw a graphical representation of the data in the hierarchical thesaurus example (section 5.4). Discuss which types of arc should be considered to be transitive and which not.


## Major exercise

Consider the following application model.

A university offers to students courses leading to degrees. A course is offered by exactly one faculty. To qualify for a degree, a student must pass a number of subjects. Each course has two schedules, or lists of subjects: a compulsory schedule and an elective schedule. A student qualifies for a degree if he/she passes all the subjects in the compulsory schedule and obtains a nominated number of credit points from the elective schedule. No more than a nominated number of credit points can be obtained from subjects whose result is "conceded pass". Both the elective credit points and the "conceded pass" credit points can vary between courses.

Subjects are offered by departments which are attached to the faculties. A subject has the characteristics described in the Department Handbook. A student enrolled in a subject can obtain three possible results: "pass", "conceded pass" or "fail". The student is enrolled in a subject before the result is available: the enrolment record will have a result "not available" during this period. (Note that the student may enrol for subjects to be studied in subsequent semesters. For example, a student may enrol in the entire sequence of subjects necessary for a degree at the beginning of the first semester.)

A student is eligible to enrol in a subject if she/he has enrolled in its prerequisite and co-requisite subjects, provided that the result is neither "fail" nor "conceded pass", and is not enrolled in an incompatible subject.

A subject is a "foundation" subject if it appears as a prerequisite to a subject which is itself a prerequisite for a subject. A subject is a "service" subject if it appears on a schedule for a course offered by a faculty other than the faculty to which the department offering it is attached. A subject is "obsolete" if it appears on no schedule. One subject "contributes to" another if it is a prerequisite or co-requisite to the second subject, either directly or indirectly.

No subject may be a prerequisite for itself, either directly or indirectly. If a subject is on a schedule, all of its prerequisites must be on the schedule as well. The total number of credit points on a compulsory schedule for a course must not exceed the total number of credits points to qualify for the course. The total number of credit points in the compulsory and elective schedules for a course must be sufficient to qualify for the degree.

There may be ambiguities or incompleteness in this model. If so, make reasonable assumptions based on your knowledge of university procedures. Document these assumptions.

1  Make an information analysis of the model, using either NIAM or ERA. Include in the diagram all fact types, including derived fact types. Indicate derived fact types by "*" or other suitable means.

2  Make knowledge diagrams of all derived facts. Indicate whether any facts are non-categorical or incomplete. Integrity constraint violations will cause the predicate *bad* to be true.

3  Express the derived facts in Horn clause form.

4  Populate the tables and update type procedures with the subject cs317 and its prerequisites, below. Some tables may be empty.

5  Ensure that the quality rules of Chapter 7 apply to all derived facts, where possible. If impossible in a particular case, explain why.

Extract from the student handbook. All these subjects are compulsory for the course B. Inf. Tech.

CS114 Introduction to Information Systems
#8 (2L1T1P) 1st [For BA Pre: Sen Math 1]
Overview of Information Systems, etc.

CS115 Relational Database Systems
#8 (2L2P/2T) 2nd Pre: CS114
Further aspects etc.

CS213 Information Systems Design
#8 (2L1T) 1st Pre: (CS113 or CS115) + (ME205 or MT108) Inc. CO865
Life cycles of information systems, etc.

CS317 Advanced Database Systems
#8 (2L1T) 2nd Pre CS213 + (i) CS225 or (ii) (CS102 + CS226)
Overview of advanced architectures etc.

Abbreviations:

| | |
|---|---|
| #8 | the subject has 8 credit points |
| L | lecture hours per week |
| T | tutorial hours per week |
| P | practical session hours per week |
| 1st, 2nd | first or second semester, respectively |
| Pre | prerequisite |
| Inc | incompatible subject |

Notes:

(a)  Don't show integrity constraints on the ERA diagram.

(b)  Show integrity constraints on the knowledge diagram. Give each a meaningful name. Indicate which predicates in the knowledge diagram are ICs.

(c)  Do not show intermediate types on either the ERA or knowledge diagrams. Indicate which predicate definitions in part 3 are intermediate.

(d)  Show course rules for B Inf Tech only. Note that the actual rules are considerably more complex than the rules in the assignment. Use the rules in the assignment with parameters elective subjects at least #144, maximum conceded pass #30.

## CHAPTER SIX

# Building a knowledge base

In this chapter, we look at methods and tools to assist in building a knowledge base, with emphasis on the design and use of a computer-aided software engineering tool based on a repository implemented as a deductive database, i.e. use of a deductive database to help build a deductive database.

## 6.1 KNOWLEDGE ACQUISITION

A knowledge-based system, be it an information system or an expert system, is generally constructed by computer specialists in order to meet the needs of a separate user community. The requirements for the system, including the knowledge it contains, are provided by specialists from the user community, which we will call **domain experts**. The domain experts communicate with computer specialists to produce the requirements in a form which can be understood by both parties. The computer specialist is called a **systems analyst** by the information systems community and a **knowledge engineer** by the expert systems community. We will call the practitioner a knowledge engineer, and the process **knowledge acquisition**.

The knowledge engineer has access to a number of sources of knowledge, including interviews with domain experts and documents used by the client organization. This knowledge is usually incomplete, inconsistent, and not structured in a way useful for computer implementation. The knowledge acquisition task is to assemble the knowledge in an implementable form, suitably structured, complete and consistent. The usual procedure is to gather the knowledge informally at first, then to formalize it with the aid of various tools. During the formalization process, the knowledge engineer will usually find gaps and inconsistencies, and will resolve these in discussion with the domain experts. A systematic approach is essential to achieve a suitable representation in a reasonable time.

The first product of knowledge acquisition is the requirements specification, which is a natural language, and therefore informal, statement of what is expected of the system. Part of the requirements specification is the application model, which was described in Chapter 5. The application model goes through several drafts. The first draft is fragmentary and extremely informal. The final draft is in the semi-formal language of Chapter 5, and is in essence a natural language representation of the formalized knowledge.

The ultimate system is an implementation of the requirements specification, so that each element of the final formal knowledge structure must be tied to something in the application model. To facilitate this linkage, the requirements specification is divided into fairly small sections with identifiers. The sections of the application model will be called **bundles** (of statements), and each bundle will be identified by a **bundle identifier**. A bundle therefore is an interrelated collection of application model statements. The hierarchical thesaurus example of Chapter 5 has four bundles.

The formalization process works from (drafts of) bundles in the application model. The knowledge engineer should work systematically. Starting from a given fact in one of the bundles, the engineer should:

■ make sure all thing populations have identifying name populations;

■ identify the population for all labels;

■ generalize particular facts;

■ if a fact is derived, determine how it is derived;

■ define subtype relationships between the populations.

For example, the hierarchical thesaurus application is about relationships between words or phrases, which are labels. Therefore, all the thing populations are also name populations and are identified by themselves. In bundle 1, the labels *broader term* and *narrower term* are names of populations. The labels *is-a*, *instance-of* and *ingredient-of* are instances of the population *broader type*. The definition of the *is-a* relationship is a particular fact, which is generalized by the fact that there are a number of specialized broader term classes, whose names are instances of the population *broader type*. These specialized broader term classes are subtypes of the general *broader term*. In this bundle, there are no instances of derived facts. Bundle 3 has two derived facts and sufficient information about how they are derived to produce a formal specification.

A systematic approach is to clarify all the statements in a bundle before proceeding to others. Within a bundle, find out all you can about one thing before moving to another.

This chapter shows how some of the tools of information and knowledge analysis can be used to assist knowledge acquisition, and also demonstrates one way to build an information system to implement the tools.

**Table 6.1**  Product of information analysis: data

| Properties | | Sample data terms | |
|---|---|---|---|
| Thing population | term | related type | broader type |
| Name population | term | related type | broader type |
| Subtype of Labels | | source-of | is-a |
| | | similar-to | instance-of |
| | | | ingredient-of |
| Fixed labels? | no | yes | yes |
| Pop. constraints | none | defined | defined |
| Label constraints | none | none | none |
| Bundle | 1 | 2 | 1 |

## 6.2  PRODUCT OF DATA AND INFORMATION ANALYSIS

### 6.2.1  Data

The information analysis produces a set of facts about the data and information in the application. This set of facts is frequently represented as a diagram, such as an Entity/Relationship/Attribute diagram or a NIAM diagram such as Figure 5.7. The facts about the data and information can be expressed in a tabular form, which is interchangeable with the diagrammatic form.

The data is described in terms of:

■  thing population (entity type);

■  name population (identifying label type);

■  subtype relationships.

In addition, we need to record whether the name population is fixed or variable, and in some cases exhibit the name population. The labels may be constrained (for example they must be positive integers, or must consist entirely of upper case alphabetic characters). The user may or may not be allowed to update the name population. Finally, the bundles in the application model from which the facts about the data are derived should be recorded.

Table 6.1 shows the data analysis product of information analysis for the hierarchical thesaurus example (section 5.4). There are three thing populations, each of which is its own name population. There are no subtype relationships in the data as represented. (Note that the application model could have been represented with typed broader term and typed related term as subtypes of term. The design choice made was to not employ subtyping in this instance.) The populations *related type* and *broader type* both have known sets of labels, which are *defined*, that is they are the only labels allowed, and the user is not allowed to update them. (They are built into the knowledge, so that a change to the labels for those two populations would require changes to the knowledge, which we assume the user is not permitted to do.) We impose no constraints on any of the labels: in other words, any string of characters is a valid label. This by default applies only to the population *term*, since the other two populations are pre-defined. Finally, the populations *term* and *broader type* are derived from bundle 1, while *related type* is derived from bundle 2.

### 6.2.2  Information

The same information analysis provides facts about the predicates relevant to the application, what is called in this text the information. The information is described as a set of relational schemas, containing

- name of the relation;
- key and other domains;
- possible tuple population;
- any relational constraints, such as foreign keys;
- any tuple constraints, such as maximum number of tuples;
- whether derived or not;
- related bundle.

Some of the relation schemas derived from Figure 5.7 are shown in Table 6.2. Illustrated are two base relations *related* and *broader_term_has_type*; and one derived relation *subtype_of*. All three describe relationships between terms, so each has as compound key two attributes from the *term* domain. The base relation *broader_term _has_type* has in addition a non-key attribute from the domain *broader_type*. These key and non-key attributes are derived from the transformation of the information model to a relational schema. The transformation is not necessarily complete or optimal, but just sufficient to find the identification scheme for each fact type. In this way, the information predicates are as close as possible to the information model. Neither base relation has any constraints on its population or on the content of its tuples shown on the information model. However, the many-to-many relationship

**Table 6.2**  Product of information analysis: information

| Properties | | Sample relation schemas | |
|---|---|---|---|
| Relation | related | broader_term_has_type | subtype_of |
| Key domains | term × term | term × term | term × term |
| Other domains | nil | broader_type | nil |
| Derived? | no | yes | no |
| Tuples | | | |
| Relation constraints | | term × term in broader | |
| Tuple constraints | | | |
| Bundle | 2 | 1 | 4 |

from which *broader_term_has_type* is derived implies that every key for that relation is also contained in the relation *broader* (foreign key). The predicate *related* derives from bundle 2 in the application model, *broader_term_has_type* from bundle 1, and *subtype_of* from bundle 4.

## 6.3  BUILDING THE KNOWLEDGE MODEL

A knowledge engineer will typically use an information analysis tool to assist in constructing the data and information models. The information analysis tool will generally include diagrammatic representations of aspects of the model. The diagrams help to visualize the various constructs and to record various constraints such as mandatory relationships. The diagrams are also used to suggest possible questions of the domain experts: for example, an entity participating in several non-mandatory roles might have a useful subtype structure.

Knowledge in this text consists of derived facts and integrity constraints. Chapter 5 suggests that a suitable way of recording knowledge is as Horn clauses: a textual representation rather than a graphic representation, since the details of derivation rules are potentially complex and diverse in structure. It, however, suggests a coarse representation of the relationship between derived and base predicates, such as is shown in Figure 5.8. In that chapter, it was suggested that the knowledge diagram was a suitable place to record whether a predicate was computational or not, and whether a clause body predicate was either negated or used in an aggregation. The knowledge diagram can be annotated with negation and aggregation, and can be used to identify knowledge structures which are not stratified.

The structure of the knowledge diagram can also suggest possible redundancies. Figure 6.1 shows two fragments which might have appeared on earlier drafts of the knowledge diagram of Figure 5.8. The upper fragment shows two predicates, *broader* and *narrower*, which are defined solely in terms of each other. This suggests that they might be equivalent, which is in fact the case. The redundant predicate *narrower* was discarded in favour of *broader*. The lower fragment shows the predicates *source-of-ingredient* and *possible-use-for*. Each of these predicates depends on both *instance-of* and *has-ingredient*. The possibility is that there is a concept expressed in the knowledge which is being computed redundantly, for example *an-ingredient-of-one-of-the-members-of-a-set*. (See Chapter 7 for further discussion of this point, particularly the discussion of knowledge quality principles K.3 and K.4.) We investigate the detail of the definitions of the two consequent predicates (from Chapter 5), and see that in fact the two consequent predicates depend on the two antecedent predicates in different ways, so that there is in fact no redundancy.

When we complete the knowledge model, we have a representation of the knowledge in terms of groups of clauses. Some of these groups are integrity constraints. We identify the update and query types. Finally, we classify the knowledge groups according to whether they are update types, query types or integrity constraints. (Recall that a predicate can be both a query and update type.) Some of the knowledge may not be in any of these classifications. Knowledge which the domain expert

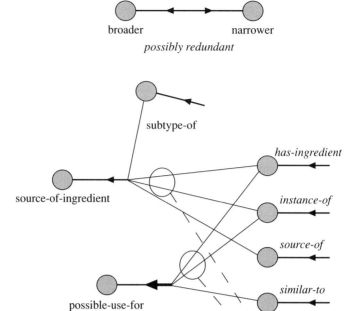

**Figure 6.1**    Use of knowledge diagram to show possible redundancies.

wants neither to change or to view, and which does not constrain the system, is knowledge which is not required for the immediate purpose, so we will classify it as *dormant*. This is kept in the model for possible future use.

### 6.4   CASE TOOL FOR THE KNOWLEDGE MODEL

#### 6.4.1   Overview

We have seen that development of a model for a knowledge-based system requires the knowledge engineer to keep track of a large amount of complexly structured data. It therefore makes sense to consider providing an information system to assist: after all, that is what an information system is for, to help people keep track of large amounts of complexly structured data.

A computer system to support software engineers in constructing systems is generally called a **Computer-Aided Software Engineering (CASE) tool**. CASE tools generally will do things like draw information model diagrams, maintain control of different versions of an evolving software product, and integrate documentation with the design. The core of a CASE tool is generally a database, which is frequently called a **repository**. We will show the main features of a repository which can be the basis of a CASE tool to help the knowledge engineer build and maintain a knowledge-based system along the lines described in this text.

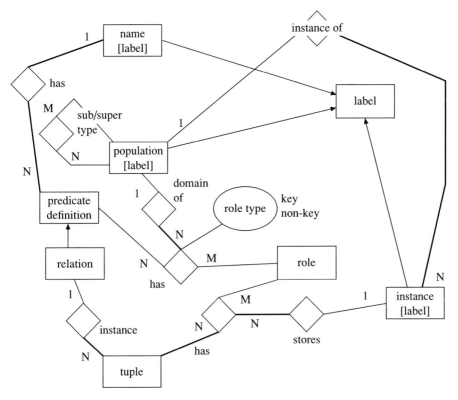

**Figure 6.2** Model for data and information.

### 6.4.2 Information repository

An early stage in the design of an information system is construction of an information model. Figure 6.2 shows an information model which describes the main features of data and information as they are represented in the knowledge model. The
key structures are that a predicate definition has roles, a predicate definition has
instances, and tuple instances have roles. Note that not all predicate definitions need
to have roles: propositional predicates do not.

Expressed as a relational predicate, the fact type *predicate definition has role* is

$$\text{pred/role}(\underline{\text{Predicate, Role}}, \text{Domain, Type}) \tag{6.1}$$

while the fact type *tuple has role* is

$$\text{tuple/role}(\underline{\text{Predicate, Tuple, Role}}, \text{Instance}) \tag{6.2}$$

A population of *pred/role* based on the EDB definitions *broader* and *typed-broader*
from the EDB derived from Figure 5.7 is given in Table 6.3. There is one row in
the table for each role in each predicate definition.

**Table 6.3**   Sample population of *pred/role*

| Predicate | Role | Domain | Type |
|---|---|---|---|
| broader | broader | term | key |
| broader | narrower | term | key |
| typed-broader | broader | term | key |
| typed-broader | narrower | term | key |
| typed-broader | type | broader-type | non-key |

**Table 6.4**   Sample population of *typed-broader*

| Broader | Narrower | Type |
|---|---|---|
| food product | dairy food | is-a |
| dairy food | butter | instance-of |
| vegetable | onion | instance-of |
| onion soup | onion | ingredient-of |

**Table 6.5**   Sample population of *tuple/role*

| Predicate | Tuple | Role | Instance |
|---|---|---|---|
| typed-broader | food product/dairy food | broader | food product |
| typed-broader | food product/dairy food | narrower | dairy food |
| typed-broader | food product/dairy food | type | is-a |
| typed-broader | dairy food/butter | broader | dairy food |
| typed-broader | dairy food/butter | narrower | butter |
| typed-broader | dairy food/butter | type | instance-of |
| typed-broader | vegetable/onion | broader | vegetable |
| typed-broader | vegetable/onion | narrower | onion |
| typed-broader | vegetable/onion | type | instance-of |
| typed-broader | onion soup/onion | broader | onion soup |
| typed-broader | onion soup/onion | narrower | onion |
| typed-broader | onion soup/onion | type | ingredient-of |

A sample population for the predicate *typed-broader* from the hierarchical thesaurus example of section 5.4 is given in Table 6.4. This population is used to
populate the predicate *tuple/role* in Table 6.5.

Notice that there is a row in Table 6.5 for each label in each tuple in Table 6.4.
The entries in the *Tuple* column of Table 6.5 are identifiers of the tuples (in this
case the key, which is concatenated).

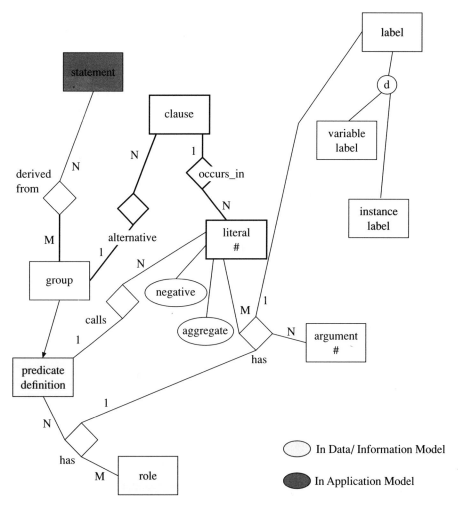

**Figure 6.3**  Model for knowledge.

### 6.4.3  Repository for knowledge

Our repository information system at this point has the capability to store the information model for an application. We will now extend it to be able to store the knowledge model. The information model for the repository able to store the knowledge model is shown in Figure 6.3. The new elements include a new subtype of label (*variable label*) and the structures needed to represent the body of a clause. A clause head is a subtype of predicate definition, which is in the model of Figure 6.2. The entity type *literal* includes both the clause head literal and the literals in the clause body, so that *literal* is an optional role in the *calls* fact type (the clause head does not call a subgoal). However, each literal argument corresponds to a role in a predicate definition. For the head predicate, the correspondence is with the group's predicate definition, whereas for a body literal, the correspondence is with the definition of the group called by the subgoal.

In addition to the relational predicates (6.1) and (6.2), there are two important predicates defined by the information model for knowledge: *literal/calls* which gives the predicate dependency relationship (refer to Chapter 4), and *literal/argument*, which stores the labels contained in the predicate definition. The schema for *literal/calls* is

literal/calls(<u>Group, Clause, Literal#</u>, Called_Predicate, Negative)          (6.3)

while the schema for *literal/argument* is

literal/argument(<u>Group, Clause, Literal#, Argument#</u>,          (6.4)
    Label, Called_Predicate, Role)

In definition (6.4), the attributes *Called_Predicate* and *Role* have a referential integrity constraint to the corresponding key attributes of *pred/role* (6.1). The information in *literal/calls* is used to construct the knowledge diagram.

Table 6.6 contains a population for the predicate *literal/calls* derived from the *Other IDB* definitions of the hierarchical thesaurus example of section 5.4. Notice that we only store body literals, since head literals do not particpate in the *calls* fact type. We will identify the head literal as *literal#* 0, and number the body literals from 1. Notice that some of the predicates are recursive (*Group* has the same value as *Called_Predicate*), and that there are no negative literals. Some of the predicates have only one clause in their definition and some two. The number of body literals ranges from one to three.

We show in Table 6.8 a population for *literal/argument* (6.4) derived from the predicate *subtype-of* from the hierarchical thesaurus IDB of Chapter 5, repeated in (6.5) for convenience:

subtype-of(Supertype, Subtype) :- is-a(Supertype, Subtype).          (6.5)
subtype-of(Supertype, Subtype) :-
    is-a(Supertype, Term), subtype-of(Term, Subtype).

We first exhibit in Table 6.7 some additional tuples for the predicate *pred/role* of Table 6.3 which represent the schema for the definition of the clause group *subtype-of*. Recall that a clause head is the schema of a view definition, and is therefore a relation schema.

Table 6.8 shows that there are two variable labels used in the first clause of *subtype-of*, namely *Supertype* and *Subtype*, while the second clause has three labels: *Supertype*, *Subtype* and *Term*. The join between *is-a* and *subtype-of* in the second clause is shown by the second argument of literal 1 and the first argument of literal 2 both having the label *Term*. That the two arguments are join compatible is shown in the population of *pred/role*. The value of the attribute *Domain* is *term* in the row where *Predicate* is *is-a* and *Role* is *narrower*, and also in the row where *Predicate* is *subtype-of* and *Role* is *supertype*.

**Table 6.6**  Sample population of *literal/calls* for hierarchical thesaurus application

| Group | Clause | Literal# | Called_Predicate | Negative | Aggregate |
|---|---|---|---|---|---|
| is-a | 1 | 1 | typed_broader | no | no |
| has-ingredient | 1 | 1 | typed_broader | no | no |
| instance-of | 1 | 1 | typed_broader | no | no |
| source-of | 1 | 1 | typed_related | no | no |
| similar | 1 | 1 | typed_related | no | no |
| similar | 2 | 1 | typed_related | no | no |
| similar-to | 1 | 1 | similar | no | no |
| similar-to | 2 | 1 | similar | no | no |
| similar-to | 2 | 2 | similar-to | no | no |
| subtype-of | 1 | 1 | is-a | no | no |
| subtype-of | 2 | 1 | is-a | no | no |
| subtype-of | 2 | 2 | subtype-of | no | no |
| source-of-ingredients | 1 | 1 | has-ingredient | no | no |
| source-of-ingredients | 1 | 2 | source-of | no | no |
| source-of-ingredients | 2 | 1 | has-ingredient | no | no |
| source-of-ingredients | 2 | 2 | one-of | no | no |
| source-of-ingredients | 2 | 3 | source-of | no | no |
| one-of | 1 | 1 | instance-of | no | no |
| one-of | 2 | 1 | instance-of | no | no |
| one-of | 2 | 2 | subtype-of | no | no |
| possible-use-for | 1 | 1 | similar-to | no | no |
| possible-use-for | 1 | 2 | has-ingredient | no | no |
| possible-use-for | 1 | 3 | instance-of | no | no |

**Table 6.7**  Additional sample population of *pred/role*

| Predicate | Role | Domain | Type |
|---|---|---|---|
| subtype-of | supertype | term | key |
| subtype-of | subtype | term | key |

Recall that the reason we need both *literal/calls* and *literal/argument* is that propositional predicates cannot have any arguments. A fully propositional knowledge-based system will have an empty *literal/argument*. Table 6.9 contains the population of *literal/calls* for the barbecue planner application in Example 10.1. Note that some of the body predicates are negative. Note that *literal/argument* does not

**Table 6.8** Sample population of *literal/argument*

| Group | Clause | Literal# | Arg# | Label | Called_Predicate | Role |
|-------|--------|----------|------|-------|------------------|------|
| subtype-of | 1 | 0 | 1 | Supertype | — | — |
| subtype-of | 1 | 0 | 2 | Subtype | — | — |
| subtype-of | 1 | 1 | 1 | Supertype | is-a | broader |
| subtype-of | 1 | 1 | 2 | Subtype | is-a | narrower |
| subtype-of | 2 | 0 | 1 | Supertype | — | — |
| subtype-of | 2 | 0 | 2 | Subtype | — | — |
| subtype-of | 2 | 1 | 1 | Supertype | is-a | broader |
| subtype-of | 2 | 1 | 2 | Term | is-a | narrower |
| subtype-of | 2 | 2 | 1 | Term | subtype-of | supertype |
| subtype-of | 2 | 2 | 2 | Subtype | subtype-of | subtype |

**Table 6.9** Sample population of *literal/calls* for barbecue planner application

| Group | Clause | Literal# | Called_Predicate | Negative | Aggregate |
|-------|--------|----------|------------------|----------|-----------|
| call_off | 1 | 1 | rain_forecast | no | no |
| all_foods | 1 | 1 | bob | no | no |
| vegetarian_fish | 1 | 1 | mary | no | no |
| meat | 1 | 1 | jim | no | no |
| lentil_burgers | 1 | 1 | vegetarian_fish | no | no |
| lentil_burgers | 1 | 2 | meat | yes | no |
| steak | 1 | 1 | meat | no | no |
| steak | 1 | 2 | vegetarian_fish | yes | no |
| fish | 1 | 1 | meat | no | no |
| fish | 1 | 2 | vegetarian_fish | no | no |
| hot_dogs | 1 | 1 | all_foods | no | no |

contain sufficient information to support aggregations and other built-ins. These and other necessary facilities have been omitted in the interests of clarity.

### 6.4.4   Repository for application model

Finally, everything in the knowledge and information models for an application must refer back to the application model for that application. It is therefore a good idea to store the application model in the repository so that the links between the parts of the other models and the application model can be represented. An information model for the area of the repository which holds the application model is shown in Figure 6.4. The central fact type is *statement establishes/derived from model entity*. The entity type *model entity* is a supertype (strictly, a generalization) of all of the entities in the repository which could be derived from the application model. These subtype entities include *group*, *relation*, *role* and *instance label*, among others.

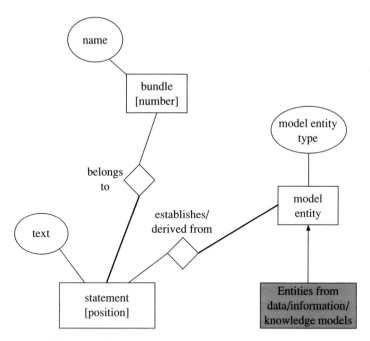

**Figure 6.4**  Model for application model.

**Table 6.10**  Sample population for *establishes*

| Bundle | Statement | Model_Entity | Type |
|--------|-----------|--------------|------|
| 4 | 1 | subtype-of | group |
| 1 | 3 | broader | predicate role |
| 1 | 2 | term | population |

A predicate containing the *establishes/derived from* relationship is

establishes(Bundle, Statement, Model_Entity, Type)                   (6.6)

Table 6.10 shows the connection to the application model for three of the model entities in the hierarchical thesaurus example (section 5.4), namely the group *subtype-of*, the predicate role *broader*, and the population *term*.

### 6.4.5   Discussion

In the previous sections, we have described the main outlines of a repository for storing the knowledge model for an application under construction. The repository will store

■ the application model;

■ schemas for the EDB;

■ populations for EDB predicates;

■ the IDB.

It should be clear that it is not difficult to extend the model to store all the material in Tables 6.1 and 6.2. For example, to better manage foreign key constraints the *predicate/role* relation needs to distinguish between different concatenated candidate keys, and to be able to group together attributes which are concatenated foreign keys. It is also not difficult to extend the model to store structures, which would be required for knowledge bases which included paths in transitive closure predicates, for example.

We should note that the repository so far defined does not help at all with the information modelling part of the knowledge acquisition task: information in the model is represented as relational schemas. A similar exercise must be undertaken to construct a repository suitable for managing an ERA diagram or a NIAM diagram.

We should also note that although the repository allows us to store and make enquiries about a deductive database, it is itself only a database, at least at this stage. So far, we have designed a database to help us manage a deductive database. Below, we will sketch some of the ways in which the repository can be extended to be a deductive database, and what benefits that extension might bring.

### 6.5   THE CASE TOOL

The repository described in the previous section is the core of the CASE tool. The tool itself consists of a set of applications built on the repository. Figure 6.5 illustrates a prototype tool, called the **Knowledge Analyst's Assistant** or **KAA**, designed to support construction of knowledge base systems using the methods of this text. The user has access to three classes of functions:

■ **model definition**, through which the repository is populated and updated;

■ **browser**, through which the structure of the application can be explored and the possible effects of changes examined;

■ **program generator**, through which the knowledge base can be turned into executable programs, for example in Prolog or SQL embedded in C.

The model definition functions of the KAA make use of the repository's data structure given in Figures 6.2–6.4 to make sure that the application specification is valid, mainly by enforcing foreign key dependencies between the repository's tables. These structural dependencies, illustrated in Figure 6.6, are employed by the browser to permit the knowledge engineer user to formulate queries, such as

■ **label occurrence**: Where does a given label appear in the specification? This can be interpreted as "what structures in the application would be affected if

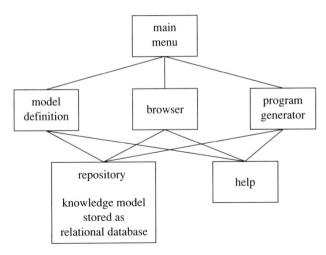

**Figure 6.5** The knowledge analyst's assistant.

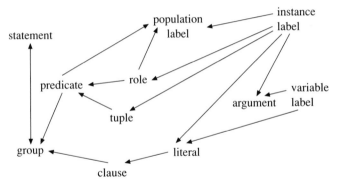

**Figure 6.6** Some structural dependencies in the repository.

that label were removed?". The first step in this query would be to find out what type the label is, then to search the tables containing labels of that type. If the label were a population label, then it might be found in the *Domain* attribute of the *pred/role* relation. If it were an instance label, it might be found in the *Label* attribute of the *literal/argument* relation.

■ **predicate relationship**: What attributes in one given derived predicate are dependent on which attributes from another given base predicate? This would involve joining *literal/argument* with the tuples of *pred/role* containing the EDB predicate schema, where the join attributes are *Predicate* and *Role* in *pred/role* and *Called_Predicate* and *Role* in *literal/argument*.

■ **grounding**: From what statements in the application model does a given label derive? To answer this query, one would first find out what model entities contain that label, then query the predicate *establishes*.

■ **join populations**: What populations appear as join attributes? This query requires a self-join on *literal/argument* to identify predicates and roles used as join attributes, then a join with *pred/role* to identify the populations via the *Domain* attribute.

Code can be generated from the repository by traversing the data structures and performing appropriate transliterations, or translations in some cases. For example, generation of Prolog code for the IDB can be done by a simple process from *literal/argument*. A propositional expert system shell can be populated from *literal/calls*. SQL *CREATE TABLE* statements can be generated from *pred/role*. Information necessary to generate SQL view definitions is contained in *literal/argument*, but creation of the SQL statements requires a more complex process than that which creates statements in Prolog. All of these translators are applications in the CASE tool which work¯from the repository.

Having a CASE tool based on a rich data structure such as we have described is a great advantage to the knowledge engineer. The application can be specified in the tool, and the tool's browsing and query capabilities used to ensure the consistency of the specification. When the engineer is satisfied with the specification, the code generator can produce a version of the system which can run in the appropriate execution environment.

Further, since the knowledge is represented in a Horn clause form, one of the applications in the CASE tool can be a Horn clause interpreter such as described in Chapter 2 or Chapter 4, which can execute the specification. The interpreter can be instrumented to allow the knowledge engineer to follow the dynamic behaviour of the specification in some detail. The system can be not only developed, but largely tested in a maintenance environment using the CASE tool.

Since the code executed in the production environment is derived from the same data structures as used by the interpreters in the maintenance environment, accuracy of testing can be ensured. Further, the maintenance environment can be used to help identify errors discovered in the production environment, without requiring the knowledge engineer to examine the production code. It is necessary only to populate the maintenance environment with sufficient data to reproduce the problem.

## 6.6   REPOSITORY AS A DEDUCTIVE DATABASE

The repository described so far in this chapter has been a database, used to assist in building a deductive database application. However, a CASE tool is an information system, and, like any other, can be at least partly specified as a deductive database, using the methods of Chapter 5.

First, the queries of the previous section can be pre-packaged for the knowledge engineer as view definitions, rather than having the knowledge engineer use the query language to pose them as *ad hoc* queries. The views *label occurrence*, *predicate relationship*, *grounding* and *join populations* could be expressed in SQL in the conventional way, or alternatively in datalog.

Secondly, the repository has recursive data structures, including *subtype/supertype* and the *calls* relationship, so that a recursive view definition would be needed, for example, to determine whether two roles were join compatible or what predicates were dependent directly or indirectly on a given predicate.

Finally, there are a number of important integrity constraints which are naturally expressed in a deductive database. One is the requirement that the IDB be stratified. This constraint can be expressed on the transitive closure of the *literal/calls* predicate as

calls_closure(Predicate, Clause, Literal, Called, Negative) :-       (6.7)
    literal/calls(Predicate, Clause, Literal, Called, Negative).
calls_closure(Predicate, Clause, Literal, Called, Negative) :-
    literal/calls(Predicate, Clause, Literal, Intermediate, Negative1),
    calls_closure(Intermediate, Clause1, Literal1, Called, Negative2),
    negation_dominates(Negative1, Negative2, Negative).
    negation_dominates(yes, _, yes).
    negation_dominates(_, yes, yes).
    negation_dominates(no, no, no).

    non_stratified :- calls_closure(Predicate, _, _, Predicate, yes).

The predicate *calls_closure* of (6.7) is the transitive closure of the *literal/calls* predicate. Since in the definition of stratification given in Chapter 4, an arc in the dependency graph is negative if any of the occurrences of the second predicate are in negative literals in the body of any of the clauses of the first predicate, the recursive clause for *calls_closure* uses the subsidiary predicate *negation_dominates* to ensure that the variable *Negative* is bound to *no* only if neither arc is negative. Finally, the integrity constraint predicate *non_stratified* is true only if a predicate appears negatively in its own definition, directly or indirectly.

Other integrity constraints, all of which involve recursive predicates, include:

■ joins must be on type-compatible roles;

■ subgoal literals must agree in number and type-compatibility of argument roles;

■ clauses must be numbered consecutively in a group and literals numbered consecutively in a clause;

■ stratification for negation and aggregation.

## 6.7 SUMMARY

This chapter has argued that a systematic approach to knowledge acquisition is made easier by the use of a CASE tool. It has then sketched a CASE tool to support the knowledge representation strategy of Chapter 5. This CASE tool is an information system which is a tool for building information systems. More particularly, the CASE tool sketched is a deductive database which is a tool to help build a deductive database.

## 6.8   FURTHER READING

The material in this chapter is drawn partly from Debenham (1989), and partly adapted from Debenham and Lindley (1990), Lindley (1990) and Lindley and Debenham (1990).

## 6.9   EXERCISES

6.1   What fact types in the model for data and information of Figure 6.2 have roles which can be populated by entities of type *label*?

6.2   Create a relational scheme for the entity type *label* of Figure 6.2 which supports the indicated subtype structure, showing the attributes from which the definitions of the subtypes are derived.

6.3   Write down a datalog query and the corresponding SQL query which will identify all tuples stored in the repository derived from Figure 6.2 which contain entity instances of type *label*.

6.4   Populate the schema of *literal/argument* (Table 6.8) with the predicate definition

    ancestor(Older, Younger) :- parent(Older, Younger).
    ancestor(Older, Younger) :-
                    parent(Older, Intermediate),
                    ancestor(Intermediate, Younger).

6.5   Translate the following population of *literal/argument* to standard Prolog notation:

| Group | Clause | Literal# | Arg# | Label | Called_Predicate | Role |
|-------|--------|----------|------|-------|------------------|------|
| sg | 1 | 0 | 1 | X | — | — |
| sg | 1 | 0 | 2 | X | — | — |
| sg | 2 | 0 | 1 | X | — | — |
| sg | 2 | 0 | 2 | Y | — | — |
| sg | 2 | 1 | 1 | P | parent | older |
| sg | 2 | 1 | 2 | X | parent | younger |
| sg | 2 | 2 | 1 | Q | parent | older |
| sg | 2 | 2 | 2 | Y | parent | younger |
| sg | 2 | 3 | 1 | P | sg | person-1 |
| sg | 2 | 3 | 2 | Q | sg | person-2 |

6.6   How would you identify a join in *literal/argument*?

6.7   Write a query in datalog and in SQL which would identify the populations which appear as join attributes. How would you test for join compatibility?

CHAPTER SEVEN

# Knowledge quality

In this chapter, we look at knowledge-based systems from a software engineering viewpoint, emphasizing factors which make them easier to maintain over the entire software life cycle. These factors are organized as a number of quality principles.

## 7.1 QUALITY AND MAINTAINABILITY

As engineers, we wish to construct information systems which are of high quality. There are several aspects to quality. First of all, it must be suitable for its purpose. Suitability for purpose depends on understanding the work processes of the organizations and people who are intended to use the system, and is captured in the system specifications. This aspect of quality is addressed by the systematic procedures recommended in Chapters 5 and 6 for constructing the application model. An important aspect closely related to suitability for purpose is ease of use. Ease of use is largely in the province of human–computer interaction (HCI). HCI principles are generic across information technology, and are not addressed specifically in this text.

Once a system has been specified, then it must be constructed. Quality in this aspect is manifested as correctness of implementation – the system actually behaves as the specification says it should. An important way to achieve correctness is to implement the system using high-level data structures, with a rich set of mathematically well-understood operations on them. The use of deductive database technology assists correctness in this way. Further assistance is provided by the use of software tools (CASE) to assist in the construction and verification of the implementation. A good high-level language supported by a good CASE tool can automatically generate the lower-level implementations needed actually to execute the application on the chosen platform, so that the object program is correctly derived from a high-level description. A second aspect of quality closely related to the implementation is resource consumption. A system to be effective must respond quickly enough and consume an economically justified amount of memory and computing power. The long-continued decline in costs of computing power has meant that resource consumption, particularly response time, is relevant for only a small fraction of the functions of the application. Often the programs which convert the high-level specification to a low-level implementation can be instructed to optimize the implementation. For example, database systems can construct indexes to speed processing of certain classes of queries.

A system which passes the suitability for purpose and correctness/efficiency quality criteria is then subject to the problem of maintainability. It is well-established that a successful computer system becomes deeply embedded in the organization using it, and therefore must adapt as the organization evolves. Even if it does not change in functionality, it must adapt as the underlying technology changes. A major thrust of the discipline of software engineering is the design of systems in such a way as to facilitate change. This chapter is devoted to quality principles related to maintainability.

A piece of knowledge from the application domain is frequently represented as a complex object in the computer domain, for example as a group of clauses or even several inter-defined predicates, each of which is a group of clauses. In the computer domain, a complex object is represented by a set of **structural links** between primitive objects. Primitive objects are things like predicate names, roles, subgoals, variable names; while the structural links are given by the syntax of the knowledge expressions: the predicate name in the clause head determines the predicate being defined, variables of the same name in the same clause show equality relationships between roles, the predicate name in a subgoal is a link to the predicate definition. The syntactic structure for Horn clauses is detailed in Chapter 2. A more detailed representation of this syntax as a relational schema is given in Chapter 6.

The operator of a knowledge-based system, or any system for that matter, performs operations whose meaning lies in the application domain. The objects in the computer domain upon which the operator acts therefore take their meaning from the application domain, and the application domain determines a set of semantic relationships or **semantic links** between the computer objects. A change in the computer system originating in a change in the organization will be expressed in terms of the application domain, while a change originating in a change of technology must preserve the semantic relationships between the computer objects.

The programmers who create and change computer systems have the assistance of computer-based tools which help manage the structural links between the primitive computer objects. These tools are at least editors and compilers, and can be very elaborate integrated programming support environments, such as described in Chapter 6.

If changes are requested in terms of semantic links and the programmer has tools to manage structural links then the potential for error is high where there are semantic links not represented by structural links. We will call such semantic links **unsupported**. Unsupported semantic links are a maintenance hazard. We will say that knowledge is of high quality from a maintainability point of view if it has no unsupported semantic links. The general principle is:

Represent one piece of knowledge in one structure and in one structure only.

## 7.2 NORMALIZED INFORMATION

The reader is assumed to be familiar with the concept of normalized relational schemas. Relational schemas are normalized to avoid **update anomalies**, in which an update to the relational tables fails to preserve semantic properties of the data. We will review the standard normal forms for information as an introduction to the concepts of this chapter. These normal forms are properties of the relational schema, which in a CASE tool are represented by (are stored in) tables in the repository. The functional associations are between what are called **domains** in Chapter 6, and the structures which represent the functional associations are stored in the EDB predicate *pred/role*.

### 7.2.1 First normal form: an association must be functional

A table is in first normal form if it is flat. The primary key determines exactly one value for each of the attributes. For example, if a student has grades for several subjects, each subject is represented in the table. The schema

student(Student#, List_of_Grades) (7.1)

is not in first normal form. A first normal form representation is

student(Student#, Subject, Grade) (7.2)

If an object in the application domain is represented as a set of functional associations, then each of these associations must be explicitly represented in the tables. The semantic links represented by the functional associations between computer objects are therefore supported by the table structure. The semantic object in (7.1) and (7.2) is the relationship between students and their grades, which in (7.2) is supported by the *Subject* attribute being part of the relation's primary key.

### 7.2.2 Second normal form: no sub-functional associations

A relational schema is in second normal form if every non-key attribute is functionally dependent on the entire primary key. This normal form is of course relevant only to relations whose primary key is composite. For example, the schema

student(Student#, Student_Name, Subject, Grade) (7.3)

has the composite key (Student#, Subject), but the attribute *Student_Name* is functionally dependent only on Student#. A second normal form representation of (7.3) is

student(Student#, Student_Name)                                              (7.4)
studies(Student#, Subject, Grade)

The relevant semantic link is that, for a given student identified by *Student#*, there must be a unique value for *Student_Name*. In the unnormalized form (7.3), there may be several instances of *Student_Name* associated with a single value of *Student#*. The requirement that these instances all be the same is not supported by structural links in the relational model. In (7.4), there is only one instance of *Student_Name* for each instance of *Student#*.

## 7.2.3   Third normal form: no transitive dependencies

A relational schema is in third normal form if there are no functional associations between non-key attributes. For example, consider the schema

enrolled(Student#, Subject, InCharge)                                        (7.5)

where *InCharge* indicates the lecturer-in-charge. There may be many students enrolled in a subject, but only one lecturer-in-charge. An equivalent normalized schema is

enrolled(Student#, Subject)                                                  (7.6)
inCharge(Subject, Lecturer)

The semantic link in (7.5) is that there is only one lecturer-in-charge for a subject, which is unsupported by structural links since there are many copies of it which are unconnected in the relational model. In (7.6), there is only one copy, so the semantic link is supported by a structural link.

## 7.2.4   Fourth normal form: no multi-valued dependencies

A relation is in fourth normal form if it has a composite key and its key attributes have no multi-valued dependencies. This is equivalent to saying that the projection of the relation onto its key attributes cannot be decomposed into the join of two relations. For example, suppose in an educational establishment we were to build a database allowing us to contact a student at any hour of the day if an emergency occurs. This relationship might be expressed as a ternary fact type in NIAM as *Student might be found at Hour attending Subject*. Suppose in addition that we knew the hours that the student was attending and the subjects in which the student was enrolled, so that for each hour the student was in attendance we generated a tuple for each subject in which the student was enrolled. This situation could arise in early stages of scheduling tutorial groups for a group of subjects: the students would nominate hours they are available for tutorials in the subjects in which they are enrolled, but the subjects have not yet been allocated to tutorial hours. This relation could be expressed as

(Student, Hour, Subject) = (Student, Hour) $\bowtie$ (Student, Subject)          (7.7)

and if it could be so expressed, it should be.

Here, the semantic links are that for each student and hour there must be a tuple with that student, hour and each different subject, which is clearly easily violated on update. In the decomposed form, this semantic link is supported by a structural link: any update to either of the two relations will preserve the semantic property.

### 7.2.5  Fifth normal form: eliminate join dependencies

Fifth normal form is a generalization of fourth normal form. A multiple-valued dependency is a join dependency between two relations. Some relations exist which can be decomposed into the join of three or more relations, but not two. The example in (7.7) can be extended. Suppose that in addition to the hours the student is available and the subjects in which the student is enrolled, we know what hours each subject is scheduled. For example, we may have now allocated tutorial times to subjects by choosing schedules which satisfy as many students as possible, but have still not allocated students to tutorial sessions. The example is now decomposed as:

(Student, Hour, Subject) =                                        (7.8)
   (Student, Hour) $\bowtie$
   (Student, Subject) $\bowtie$
   (Subject, Hour)

Fifth normal form states that if a relation can be decomposed into the lossless join of several relations, then it should be so decomposed. It is thus a generalization of fourth normal form.

The semantic links are constraints on student, hour and subject: not all populations for the table are permissible. The structural links provided by the decomposition support the semantic links in the same way as those in fourth normal form do: any update to the decomposed relations will preserve the semantic constraint.

### 7.3  QUALITY PRINCIPLES FOR DATA, INFORMATION AND KNOWLEDGE

Deductive database technology is an extension of relational database technology with respect to aspects which are conventionally implemented in imperative programming languages. Design for maintainability in the world of programming is part of the discipline of **software engineering**. There is a variety of principles in software engineering which are analogous to normalization in the database world. These principles can be applied to the design of knowledge bases. Some of them are like data normalization in that they are syntactic representations of constraints imposed by the application on the primitive computer objects (data normalization is largely about design of tables to take into account functional associations). Others are more semantic in nature: making sure that a concept in the application domain is supported in the computer domain.

In Chapter 5, we described the design of an information system in terms of data, information and knowledge. In this section, we look at software engineering aspects of this design, under the guise of principles for quality of data, information and knowledge.

### 7.3.1  Quality principles for data

*Principle D.1: One object, one label*

An object in the application domain should be represented in the computer domain by a single label, or a unique structure of labels if the object is not represented primitively. Conversely, a label or structure of labels in the computer domain should always refer to the same object in the application domain. This principle applies to relation and predicate names, as well as instance labels. The semantic link supported by this structure is the preservation of the correspondence between the computer objects and the domain objects.

*Principle D.2: Labels should be minimal*

The primitive labels used should not be decomposable into semantically meaningful parts. For example, if a university subject code is *CS317*, where the parts have the meaning

CS – Department of Computer Science
3 – third-year subject
1 – information systems subject
7 – identifier

the code should be represented as a tuple of the more primitive labels.

The same principle applies to relation and predicate names. If a predicate has one form which applies to undergraduate students and (possibly) other forms applying to other types of student, it should be called something like

pname(undergraduate, . . . )                                          (7.9)

rather than something like

undergraduate_pname                                                   (7.10)

The situation illustrated in (7.9) and (7.10) is similar to the justification for tagged variant records in Pascal.

The semantic link supported by this structure is that primitive objects in the application domain are represented by primitive objects in the computer domain.

*Principle D.3: Compound keys should be minimal*

If there are several candidate keys for a relation, unless there is compelling reason to the contrary, the one with fewer attributes should be chosen. The semantic link supported here is economy of object representation.

## 7.3.2 Quality principles for information

Besides the principle that all relations should be normalized according to the standard normal forms, there are several additional, more semantic, principles.

*Principle I.0: Labels and population names satisfy data quality principles*

We must get the data right before we can design the information.

*Principle I.1: No redundant domains*

The head of a clause in a predicate definition should contain no variables which do not appear in its body. In Chapter 4, a clause fulfilling this principle was called **safe**. Most of the results in deductive database theory assume that the predicates are all defined using safe clauses. This ensures that any tuples generated for that predicate in its bottom-up evaluation have ground values for all attributes.

More prosaically, predicates should follow the second standard normal form in their arguments. This is not a hard and fast rule, since predicate definitions are frequently used to define views, which are often not normalized. However, in this case the definition of the predicate should reflect the joins made in the definition of the de-normalized view. For example, the relation schema

$$\text{student/result(St\#, Sname, Sub\#, Grade)} \tag{7.11}$$

would be rejected in the information model as it is not in second normal form (*Sname* is functionally dependent only on *St#*). On the other hand, that set of attributes would naturally appear on an output report. Suppose that schema (7.11) were a predicate whose definition is

$$\text{student/result(St\#, Sname, Sub\#, Grade) :-} \tag{7.12}$$
$$\text{student(St\#, Sname),}$$
$$\text{result(St\#, Sub\#, assignment, Mark1),}$$
$$\text{result(St\#, Sub\#, exam, Mark2),}$$
$$\text{Grade is Mark1 + Mark2.}$$

Definition (7.12) should be rejected in favour of

$$\text{student/result(St\#, Sname, Sub\#, Grade) :-} \tag{7.13}$$
$$\text{student(St\#, Sname),}$$
$$\text{total\_result(St\#, Sub\#, Grade).}$$

```
total_result(St#, Sub#, Grade) :-
    result(St#, Sub#, assignment, Mark1),
    result(St#, Sub#, exam, Mark2),
    Grade is Mark1 + Mark2.
```

The semantic link supported here is that relationships which are meaningful in the application domain are explicitly represented in the computer domain. This principle is closely related to the knowledge quality principle K.4 described below.

### Principle I.2: Real object represented once only

This principle is an elaboration of principle D.1 (one object/one label). Its point is that if there is a semantic relationship between labels, it should be explicitly represented. For example, in a payroll application, it is usually necessary to deduct income tax from a person's wage. This leads to an output report defined by a predicate looking something like

$$emp/pay(Emp\#, Gross\_pay, Tax, Net\_pay) \qquad (7.14)$$

In a manual payroll system, the tax is frequently (at least partly) calculated using a table whose schema is something like

$$pay/tax(Gross\_pay, Tax) \qquad (7.15)$$

Table (7.15) is created from a rule provided by the taxation office which involves application objects such as thresholds and marginal tax rates. This rule expresses the implicit functional association between *Gross_pay* and *Tax*. In the sense of this principle, *Gross_pay* is represented twice, the second time in the value of *Tax*.

If one of the underlying application objects changes, the table must be re-created. There is much less possibility of error if the knowledge used in calculating tax is explicitly represented as a computation rule. If for reasons of computational efficiency in the final implementation the tax is computed using a table such as in (7.15), this table should be computed from the knowledge in the rule. The table thus does not appear in the conceptual design of the system as considered in this text.

This principle applies to complex structures such as the *ancestor* relation described in Chapter 2 as the transitive closure of the *parent* relation. Even if in the final implementation the tuples of *ancestor* are explicitly represented, the predicate should be expressed in the manner described in Chapter 2.

### Principle I.3: Predicate should not be semantically decomposable

In the relational schema, it sometimes happens that there are attributes from semantically different classes which are functionally associated with one attribute. For example, the University information system might have both academic and extra-curricular information about a student. It is better to represent the student in two distinct tables, one for each class of attribute. There may, of course, be query-type predicates which combine information from these semantically different classes.

These predicates should be represented as joins, in a similar way to the illustration in principle I.1 above. The semantic link supported is that distinctions visible in the application domain should be explicitly represented in the computer domain.

### Principle I.4: Keep subtypes separate

An entity type frequently has a relationship with another entity type, but only a subset of the population named by the entity type can participate. This situation is recognized in conceptual modelling by the use of *subtypes* to designate the relevant populations. For example, a University database may have an entity type *Person*, which has subtypes *Student* and *Staff*. Those persons who are students have, for example, course enrolment, while those persons who are staff have, for example, academic rank. It is common in the relational implementation of conceptual models to absorb subtypes into the supertype, resulting in optional attributes. For example, the situation described in this paragraph might result in the schema

person(ID#, Student/Staff, Course, Academic_Rank)                (7.16)

where Course and Academic_Rank are both optional.

This procedure results in a predicate definition which contains an implied if-then-else. Recall that the concern of this chapter is not the implementation of the knowledge-based system, but its specification. We are therefore essentially extending the conceptual model. The EDB predicate definitions used in the knowledge analysis are condensations of the conceptual model, not proposed implementations. We would therefore not use a representation like (7.16), but rather keep the subtypes separate, as in

person(student, ID#, Course)                (7.17)
person(staff, ID#, Academic_Rank)

Most database systems permit view definitions, so that even if the internal scheme of *person* is (7.16), its external scheme can be (7.17).

In general, under this principle predicate definitions should not contain optional arguments which have any systematic basis. However, similarly to the other information quality principles, a query type may contain systematic optional arguments, but its definition should reflect the semantically significant structure.

This principle is related to data quality principle D.2. The semantic link supported is that distinctions important in the application domain are explicitly represented in the computer domain.

## 7.3.3 Quality principles for knowledge

Knowledge is represented as predicate definitions which consist of clause groups. There are several kinds of functional associations connected with knowledge, so that there are several different sorts of quality principles.

First, the predicate has a perfect model, so can be viewed as a relation.

Secondly, we saw in Chapter 5 that the predicate defines a function from the tuple spaces of the predicates occurring in the clause bodies into the tuple space of the clause head. This is the function computed by the semi-naive algorithm in the course of computing the perfect model, as described in Chapter 4.

Thirdly, a theorem proving mechanism based on, for example, the resolution principle, of which the Prolog inference engine described in Chapter 2 is a specialization, can map one expression of a clause group into another. Some of these are considered systematically in Chapters 8, 9 and 10.

Knowledge quality principles are divided into two classes: one relating to individual clauses (principles K.0–K.4) and one relating to clause groups (principles G.0–G.4).

### Principle K.0: Predicates should satisfy information quality principles

Since a clause head defines a relation and can therefore be viewed as information, all the information quality principles apply.

### Principle K.1: No "magic number" labels

A fundamental principle of programming is that a constant should be assigned to a variable with a descriptive name whose scope is co-extensive with its scope in the application domain. All uses of that constant should be instances of that variable label. This is recommended even if the constant is used only once. The possibility always exists that as the software changes, it may need to be altered, or used again.

For example, the clause (7.18) expressing the relationship between selling price and buying price:

```
item/sell(Item#, Selling_Price) :-                           (7.18)
    item/buy(Item#, Buy_Price),
    Selling_Price is Buying_Price * 1.2
```

should be expressed as

```
item/sell(Item#, Selling_Price) :-                           (7.19)
    item/buy(Item#, Buy_Price),
    markup_factor(Markup),
    Selling_Price is Buying_Price * Markup

markup_factor(1.2).
```

The constant 1.2, which is the markup factor, is globally available in (7.19), and is also clearly documented.

There is sometimes a need for constant labels in clause definitions, however, as the clause may be functionally dependent on the label. In (7.20), the clause is specific to the class of product designated by the label *spare_part*:

```
item/sell(Item#, Selling_Price) :-                                    (7.20)
    item/type(Item#, spare_part),
    item/buy(Item#, Buy_Price),
    markup_factor(Markup),
    Selling_Price is Buying_Price * Markup

markup_factor(1.2).
```

Other types of product may have different formulas for computing selling price. This use is analogous to the use of tags in variant types in *Pascal*.

The semantic link supported is the explicit representation of application domain semantics in the computer domain.

## Principle K.2: No redundant predicates

A typical clause body consists of several goal predicates. It is possible that some of them are redundant in the sense that their removal has no effect on the perfect model. This redundancy can have several sources. One predicate may be implicit in another. For example, in (7.21) the type predicate *student(Student#)* is implicit in the predicate *studies(Student#, cs317)* if there is a referential integrity constraint on the *Student#* attribute of the *studies* relation. The expression in (7.22) is preferred:

```
my_student(Student#) :-                                               (7.21)
    student(Student#),
    studies(Student#, cs317).

my_student(Student#) :-                                               (7.22)
    studies(Student#, cs317).
```

A predicate may be semantically redundant. For example, in (7.23) if the *studied* predicate is true, it is expected that both of the other predicates are true. Furthermore, it would be expected that if someone understood perfect models and magic sets, then that person would be able to pass the subject *cs317*. Although there is no logical necessity, the *studied* predicate contributes nothing from the domain point of view. The form (7.24) is preferred:

```
understands_deductive_database(Student#) :-                           (7.23)
    studied(Student#, cs317)
    understands_perfect_models(Student#),
    understands_magic_sets(Student#).

understands_deductive_database(Student#) :-                           (7.24)
    understands_perfect_models(Student#),
    understands_magic_sets(Student#).
```

The principle is to avoid representing semantic links which are redundant in the application domain.

*Principle K.3: Use defined knowledge where it exists*

In a complex application domain, knowledge is generally built up by aggregating elementary knowledge into larger and larger chunks. Particularly if the knowledge comes from a number of different sources it often happens that the same aggregate is defined several times, sometimes explicitly and sometimes implicitly. Care should be taken to ensure that each definition appears once only. As knowledge is added to the model, the analyst should take advantage of already existing definitions. In particular, a complex aggregate of knowledge might be suspected to have sub-aggregates which are already defined. For example, if we have the definition (7.25), then the knowledge (7.26) should take advantage of (7.25), resulting in the preferred definition (7.27):

    account/balance(Account#, Balance) :-                                (7.25)
        account/revenue(Account#, Revenue),
        account/expenses(Account#, Expenses),
        Balance is Revenue – Expenses.

    account/tax(Account#, Tax) :-                                        (7.26)
        account/revenue(Account#, Revenue),
        account/expenses(Account#, Expenses),
        Tax is (Revenue – Expenses) * Rate.

    account/tax(Account#, Tax) :-                                        (7.27)
        account/balance(Account#, Balance),
        Tax is Balance * Rate.

The principle is that each semantic link should be supported once only.

*Principle K.4: Express implicit knowledge*

It often happens in a complex application domain that a piece of knowledge is expressed as an aggregate of a large number of smaller pieces. It is common in this situation that the aggregate has sub-aggregates which are meaningful in the application domain, but which have not been articulated by the domain experts. Since changes in the application domain are generally expressed in terms of existing knowledge, it is an advantage if the meaningful sub-aggregates are made explicit. For example, if we have the expression (7.26), it is probably better to create the sub-aggregate (7.25) so that (7.26) can be expressed as (7.27). This differs from principle K.3 in that the sub-aggregate (7.25) must have already been recognized in order to apply principle K.3, whereas to use principle K.4 the knowledge expressed in (7.25) must not have been explicitly recognized previously.

The principle is that every semantic link should be made explicit and supported.

*Principle G.0: The clauses in a group satisfy the knowledge clause quality principles*

This and following principles apply to the entire clause group comprising a predicate definition. Each clause in the group should satisfy all the previous quality principles.

## Principle G.1: No redundant clauses

If a clause in a group can be removed without changing the perfect model, then it should be removed. For example, consider the definition (7.28) of the *same_generation* predicate, which is true if two persons are the same distance from a common ancestor, with the proviso that a person is of the same generation as him/herself:

same_generation(Person, Person) :- person(Person).  (7.28)
same_generation(Person1, Person2) :-
    parent(P, Person1),
    parent(P, Person2).
same_generation(Person1, Person2) :-
    parent(P1, Person1),
    parent(P2, Person2),
    same_generation(P1, P2).

Some reflection should satisfy the reader that the second clause is redundant. Bindings of *Person1, Person2* and *P* satisfying this clause will also satisfy the third clause, taking into account the first. The knowledge in (7.28) should therefore be expressed as:

same_generation(Person, Person) :- person(Person).  (7.29)
same_generation(Person1, Person2) :-
    parent(P1, Person1),
    parent(P2, Person2),
    same_generation(P1, P2).

This sort of situation often occurs in the early stages of expressing knowledge involving navigation through complex structures. When an expression is found which is correct, it should be examined for redundancy.

The principle is that each piece of domain knowledge should be supported once only in the computer domain.

## Principle G.2: Each tuple derived from the group should have a unique derivation

Recall that the perfect model of a predicate is a relation, each of whose tuples is a set of bindings of the variables in the head predicate. If each set of bindings is generated in only one way (has only one proof tree), then the built-in *bagof* described in Chapter 2 returns a set of solutions, so has the same effect as *all_solutions*.

One way in which a tuple could have several derivations is if the group violates principle G.1. We have already noted that every solution for the second clause of (7.28) is also a solution for the third. Principle G.1 is not strong enough, however. Consider (7.30), which might be used to generate a mailing list for a University library combining the student and staff databases:

library/mail(Name, Address) :-  (7.30)
    student(_, Name, Address).
library/mail(Name, Address) :-
    staff(_, Name, Address).

Neither clause can be removed, so principle G.1 is satisfied. However, if a person happens to be both a student and a member of staff, then that person will receive the mailing twice, since that person's name and address is derived from each clause. In practice, violation of this principle is often subtle and frequently due to semantic redundancies. One way to resolve the problem in (7.30) is shown by

> library/mail(Name, Address) :-                                                        (7.31)
>     student(_, Name, Address).
> library/mail(Name, Address) :-
>     staff(X, Name, Address),
>     not student(X, Name, Address).

Principle G.2 applies only in groups in which, for each clause, all variables occurring in the clause are functionally dependent on the variables occurring in the clause head. For example, if each person has exactly one parent, then (7.29) satisfies principle G.2. Otherwise, (7.29) is a projection onto non-key attributes, and one would expect that a tuple would occur more than once. Principle G.2 does not apply.

Principle G.2 always applies to negative predicates, since a negative predicate in a clause contributes to the perfect model only if it has no solutions at all. Negative predicates therefore always satisfy principle G.2 vacuously.

The principle is similar to the principle governing G.1, i.e. that each piece of domain knowledge should be supported once only in the computer domain.

## Principle G.3: Group should be logically irreducible

A group could satisfy principle G.1 but still be logically redundant. A clause group is a statement in the first-order predicate calculus, and there are many ways of simplifying such statements using automatic theorem proving principles, usually based on a more general form of the resolution principle touched on in Chapter 2. A clause group satisfies principle G.3 if it cannot be transformed into another equivalent group with fewer clauses.

This principle should be thought of as an in-principle rather than in-practice rule, since there does not exist any general method guaranteeing to prove that a group cannot be simplified. There are a number of specific classes of transformation, for which it is possible to prove that a group cannot be simplified by that particular class. Many of these classes require an exponential amount of computation, however, and in any case most of them are outside the scope of this text.

One useful and fairly straightforward class of transformations is *folding* and *unfolding*, described in Chapter 9. By way of illustration, we show the simplification of a different representation of the *same_generation* predicate. The representation in (7.32) assumes that there are at most three generations, and is non-recursive:

> 1. same_generation(Person, Person) :- person(Person).                                 (7.32)
> 2. same_generation(Person1, Person2) :-
>        parent(P, Person1),
>        parent(P, Person2).

3. same_generation(Person1, Person2) :-
   grandparent(P, Person1),
   grandparent(P, Person2).
4. grandparent(Older, Younger) :-
   parent(Older, Intermediate).
   parent(Intermediate, Younger).

The principle of unfolding allows us to replace clauses 3 and 4 of (7.32) by

5. same_generation(Person1, Person2) :-                                    (7.33)
   parent(P, Intermediate_1), parent(Intermediate_1, Person1),
   parent(P, Intermediate_2), parent(Intermediate_2, Person2).

The principle of folding then allows us to combine (7.33) with clause 2 of (7.32), resulting in the group (7.34), which is logically equivalent to (7.32), but has fewer clauses:

1. same_generation(Person, Person) :- person(Person).                      (7.34)
6. same_generation(Person1, Person2) :-
   parent(Intermediate_1, Person1),
   parent(Intermediate_2, Person2),
   same_generation(Intermediate_1, Intermediate_2).

Note by the way that (7.34) is exactly the same as (7.29), except that the variables have different names. The logical transformations have changed a non-recursive definition into a recursive one.

The principle is similar to that governing G.1 and G.2, i.e. that each piece of domain knowledge should be supported once only in the computer domain.

## *Principle G.4: A group should be semantically coherent*

This principle is analogous to principles K.4, I.3 and I.4. If a predicate definition has a number of clauses, it is often the case that the clauses form semantically significant subgroups. For example, in (7.35) two of the clauses relate to students and the other two to staff:

library_loan_term(ID#, Weeks) :-                                           (7.35)
   student(ID#, undergraduate), Weeks = 2.
library_loan_term(ID#, Weeks) :-
   student(ID#, graduate), Weeks = 4.
library_loan_term(ID#, Weeks) :-
   staff(ID#, academic), Weeks = 13.
library_loan_term(ID#, Weeks) :-
   staff(ID#, general), Weeks = 2.

The fact that the subgroups are semantically significant indicates a semantic link. This link should be supported by expressing (7.35) as, for example, (7.36), where the subgroups are explicit:

library_loan_term(ID#, Weeks) :-                                            (7.36)
   loan_term(student, ID#, Weeks).
library_loan_term(ID#, Weeks) :-
   loan_term(staff, ID#, Weeks).

loan_term(student, ID#, Weeks) :-
   student(ID#, undergraduate), Weeks = 2.
loan_term(student, ID#, Weeks) :-
   student(ID#, graduate), Weeks = 4.
loan_term(staff, ID#, Weeks) :-
   staff(ID#, academic), Weeks = 13.
loan_term(staff, ID#, Weeks) :-
   staff(ID#, general), Weeks = 2.

The principle is that semantic links should be supported. Note that the revision of (7.35) has also altered the predicate names to satisfy principle D.2.

## 7.4   EXAMPLE

The hierarchical thesaurus example of section 5.4 satisfies these quality principles. Some comments on it may make the principles clearer.

First, the data. Even though the data labels are sometimes phrases (e.g. *onion soup*), they are treated as atomic by the system, so satisfy principle D.2.

Most of the information quality principles, especially principles I.2 and I.3, tend to be satisfied because the information modelling methods encourage simple and non-redundant representations. Principle I.4 is the reason why the design kept the typed broader and related terms separate from the general untyped broader and related terms.

The only labels which appear in the knowledge are the type names which appear in *is-a*, *has-ingredient*, etc. These predicates make the data labels more accessible for the construction of more complex knowledge. The definitions are functionally dependent on them, so the knowledge satisfies principle K.1.

These predicates, as well as the predicates *similar* and *one-of* which do not appear on the knowledge diagram, are needed to satisfy principle K.4. Further, *generally-broader*, *has-ingredient* and *instance-of* appear on the knowledge diagram since they satisfy principle K.3, being actually used more than once. The predicates *is-a*, *source-of* and *similar-to* appear on the knowledge diagram even though they are used only once since they are conceptually so similar to *has-ingredient* and *instance-of* that it seems natural to represent them in the same way. On the other hand, *similar* and *one-of* seem to be specific to the definition of *similar-to* and *source-of* respectively, so they were left off the knowledge diagram to avoid clutter.

## 7.5   DISCUSSION

Maintainability quality is a process occurring logically after knowledge has been acquired and verified: a system must be suitable and correct before maintainability is a problem. In addition, most of the principles D.x, I.x, K.x and G.x are not algorithmically verifiable. Like most principles of software engineering, their satisfaction is a matter of judgment by the analyst or knowledge engineer with the cooperation of the domain experts where semantic issues are relevant.

As a rule of thumb, one should be suspicious if any of the following situations is observed in the evolving knowledge base (relevant principles indicated):

- complicated labels for data, relations or predicates (D.2);
- relations with lots of attributes (I.3, I.4);
- lots of relations with similar attributes (I.3, I.4);
- labels appearing in clauses (K.1);
- clauses with lots of subgoals (K.3, K.4);
- collections of subgoals appearing in more than one clause (K.4);
- groups with lots of clauses (G.1, G.4).

All of these situations can be identified in the CASE tool by queries on the repository, so that although the quality principles cannot be applied automatically, the tools used to assist the knowledge engineer in designing a knowledge-based system can be of some help in achieving a high-quality design.

Keep in mind that knowledge (and information) modelling is the representation of functional associations between populations of atomic data.

- The atomic data should be simple, otherwise they are likely not to be atomic.
- Domains of functions should be minimal. This is supported by a type hierarchy on the populations.
- If a functional association can be derived, it should be.

In general, avoid redundancy.

Note that quality principles may be incompatible. Improving quality of information often complicates data by introducing identifiers which have no meaning to the users. Improving quality of knowledge often complicates information by introducing predicates (intermediate types) which may be seen as unnecessary by the users. The predicates *similar* and *one_of* in the hierarchical thesaurus application of section 5.4 are examples of this phenomenon.

Maintainability quality requires design trade-offs.

## 7.6 SUMMARY

Knowledge is represented as complex structures. There are semantic links between the objects in the application domain. Each object in the application domain is represented in some way in the computer domain. The semantic links between the domain objects therefore induce semantic links between the computer objects. The computer objects are linked in the computer system by structural links. Every semantic link should be supported by structural links. Moreover, a semantic link should be supported in only one way.

Unsupported links are a maintenance hazard.
Redundantly supported links are a maintenance hazard.

## 7.7 FURTHER READING

The material in this chapter is taken largely from Debenham (1989). There are many books on software engineering principles. Yourdon and Constantine (1978) is a classic which considers concepts relevant to this chapter.

## 7.8 EXERCISES

Consider some plausible changes to the hierarchical thesaurus example from section 5.4. Sketch their implementation. Discuss whether and how the quality principles make these changes easier to make.

## CHAPTER EIGHT

# Magic sets

In this chapter we describe optimization techniques which make the semi-naive algorithm a practical basis for deductive database system applications.

## 8.1 BOTTOM-UP EVALUATION AS A PRACTICAL METHOD

The bottom-up evaluation of a datalog program gives a definite meaning to any program, and also provides a decision procedure for any query. To have a decision procedure means firstly that we can always tell whether a statement in datalog is a conclusion of a given program by testing whether it is present in the perfect model computed by the semi-naive bottom-up algorithm starting with the given EDB. Secondly, for an algorithm to be a decision procedure, it must always terminate. The semi-naive bottom-up algorithm for datalog always terminates.

Unfortunately, the semi-naive algorithm can perform a large amount of unnecessary computation. For example, consider a bill of materials database for an aircraft carrier, which would have an IDB with *ancestor*-style predicates, as were described in Chapter 4. There are tens of millions of parts in tens of thousands of subassemblies. The depth of sub-sub- . . . -subassemblies might be as many as 20. Suppose we wish to find out how many of a particular chip are used in a radar unit on one of the types of aircraft on board. Say there are four levels, each with 20 parts. To answer this query by top-down inference, we would need to examine up to $20^4 = 160\,000$ tuples, while the perfect model for the *ancestor* predicate might have billions of tuples. Selecting a result from the perfect model might in this case involve $10\,000$ times more work.

In order to make the perfect model semantics for datalog into a useful deductive database system, we must have ways to compute only as much of the perfect model as is required for a particular query. After all, we can't actually *look at* billions of tuples, so it makes sense to compute the perfect model *lazily*, that is only the parts needed when they are needed. The fundamental tool to this end is the *magic sets* transformation of the IDB.

If the query is unrestricted (all its variables are free), then the result is the entire perfect model. We can only gain from lazy evaluation if there are some selection conditions in the query (some of the variables in the query are bound). In the terms of Chapter 5, we can give up information goal independence in order to gain speed of execution. The magic sets transformation essentially makes the bound variables in the query part of the EDB. Magic sets is a generalization of the database optimization technique of pushing selections and projections into relational expressions so as to evaluate them as soon as possible.

We will describe the transformation after reviewing the relationship between the datalog syntax and the relational algebra. Part of this review will be the introduction of some necessary concepts.

## 8.2  DATALOG AND RELATIONAL ALGEBRA REVISITED

The bottom-up computation strategy treats a datalog program as a set of (possibly recursive) database views. We saw in Chapter 3 that the prolog syntax expresses operations which are equivalent to expressions involving the relational operations select, project and join. For example, consider the clause

$$p(X, Y) \; :- \; q(X, W), \; r(W, Z), \; s(Z, Y). \tag{8.1}$$

Assume that when clause (8.1) is evaluated, the variable in the goal corresponding to $X$ will always be bound to some constant $c$, while the variable in the goal corresponding to $Y$ will always be bound to a constant only on completion of the computation.

The Prolog syntax is expressed in the relational algebra as follows, following the correspondence established in Chapter 3: There are four relations, $P$, $Q$, $R$ and $S$ with names $p$, $q$, $r$ and $s$, respectively. Each relation has two roles. Relation $P$ has roles which we will call $p1$ and $p2$, $Q$ has roles $q1$ and $q2$, $R$ has roles $r1$ and $r2$, $S$ has roles $s1$ and $s2$.

The predicate $p(X, Y)$ refers to the relation $P$. The argument positions of $p$ refer to the roles $p1$ and $p2$: the first position refers to the role $p1$ and the second to the role $p2$. Similarly for $Q$, $R$ and $S$. The variables $W$, $X$, $Y$, $Z$ take values from the domains from which the populations are drawn which fill the various roles. The variable $X$ therefore takes values from the domain from which role $p1$ of relation $P$ is drawn, and also from the domain from which role $q1$ of relation $Q$ is drawn. That the variable is used in both roles expresses the condition that the two roles must be domain-compatible. Similarly for $Y$.

The variable $W$ takes values from the domain from which role $q2$ of relation $Q$ is drawn and also from the domain from which role $r1$ of relation $R$ is drawn. The two roles must therefore be domain compatible. Also, the presence of the same variable in both relations denotes that the two relations participate in an equijoin, with the join condition being $q2 = r1$. Similarly for $Z$.

The symbol ":-" denotes that the relation $P$ is computed as the join of the relations $Q, R$ and $S$. Finally, the fact that the relation $P$ has only two roles indicates that the join must be projected onto the roles $q1$ and $s2$.

The relational algebra equivalent to (8.1) is therefore

$$P = \sigma_{q1=c \quad q2=r1 \quad r2=s1} Q \bowtie R \bowtie S \,[q1, s2] \tag{8.2}$$

The fact that the join operator commutes means that we can permute the predicates in the body of a clause, so that (8.1) is equivalent, for example, to

$$p(X, Y) :\text{-} \ r(W, Z), \ s(Z, Y), \ q(X, W). \tag{8.3}$$

A join operation involves selection. We can therefore use joins to perform selections. A selection on a role of a relation defines a subset of the tuples in the relation for which the value of the role for that tuple meets the selection criterion. We can define a new *selection relation* having only one tuple and a role for each selection criterion involving a constant. The value of each role for the tuple in the selection relation is the corresponding constant in the selection criterion. The selection can be computed by joining the original relation to the new single-tuple selection relation. For a selection involving equality tests only, the join condition is that the roles in the selection relation are equal to the corresponding roles in the relation upon which the selection is to be performed. Accordingly, if we define a selection relation $C$ having only one role $c1$, and agree to populate it with the constant $c$ supplied for the selection, then (8.1) is also equivalent to

$$P = C \bowtie Q \bowtie R \bowtie S \,[q1, s2] \tag{8.4}$$
$$\phantom{P = } {\scriptstyle c1=q1 \quad q2=r1 \quad r2=s1}$$

In practice we compute a sequence of joins one pair at a time. If we follow the convention that we compute the joins from left to right, we can assign names to the partial results, as follows:

$$
\begin{aligned}
&\text{sup0} = C \\
&\text{sup1} = \text{sup0} \bowtie Q \\
&\text{sup2} = \text{sup1} \bowtie R \,[q1, r2] \\
&P = \text{sup2} \bowtie S \,[q1, s2]
\end{aligned}
\tag{8.5}
$$

The projection in the computation of *sup2* expresses the fact that we only require distinct pairs of values from the roles $q1$ and $r2$ in the subsequent join.

This relational algebra set of partial solutions is expressed in Prolog syntax as follows: We define a predicate $sup0(X)$ which has a single solution $X = c$. The partial results for clause (8.1) become

$$
\begin{aligned}
&\text{sup1}(X, W) :\text{-} \ \text{sup0}(X), q(X, W). \\
&\text{sup2}(X, Z) :\text{-} \ \text{sup1}(X, W), r(W, Z). \\
&p(X, Y) :\text{-} \ \text{sup2}(X, Z), s(Z, Y).
\end{aligned}
\tag{8.6}
$$

The partial results are called **supplementary predicates**. Supplementary predicate *sup0* carries the bound variables from the head of the clause, while *supj* is the result after evaluating the *j*th predicate in the clause body. Supplementary predicates are an important part of magic sets, and will be defined formally below.

If we have query (8.4) reformulated as (8.6), then it should be apparent that the bottom-up computation strategy will generate only tuples for *p* having the first argument bound to the constant *c*. Therefore, all the tuples generated will satisfy the selection. No superfluous tuples will be generated.

The tricky part is how to establish the predicate *sup0*. This predicate is inserted into the program as part of the processing of the query *p(c, Y)?* using extra-logical means, for example by creating the predicate and inserting the tuple into it by an update. Since this process is outside the logic implemented by the interpreter, it is referred to as **magic**. The machinery used to do this is referred to as **magic sets**.

## 8.3   PRELIMINARIES: TRANSFORMING THE DDB INTO CANONICAL FORM

The magic sets transformation of a DDB is a syntactic transformation of the clauses. It assumes that the clauses have two properties: subgoal-rectified and unique binding, which we define in this section. Any datalog program can be transformed by syntactic methods into a program with these two properties, so there is no loss of generality. Recall that we require that all datalog clauses be safe.

### 8.3.1   Subgoal rectification

A clause is **subgoal-rectified** if no variable occurs more than once in a subgoal predicate. For example, in the clause

$$p(X, Y) :- q(X, X), r(X, Y). \tag{8.7}$$

the variable *X* appears twice in the subgoal *q*. Assume that the definition of *q* is

$$q(X, Y) :- s(X, Z), t(Z, Y). \tag{8.8}$$

We can subgoal rectify clause (8.7) by defining a new predicate

$$qxx(X) :- s(X, Z), t(Z, X). \tag{8.9}$$

and modifying clause (8.7) to

$$p(X, Y) :- qxx(X), r(X, Y). \tag{8.10}$$

The general principle is to identify any subgoals in which a variable occurs more than once, then replace it with a new predicate with fewer arguments, one for each distinct variable. The definition of the new predicate is obtained from the original definition by equating the variables which were repeated in the subgoal. This definition may, in turn, not be subgoal-rectified even if the original definition was, since formerly distinct variables have been identified. The process repeats until all subgoals are rectified.

## 8.3.2   Unique binding property

We have said that the magic sets transformation is useful only if there is selection imposed on the goal. In Prolog terms, this is to say that the goal predicate will have some (possibly all) of its variables bound to constants. A specification that a particular set of arguments of a goal be bound is called a **binding pattern**. For example, we could specify that the first and third arguments be bound. This is a different binding pattern from the specification that the second and third arguments be bound. We denote a binding pattern by a sequence of letters from the set $\{b, f\}$, one letter for each argument of the goal ($b$ stands for **bound**, while $f$ stands for **free**). This sequence is called an **adornment** for the goal. That the first and third of four arguments be bound is expressed by the adornment $b\,f\,b\,f$, while that the second and third of four be bound is expressed by the adornment $f\,b\,b\,f$. Two binding patterns are the same if their adornments are the same.

The binding pattern of the goal induces a binding pattern in each subgoal appearing in the definition of the goal's predicate. For example, consider the following DDB, relating to the ranks of members of a hierarchical organization. (This predicate searches a tree.)

EDB relations

   belongs(Member): true if *Member* is a member of the organization.
   reports_to(Subordinate, Superior): true if both *Subordinate* and *Superior* are members of the organization and *Subordinate* is immediately supervised by *Superior*.

IDB predicate

   same_rank(Member_1, Member_2): true if *Member_1* and *Member_2* are the same number of reporting levels away from a common supervisor. (Compare with *nodes-removed-level* of Chapter 3.)

same_rank(Member, Member) :- belongs(Member).                              (8.11)
same_rank(Member_1, Member_2) :-
   reports_to(Member_1, Superior_1),
   same_rank(Superior_1, Superior_2),
   reports_to(Member_2, Superior_2).

Binding pattern: $f\,b$ induces the following adornments in the definition:

$$\qquad\quad f\qquad\quad b\qquad\qquad\qquad b$$
same_rank(Member, Member) :- belongs(Member).                              (8.12a)
$$\qquad\quad f\qquad\qquad b$$
same_rank(Member_1, Member_2) :-                                           (8.12b)
$$\qquad\qquad f\qquad\qquad\quad f$$
   reports_to(Member_1, Superior_1),                                        (8.12c)
$$\qquad\quad b\qquad\qquad\quad f$$
   same_rank(Superior_1, Superior_2),                                       (8.12d)
$$\qquad\quad b\qquad\qquad\quad b$$
   reports_to(Member_2, Superior_2).                                        (8.12e)

Strictly speaking, no clause should have a duplicated variable in its head. This condition is called **rectification**. Accordingly, line (8.12a) should be

$$\overset{f}{\text{same\_rank}}(\text{Member\_1}, \overset{b}{\text{Member\_2}}) :- \tag{8.13a}$$

$$\overset{b}{\text{belongs}}(\text{Member\_2}), \tag{8.13b}$$

$$\overset{f}{\text{Member\_1}} = \overset{b}{\text{Member\_2}}. \tag{8.13c}$$

Note that the original form does not interfere with the magic sets transformation, so we do not always rectify the clause head.

In the top-down method, the predicates are evaluated from left to right. When the predicate *belongs* is executed at line (8.13b), its argument *Member_2* is bound, since it was bound in the clause head. When the predicate = is executed at line (8.13c), the argument *Member_2* is bound for the same reason, while the argument *Member_1* is free, since it was free in the clause head and has not been bound by any previous subgoals. The action of the = predicate is to bind *Member_1* to *Member_2*.

We look now at the recursive clause starting at line (8.12b). In the first subgoal, line (8.12c), both arguments are free: *Member_1* since it was free in the clause head and *Superior_1* since this is its first occurrence. If the subgoal succeeds, it will generate bindings for both arguments, so any later subgoal will see them as bound. In the second subgoal, line (8.12d), the first argument *Superior_1* is bound, since it was bound during the computation of the preceding subgoal, while the second, *Superior_2*, occurs first in this subgoal, so is free. The induced binding pattern for a subgoal is the state of binding of its variables *immediately before its execution*. The last subgoal, line (8.12e), has both its arguments bound: *Member_2* in the clause head, *Superior_2* by the preceding subgoal.

To make the magic sets transformation, we require that the IDB have the **unique binding property** i.e. that all instances of an IDB predicate have the same binding pattern with respect to a given adornment of the goal. Our example *same_rank* does not have that property with respect to the given adornment $f\,b$: the instance of *same_rank* as a subgoal at line (8.12d) has the adornment $b\,f$. Note that the binding pattern of EDB goals does not matter.

We can transform an IDB to have the unique binding property in two different ways. The easiest way arises from the fact that the join operation is commutative. This means that we can permute the subgoals in a clause without changing the result of the computation, as we did to get from (8.1) to (8.6). If we exchange the subgoals at lines (8.12c) and (8.12e), we obtain the induced binding pattern

$$\overset{f}{\text{same\_rank}}(\text{Member\_1}, \overset{b}{\text{Member\_2}}) :- \tag{8.14a}$$

$$\overset{b}{\text{reports\_to}}(\text{Member\_2}, \overset{f}{\text{Superior\_2}}), \tag{8.14b}$$

$$\overset{f}{\text{same\_rank}}(\text{Superior\_1}, \overset{b}{\text{Superior\_2}}), \tag{8.14c}$$

$$\overset{f}{\text{reports\_to}}(\text{Member\_1}, \overset{b}{\text{Superior\_1}}). \tag{8.14d}$$

which does have the unique binding property (note that *reports_to* is an EDB predicate).

This transformed clause is superior in another way. The EDB predicate in line (8.12c) had the adornment *f f*, while in the transformed clause, one instance of *reports_to* has adornment *b f* and the other *f b* (lines 8.14b and 8.14d). Recall from database query optimization that we prefer to have all relations participating in a join to have some restriction, and we are able to permute the factors of a join to achieve this.

The first rule for transforming an IDB clause to achieve the unique binding property is therefore:

If you can permute the subgoals so that the IDB subgoals have the unique binding property without increasing the number of EDB predicates with all variables free, then do so.

There are cases in which it is impossible to achieve the unique binding property by permuting the subgoals. Consider the predicate *middle* defined in terms of the IDB predicate *controlled_by*

middle(Subordinate, Superior, Middle) :-                                     (8.15)
    controlled_by(Subordinate, Middle),
    controlled_by(Middle, Superior).

controlled_by(Subordinate, Superior) :-
    reports_to(Subordinate, Superior).
controlled_by(Subordinate, Superior) :-
    reports_to(Subordinate, Intermediate),
    controlled_by(Intermediate, Superior).

The predicate *controlled_by* is true if *Superior* supervises *Subordinate*, either directly or indirectly, while *middle* is true if *Middle* supervises *Subordinate* and is supervised by *Superior*, either directly or indirectly.

If *middle* has the adornment *b b f*, the binding pattern induced on the subgoals of (8.15) is

              b          b        f
middle(Subordinate, Superior, Middle) :-                                     (8.16)
                        b              f
    controlled_by(Subordinate, Middle),
                    b        b
    controlled_by(Middle, Superior).

A transformation which always results in the unique binding property defines a new predicate for each instance of an old predicate having a different adornment. For example, (8.15) would be transformed to

middle(Subordinate, Superior, Middle) :-                                     (8.17)
    controlled_by_bf(Subordinate, Middle),
    controlled_by_bb(Middle, Superior).

```
controlled_by_bf(Subordinate, Superior) :-
    reports_to(Subordinate, Superior).
controlled_by_bf(Subordinate, Superior) :-
    reports_to(Subordinate, Intermediate),
    controlled_by_bf(Intermediate, Superior).

controlled_by_bb(Subordinate, Superior) :-
    reports_to(Subordinate, Superior).
controlled_by_bb(Subordinate, Superior) :-
    reports_to(Subordinate, Intermediate),
    controlled_by_bb(Intermediate, Superior).
```

Note that the *controlled_by* subgoals in the recursive clause for *controlled_by* have also been replaced by the appropriate new version.

The principle is:

> If you can't get the unique binding property by permuting subgoals without increasing the number of EDB predicates with all variables free, then replace the predicates with new predicates specialized to the binding patterns which occur.

The unique binding property is relative to a particular predicate. More exactly, its scope is limited to the predicates necessary in evaluation of a particular class of query. Independent occurrences of the predicate need not be considered.

### 8.4   MAGIC SETS TRANSFORMATION

If our IDB is subgoal-rectified and has the unique binding property (possibly having been transformed to this canonical form), and we are given an adornment of the top-level goals, then it can be converted by the magic sets transformation into an IDB which gives an efficient bottom-up computation for the given binding pattern.

We first need to formalize the notion of *supplementary predicates* sketched in (8.6) above. We begin by assigning a number to each clause of the IDB, and by obtaining an adornment for each predicate, either from the user for the highest-level query types or induced via the process exemplified in (8.12)–(8.14) and (8.16).

There will be a number of supplementary predicates for each clause: one for the clause head and one for each subgoal except for the last. The supplementary predicate associated with the head of clause $i$ is called $sup_{i,0}$ and it has as arguments those variables which are bound in the adornment for the predicate. For example, the clauses for *same_rank* from (8.12) and (8.14) are reproduced

$$
\begin{array}{ccc}
f & b & b
\end{array}
$$

1. same_rank(Member, Member) :- belongs(Member).                    (8.18)

$$
\begin{array}{cc}
f & b
\end{array}
$$

2. same_rank(Member_1, Member_2) :-

$$
\begin{array}{cc}
b & f
\end{array}
$$

    reports_to(Member_2, Superior_2),

$$\overset{f}{\text{same\_rank(Superior\_1,}} \overset{b}{\text{Superior\_2),}}$$
$$\overset{f}{\text{reports\_to(Member\_1,}} \overset{b}{\text{Superior\_1).}}$$

The supplementary predicates associated with the clause heads (also called the **zeroth supplementary predicates**) are

$\text{sup}_{1,0}(\text{Member})$                                              (8.19)
$\text{sup}_{2,0}(\text{Member\_2})$

There are no other supplementary predicates for clause 1, since it has only one subgoal and there are therefore no intermediate results in the computation of the join. Clause 2 is the join of three relations and the bindings from the clause head, so has two supplementary predicates associated with its body (**other supplementary predicates**). These supplementary predicates carry the binding information from left to right. The $j$th supplementary predicate for rule $i$ represents the situation *after* the execution of the $j$th subgoal. It carries the binding information to the next subgoal. This passing of binding information from one subgoal to the next is sometimes called **sideways information passing**.

The supplementary predicate $sup_{i,j}$ has variables from two sources:

- variables bound in the clause head;
- variables bound in subgoals up to and including the $j$th subgoal which appear either in subgoals after the $j$th or in the clause head (variables needed later).

Variables which are bound in the subgoals up to the $j$th and not needed later are not included. Recall that the entire clause is a join which is projected onto the variables in the clause head, and that supplementary predicate $sup_{i,j}$ is the $j$th partial result of the join projected onto the variables needed either for subsequent joins or for the final projection onto the variables in the clause head.

For the IDB (8.18) the other supplementary predicates are

$\text{sup}_{2,1}(\text{Member\_2, Superior\_2})$                              (8.20)
$\text{sup}_{2,2}(\text{Member\_2, Superior\_1})$

All the supplementary predicates for (8.18) are shown below:

1. same_rank(Member, Member) :- belongs(Member).                              (8.21)
   $sup_{1,0}(Member)$
2. same_rank(Member_1, Member_2) :-
   $sup_{2,0}(Member\_2)$
       reports_to(Member_2, Superior_2),
       $sup_{2,1}(Member\_2, Superior\_2)$
       same_rank(Superior_1, Superior_2),
       $sup_{2,2}(Member\_2, Superior\_1)$
       reports_to(Member_1, Superior_1).

Besides the supplementary predicates, the magic sets transformation defines a new "magic" predicate which carries the binding from the goal to the zeroth supplementary predicate. This is in two parts: an extension which contains the bindings from the query goal, and an intension: a set of clauses which transmit the bindings for IDB predicates occurring as subgoals. We generate a name for the magic predicate for an IDB predicate by adding *m_* to the front of the name of the predicate. Thus the magic predicate for *controlled_by* is *m_controlled_by*, and the magic predicate for *same_rank* is *m_same_rank*.

The magic predicate has one argument for each variable which is bound in the adornment. It is therefore very similar to the zeroth supplementary predicate. The magic predicate transformation is an implementation of the relational algebra equivalence of selection with join as illustrated in (8.4).

The concept of magic predicates, although not difficult, is a little strange, and will be discussed in more detail after the transformation is described and the definitions of the magic predicates are presented.

The magic sets transformation of an adorned IDB has five parts:

1   Magic predicate extension
2   Magic predicate intension
3   Zeroth supplementary predicates
4   Other supplementary predicates
5   IDB predicates

We will illustrate the transformation by the *same_rank* IDB (8.21).

### 8.4.1   Magic predicate extension

The extension carries the constants provided by the user in the query, which are inserted into the tuple by the system. If there are $k$ variables bound in the adornment, then the extension of the magic predicate for predicate $p$ has a single tuple

$$m\text{-}p(\&1, \&2, \ldots, \&k). \tag{8.22}$$

Example from (8.21):

m_same_rank(&1).

where $\&i$ is the notation used for procedure parameters in some implementations of SQL.

### 8.4.2   Magic predicate intension

New tuples are added to the magic predicate whenever its IDB predicate occurs as a subgoal. If predicate $p$ occurs as the $j$th subgoal in clause $i$, we must create a tuple containing the bindings carried from the $j$-1st supplementary predicate which are used by the subgoal. Note that there may be variables in the supplementary predicate which are used by later subgoals or which appear in the clause head, so not all of the variables in the supplementary predicate appear in the magic predicate. On the other hand, all the variables in the magic predicate are bound, so must be among the variables in the supplementary predicate. If $X_1, \ldots, X_m$ are the variables occurring in the $j$-1st supplementary predicate, and $X_{i1}, \ldots, X_{ik}$ are the $k$ variables from those occurring in the subgoal, then we add the clause

$$\text{m\_p}(X_{i1}, \ldots, X_{ik}) \text{ :- } \text{sup}_{i,j-1}(X_1, \ldots, X_m). \tag{8.23}$$

Example from (8.21): The IDB predicate *same_rank* occurs as the second subgoal of rule 2:

    m_same_rank(Superior_2) :-
        supp_{2,1}(Member_2, Superior_2).

There is one magic predicate clause for each occurrence of the corresponding predicate as a subgoal in the IDB. In the case of (8.21), the predicate *same_rank* occurs only once as a subgoal, so there is only one clause in the intension for the magic predicate *m_same_rank*.

### 8.4.3   Zeroth supplementary predicates

The zeroth supplementary predicate carries the bindings from the goal into each clause in the goal's predicate. It has the same variables as the magic predicate. If clause $i$ is a clause of predicate $p$, then its zeroth supplementary predicate is

$$\text{sup}_{i,0}(X_{i1}, \ldots, X_{ik}) \text{ :- } \text{m\_p}(X_{i1}, \ldots, X_{ik}). \tag{8.24}$$

There is one zeroth supplementary predicate for each clause in the IDB.
   Example from (8.21):

    sup_{1,0}(Member) :- m_same_rank(Member).
    sup_{2,0}(Member_2) :- m_same_rank(Member_2).

Note that the variable names *Member* and *Member_2* have only mnemonic significance. Recall that the scope of a variable is the clause in which it occurs. The important thing is that both variables in each clause have the same name. The actual name is immaterial. For convenience, we choose the names which appear in the clauses from which the new clauses are derived.

### 8.4.4   Other supplementary predicates

Clauses for the other supplementary predicates are taken directly from their definition. There is one clause for each subgoal in the IDB other than the last in its clause. The $j$th supplementary predicate $(j > 0)$ in clause $i$ is the join of the $j$-1st supplementary predicate with the $j$th subgoal. A variable in the $j$th supplementary must therefore also be a variable appearing in either the $j$-1st supplementary or the $j$th subgoal. The $j$-1st supplementary and the $j$th subgoal will usually have some variables in common, though not all. They may possibly have no variables in common.

Assume there are $m$ distinct variables in the two subgoals, and collect their names in the list $X_1, \ldots, X_m$. All the variables in the two supplementaries and the $j$th subgoal will be in this list. If the $j$-1st supplementary has $ms \leq m$ variables, the $j$th subgoal is predicate $p$ with $mg \leq m$ variables, and the $j$th supplementary has $mh \leq m$ variables, then the $j$th supplementary is defined by the clause

$$\sup_{i,j}(X_{i_1}, \ldots, X_{i_{mh}}) :- \qquad (8.25)$$
$$\sup_{i,j-1}(X_{j_1}, \ldots, X_{j_{ms}}), p(X_{k_1}, \ldots, X_{k_{mg}}).$$

where all the $X_{i_j}$ are selected from the list $X_1, \ldots, X_m$.
Example from (8.21):

    sup$_{2,1}$(Member_2, Superior_2) :-
        sup$_{2,0}$(Member_2),
        reports_to(Member_2, Superior_2).

    sup$_{2,2}$(Member_2, Superior_1) :-
        sup$_{2,1}$(Member_2, Superior_2),
        same_rank(Superior_1, Superior_2).

### 8.4.5   IDB predicates

The IDB predicates, like the other supplementary predicates, generate clauses directly from their definition. The variables are named in a way similar to the other supplementary predicates. There is one clause generated for each clause in the IDB. If the IDB predicate for the $i$th clause is $p$, there are $j+1$ subgoals and the last subgoal is predicate $q$, then

$$p(X_{i_1}, \ldots, X_{i_{mh}}) :- \qquad (8.26)$$
$$\sup_{i,j}(X_{j_1}, \ldots, X_{j_{ms}}), q(X_{k_1}, \ldots, X_{k_{mg}}).$$

Example from (8.21):

    same_rank(Member, Member) :-
        sup$_{1,0}$(Member),
        belongs(Member).

    same_rank(Member_1, Member_2) :-
        sup$_{2,2}$(Member_2, Superior_1),
        reports_to(Member_1, Superior_1).

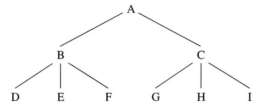

**Figure 8.1** A sample EDB for *reports_to*.

*Comments*

The complete magic sets transformation of the *same_rank* predicate from (8.21) is

1. m_same_rank(&1).                                                            (8.27)
2. m_same_rank(Superior_2) :-
     $supp_{2,1}$(Member_2, Superior_2).
3. $sup_{1,0}$(Member) :- m_same_rank(Member).
4. $sup_{2,0}$(Member_2) :- m_same_rank(Member_2).
5. $sup_{2,1}$(Member_2, Superior_2) :-
     $sup_{2,0}$(Member_2),
     reports_to(Member_2, Superior_2).
6. $sup_{2,2}$(Member_2, Superior_1) :-
     $sup_{2,1}$(Member_2, Superior_2),
     same_rank(Superior_1, Superior_2).
7. same_rank(Member, Member) :-
     $sup_{1,0}$(Member),
     belongs(Member).
8. same_rank(Member_1, Member_2) :-
     $sup_{2,2}$(Member_2, Superior_1),
     reports_to(Member_1, Superior_1).

Consider what happens to this IDB when evaluated bottom-up using the semi-naive algorithm. At the first step all the IDB predicates except for *m_same_rank* are empty. These include *same_rank* and all the supplementaries. The magic predicate *m_same_rank* has one tuple, clause 1, placed in the predicate by the query processor. The only clauses which can generate tuples at the first stage are those all of whose subgoals are EDB predicates. Only clauses 3 and 4 meet this criterion: they each have one subgoal, *m_same_rank*, which has one tuple as we have seen.

After these clauses fire, we have one tuple each in $sup_{1,0}$ and $sup_{2,0}$. Clauses 5 and 7 can now fire, putting tuples in $sup_{2,1}$ and *same_rank*. Clauses 2 and 6 can fire, and after 6, clause 8. If we keep clause 2 from firing, we see from the example below that we will fairly quickly reach a point where no new tuples can be generated.

Consider the reporting structure in Figure 8.1, assuming that the bound variable in the query is *I*, i.e. we want all people with the same rank as *I*. Looking at the graphical representation, we can see intuitively that the desired response is the bottom line, which is {*D, E, F, G, H, I*}. If we take the evaluation strategy of refraining from firing clause 2 until no other clause can fire, we can divide the

**Table 8.1**  Generation of the perfect model for *same_rank*

| Iteration | m_same_rank | sup2,1 | sup2,2 | same_rank |
|---|---|---|---|---|
| 1 | \<I\> | \<I, C\> |  | \<I, I\> |
| 2 | \<C\> | \<C, A\> | \<I, C\> | \<C, C\> |
|  |  |  |  | \<H, I\> |
|  |  |  |  | \<G, I\> |
| 3 | \<A\> |  | \<I, B\> | \<A, A\> |
|  |  |  |  | \<B, C\> |
|  |  |  |  | \<D, I\> |
|  |  |  |  | \<E, I\> |
|  |  |  |  | \<F, I\> |

evaluation into a number of iterations, one for each time clause 2 is allowed to fire. Note that these iterations are different from the $T$ operator, and at a coarser grain. A fundamental result of deductive database theory is that any sequence respecting stratification yields the same perfect model.

In iteration 1, we first get the tuple *\<I, I\>* for *same_rank* from clause 7 via clause 3 from the initial tuple *\<I\>* in *m_same_rank*. Clause 8 cannot fire since, although clauses 4 and 5 produce the tuple *\<I, C\>* for $sup_{2,1}$, clause 6 cannot fire as there is no tuple *\<C, C\>* in *same_rank* as yet. We have no alternative but to complete iteration 1 by firing clause 2, obtaining the tuple *\<C\>* in *m_same_rank*.

In iteration 2, we immediately obtain the tuple *\<C, C\>* in *same_rank* via clauses 3 and 7, which allows clause 6 to fire, producing the tuple *\<I, C\>* for $sup_{2,2}$. This tuple allows clause 8 to generate the tuples *\<G, I\>* and *\<H, I\>* for *same_rank*. Neither of the new tuples in *same_rank* allows clause 6 to fire, since none of them have *Superior_2* bound to *C*. No other clause can fire, so we must end iteration 2 by allowing clause 2 to generate the tuple *\<A\>* for *m_same_rank*.

As before, in iteration 3 clauses 3 and 7 generate the tuple *\<A, A\>* for *same_rank*. Also, in the previous iteration, clauses 4 and 5 have generated the tuple *\<C, A\>* for $sup_{2,1}$, which with the new tuple *\<A, A\>* in *same_rank* allows clauses 6 and 8 to generate the tuple *\<B, C\>* for *same_rank*. We already have the tuple *\<I, C\>* in $sup_{2,1}$, so that the new tuple *\<B, C\>* in *same_rank* allows clause 6 to generate the tuple *\<I, B\>* for $sup_{2,2}$, which now allows clause 8 to generate the remaining tuples *\<D, I\>*, *\<E, I\>* and *\<F, I\>* for *same_rank*. At this point, none of the other clauses can fire, nor can clause 2, so the fixed point has been reached and the perfect model is complete.

Table 8.1 shows the tuples generated in the perfect model in each iteration. The zeroth supplementaries are omitted for clarity. The flow of data through the clauses is shown in Figure 8.2. There are two cycles: one, labelled *A*, from clause 8 to clause 6 via the predicate *same_rank*; and one, labelled *B*, from clause 2 to clauses 3 and 4 via the magic predicate *m_same_rank*. As we have seen, loop *B* (C2→C4→C5→C2) extends the search by taking one step up the hierarchy, while loop *A* (C6→C8→C6) fills in those solutions available at a given level.

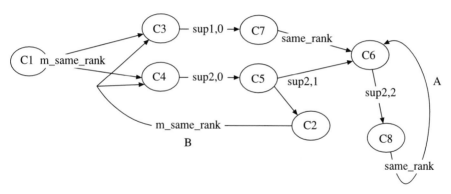

**Figure 8.2** Flow of data through the generated IDB.

*Complications*

The magic sets transformation always works if the IDB meets its conditions. There can, however, be some surprising situations arising from special cases in the supplementary predicates.

First of all, the arguments of a supplementary predicate are those variables either bound in the clause head or bound in the body and needed later. In the examples given, variables which are free in the clause head are not bound until the last subgoal. It is quite possible for a variable to be free in the clause head and bound earlier than the last subgoal. For example, if the predicate *same_rank* from (8.12) is changed slightly, reversing the order of arguments in the subgoal *same_rank* in line (8.12d), the predicate already has the unique binding property. Its supplementary predicates are shown in (8.28) in interspersed italics. A supplementary predicate records the results of a partial computation. The supplementaries in (8.28) appear below the last predicate included in the partial result which it summarized.

1. same_rank(Member, Member) :- belongs(Member).                    (8.28)
   $sup_{1,0}(Member)$
2. same_rank(Member_1, Member_2) :-
   $sup_{2,0}(Member\_2)$
       reports_to(Member_1, Superior_1),
       $sup_{2,1}(Member\_1, Member\_2, Superior\_1)$
       same_rank(Superior_2, Superior_1),
       $sup_{2,2}(Member\_1, Member\_2, Superior\_2)$
       reports_to(Member_2, Superior_2).

Note that the binding for *Member_2* in $sup_{2,0}$ is not used in the immediately following subgoal, but is passed on in $sup_{2,1}$ and $sup_{2,2}$ to the final subgoal, where it is used. The *middle* predicate (8.16) also has a variable free in the clause head which is bound before the final subgoal.

It is also possible for a supplementary predicate to have no arguments. Suppose *same_rank* has the adornment $f\,f$. IDB (8.28) would need to be modified to have the unique binding property, becoming

1. same_rank_ff(Member, Member) :- belongs(Member).                    (8.29)
   $sup_{1,0}$.
2. same_rank_ff(Member_1, Member_2) :-
   $sup_{2,0}$,
        reports_to(Member_1, Superior_1),
        $sup_{2,1}(Member\_1, Superior\_1)$
        same_rank_fb(Superior_2, Superior_1),
        $sup_{2,2}(Member\_1, Superior\_2)$
        reports_to(Member_2, Superior_2).

The magic predicate for *same_rank_ff* would also be simply a proposition *m_sr_ff*. Note that the subgoal *same_rank* now has a different binding pattern from its clause head, so has been renamed *same_rank_fb*.

Although strict datalog does not permit functions as arguments to predicates, we have seen in Chapter 4 that functions are useful in practice, and that deductive database systems often accommodate them in limited ways. This means that a magic sets transformation algorithm may be called upon to transform procedures which have structures. This does not, in fact, introduce any additional complexity in the transformation, since the supplementary predicates are employed to pass variable bindings only. The structures remain part of the original program text and are carried along with it during the transformation.

We illustrate this by transforming the transitive closure procedure for directed acyclic graphs given in Chapter 3:

1. path(Source, Target, PathSoFar, [Source | PathSoFar]) :-                (8.30)
        arc(Source, Target).
2. path(Source, Target, PathSoFar, Path) :-
        arc(Intermediate, Target),
        path(Source, Intermediate, [Intermediate | PathSoFar], Path).

with the adornment *f b b f*.
   The supplementaries are

$sup_{1,0}$(Target, Path_so_far).                                         (8.31)
$sup_{2,0}$(Target, Path_so_far).
$sup_{2,1}$(Target, Path_so_far, Intermediate).

Notice that the structure does not appear.
   The transformation is

I.     m_path(&1, &2).                                                     (8.32)

II.    m_path(Intermediate, [Intermediate | Path_so_far]) :-
           $sup_{2,1}$(Target, Path_so_far, Intermediate).

III.   $sup_{1,0}$(Target, Path_so_far) :- m_path(Target, Path_so_far).
       $sup_{2,0}$(Target, Path_so_far) :- m_path(Target, Path_so_far).

IV.    $sup_{2,1}$(Target, Path_so_far, Intermediate) :-
           $sup_{2,0}$(Target, Path_so_far), arc(Intermediate, Target).

V.  path(Source, Target, Path_so_far, [Source | Path_so_far]) :-
        $sup_{1,0}$(Target, Path_so_far), arc(Source, Target).
    path(Source, Target, Path_so_far, Path) :-
        $sup_{2,1}$(Target, Path_so_far, Intermediate),
        path(Source, Intermediate, [Intermediate | Path_so_far], Path).

Notice that the structure appears in II, where the bound variable in the magic predicate is constructed from two of the bound variables in $sup_{2,1}$, and in V, where structured literals are carried from the original predicate definition.

Another common use of structure appears in the *nodes-removed-level* predicate from Chapter 3, which performs a hierarchical search on a tree data structure. Assume the binding pattern *b f b*. In other words, we are looking for the set of nodes at a given distance from a given node. Note that the constant has been removed from the head of clause 1 to an equivalent formulation:

$$b \quad f \quad b$$
1.  nodes-removed-level(R, R, N) :- N = 0.                         (8.33)
        $sup_{1,0}(R, N)$

$$b \quad f \quad b$$
2.  nodes-removed-level(R, C, N) :-
        $sup_{2,0}(R, N)$
        $f \qquad b$
        N > 0, M is N − 1,
        $sup_{2,1}(R, M, N)$
        $b \quad f$
        arc(R, I),
        $sup_{2,2}(R, N, M, I)$
        $$b \quad f \quad b$$
        nodes-removed-level(I, C, M).

The transformation is:

I.   m_n(&1, &2).                                                   (8.34)

II.  m_n(I, M) :- $sup_{2,2}$(R, N, M, I).

III. $sup_{1,0}$(R, N) :- m_n(R, N).
     $sup_{2,0}$(R, N) :- m_n(R, N).

IV.  $sup_{2,1}$(R, M, N) :- $sup_{2,0}$(R, M), N > 0, M is N − 1.
     $sup_{2,2}$(R, N, M, I) :- $sup_{2,1}$(R, M, N), arc(R, I).

V.   nodes-removed-level(R, R, N) :- $sup_{1,0}$(R, N), N = 0.
     nodes-removed-level(R, C, N) :- $sup_{2,2}$(R, N, M, I),
         nodes-removed-level(I, C, M).

We first observe that the transformation is performed on the formulation of the problem suited to top-down evaluation, rather than its reformulation for bottom-up evaluation as shown in Chapter 4. The magic sets transformation can therefore be seen to preserve the top-down structure of predicates, but allow them to be efficiently computed bottom-up. Secondly, we observe that the computational predicate in the second clause functions as an EDB predicate. We can conclude that the presence of computational predicates does not affect the validity of the magic sets transformation.

Consider, however, what happens if the binding pattern of (8.33) is $bff$, so that the level is not known beforehand. The magic sets transformation is now

I.     m_n(&1).                                                                          (8.35)

II.    m_n(I) :- $sup_{2,2}$(R, I).

III.   $sup_{1,0}$(R) :- m_n(R).
       $sup_{2,0}$(R) :- m_n(R).

IV.    $sup_{2,1}$(R) :- $sup_{2,0}$(R), N > 0, M is N − 1.
       $sup_{2,2}$(R, I) :- $sup_{2,1}$(R), arc(R, I).

V.     nodes-removed-level(R, R, N) :- $sup_{1,0}$(R), N = 0.
       nodes-removed-level(R, C, N) :- $sup_{2,2}$(R, I), nodes-removed-level(I, C, M).

The computation of $sup_{2,1}$ in IV does not give bindings for $N$ and $M$, since there is insufficient information available for the computational predicate to proceed. The point here is that a computational predicate must have its input arguments bound, so that it behaves as an EDB predicate, otherwise the magic sets transformation is not valid. For a binding pattern where the level is unspecified, it is necessary to use the formulation of Chapter 4, and not the magic sets transformation.

## 8.5   LINEAR RECURSION

There are a number of special cases where it is possible to do better than the standard magic sets transformation. We will consider a very common case: right linear recursion, where there is a single recursive subgoal which can be the rightmost subgoal. There are a number of other kinds of linear recursion with their own special transformations, which will not be considered.

Consider the predicate *controlled_by* (8.15), with binding pattern $bf$:

1. controlled_by(Subordinate, Superior) :-                                               (8.36)
     $sup_{1,0}$(Subordinate)
        reports_to(Subordinate, Superior).

2. controlled_by(Subordinate, Superior) :-
     $sup_{2,0}$(Subordinate)
        reports_to(Subordinate, Intermediate),
        $sup_{2,1}$(Subordinate, Intermediate)
        controlled_by(Intermediate, Superior).

Its magic sets transformation is

m_c(&1).                                                                                    (8.37)

m_c(Intermediate) :- $\text{sup}_{2,1}$(Subordinate, Intermediate).

$\text{sup}_{1,0}$(Subordinate) :- m_c(Subordinate).
$\text{sup}_{2,0}$(Subordinate) :- m_c(Subordinate).

$\text{sup}_{2,1}$(Subordinate, Intermediate) :-
    $\text{sup}_{2,0}$(Subordinate),
    reports_to(Subordinate, Intermediate).

controlled_by(Subordinate, Superior) :-
    $\text{sup}_{1,0}$(Subordinate),
    reports_to(Subordinate, Superior).
controlled_by(Subordinate, Superior) :-
    $\text{sup}_{2,1}$(Subordinate, Intermediate),
    controlled_by(Intermediate, Superior).

It is difficult to see the contribution of each of the transformed clauses to the result of the query, since there are so many. The IDB can, however, be simplified by the method of unfolding and folding (to be discussed in Chapter 9), to

1. m_c(&1).                                                                                 (8.38)

2. m_c(Intermediate) :- controlled_by(Subordinate, Intermediate).

3. controlled_by(Subordinate, Superior) :-
       m_c(Subordinate),
       reports_to(Subordinate, Superior).

4. controlled_by(Subordinate, Superior) :-
       controlled_by(Subordinate, Intermediate),
       controlled_by(Intermediate, Superior).

To convince yourself that the simplified clauses are equivalent to the original, compute the perfect model for both IDBs using the EDB in Figure 8.1. You will see that the same tuples are generated in each case for the predicate *m_c* and, as well, for the predicate *controlled_by*.

What we are looking for in the query *controlled_by(&1, Superior)* is the set of bindings for *Superior* such that the tuples *controlled_by(&1, Superior)* are in the perfect model. When you evaluate the IDB (8.38) using the semi-naive algorithm, you can see that the bindings for *Superior* are generated by repeated executions of clauses 3 and 2 after the initial seeding of *m_c* in clause 1. This corresponds to searching the tree in Figure 8.1 from one of the leaves towards the root.

Notice that we have not needed clause 4 in this computation. What clause 4 does is to compute the transitive closure of the path from a leaf to the root, which is irrelevant to this particular class of query.

The class of query we have just identified is called **right linear recursive**. It is called *linear* because the only IDB predicate appearing in the clause body is the recursive appearance of the predicate defined by the clause head. It is called *right* *linear* because the recursive subgoal can appear as the rightmost subgoal and the clause still has the unique binding property. For contrast, the predicate *middle* (8.15) is not linear, while the predicate *controlled_by* (8.15) is right linear, as are the predicates *controlled_by_bf* and *controlled_by_bb* in (8.17). The predicate *same_rank* in (8.21) is linear, but not right linear with respect to the adornment $bf$, because with this adornment the recursive subgoal cannot be the last subgoal and still have the unique binding property. Right linear clauses are very common in practice.

An IDB predicate $p$ with adornment $a$ is right linear if it meets the following three conditions:

1  *Max 1 Recursive*: all clauses contain either no IDB subgoals which depend on the predicate being defined, or exactly one occurrence of the predicate $p$ being defined as a subgoal.

2  *Recursive Last*: the recursive subgoal $p$ can be the last subgoal without violating the unique binding property.

3  *Recursively Computed Output*: the free variables in $p$ indicated by the adornment $a$ are also the free variables in the recursive subgoal $p$, and these variables occur nowhere else in the clause.

A clause which contains no IDB subgoals is a basis clause for the recursion. The condition *Recursively Computed Output* means that the computation consists of several iterations of recursive clauses followed by a single basis clause. The bindings for the free variables in the original goal come from the basis clause, and are passed up to the original goal through the recursive clauses unchanged. The examples of right linear recursive systems noted above all have these three properties.

An example having properties *Max 1 Recursive* and *Recursive Last* but not *Recursively Computed Output* is the predicate *live* defined in (8.39) below. The EDB is a relation *connected(Node1, Node2)*, which describes an electrical network with a number of nodes and wires connecting some of the pairs of nodes. Nodes $a$ and $b$ have a wire between them if *connected(a, b)* is in the EDB. There is a distinguished node *powerpoint* which is a source of power for the network. A wire between two nodes is *live* if there is a path from it to *powerpoint*. Assume that the wires transmit power only from the right node to the left node in a *connected* pair of nodes. The IDB is

live(A, powerpoint) :- connected(A, powerpoint).          (8.39)
live(A, B) :- connected(A, B), live(B, C).

with the adornment $bf$. In other words, the query is to identify any live wires that terminate at node $A$.

We can take advantage of not needing to compute the transitive closure for right linear predicates by making a special case in the magic set transformation. In particular, we do not need to consider supplementary predicates. Assume that the predicate $p$ has $n + m$ variables, and that the first $n \geq 0$ of them are bound in the adornment, leaving the last $m \geq 0$ variables free. A particular recursive clause for $p$ will have a number of subgoals, with the recursive subgoal $p$ at the end. Assume there are

$k \geq 0$ subgoals other than $p$. Let the free variables in the clause head and the recursive rules be $X_1, \ldots, X_m$. Let the bound variables in the clause head be $T_1, \ldots, T_n$ and the bound variables in the recursive subgoal be $S_1, \ldots, S_n$. The general form of a right linear recursive clause is then

$$p(T_1, \ldots, T_n, X_1, \ldots, X_m) :\!- G_1, \ldots, G_k, p(S_1, \ldots, S_n, X_1, \ldots, X_m). \qquad (8.40)$$

A basis clause has a number, say $j \geq 0$, of non-recursive subgoals, and has the general form

$$p(T_1, \ldots, T_n, X_1, \ldots, X_m) :\!- B_1, \ldots, B_j. \qquad (8.41)$$

We still need a magic predicate for each IDB subgoal, so that each recursive clause will produce a single magic predicate:

$$m\_p(S_1, \ldots, S_n) :\!- m\_p(T_1, \ldots, T_n), G_1, \ldots, G_k. \qquad (8.42)$$

We also need the EDB clause for the magic predicate, having a single tuple whose arguments are the bound variables from the query

$$m\_p(\&1, \ldots, \&n). \qquad (8.43)$$

The bindings for the free variables $X_1, \ldots, X_m$ come from the basis rules. We therefore create a new *answer predicate* $a\_p$ from each basis clause

$$a\_p(X_1, \ldots, X_m) :\!- m\_p(T_1, \ldots, T_n), B_1, \ldots, B_j. \qquad (8.44)$$

Finally, the answer to the query can be constructed from the answer predicate

$$p(\&1, \ldots, \&n, X_1, \ldots, X_m) :\!- a\_p(X_1, \ldots, X_m). \qquad (8.45)$$

In summary, if the basis clauses of a right linear predicate are of form (8.41) and the recursive clauses are of form (8.40), then the magic sets transform consists of

*Recursive*:  for each recursive clause a magic predicate of the form (8.42)
*Start*:      an EDB tuple for the magic predicate of the form (8.43)
*Basis*:      for each basis clause an answer predicate of the form (8.44)
*Answer*:     the query answer of the form (8.45)

For example, consider the predicate *controlled_by* (8.15), (8.33), with adornment $bf$:

1. controlled_by(Subordinate, Superior) :-                                    (8.46)
     reports_to(Subordinate, Superior).

2. controlled_by(Subordinate, Superior) :-
     reports_to(Subordinate, Intermediate),
     controlled_by(Intermediate, Superior).

*Recursive*: clause 2 is the only recursive clause, so the magic predicate is

m_controlled_by(Intermediate) :-                                              (8.47)
     m_controlled_by(Subordinate),
     reports_to(Subordinate, Intermediate).

*Start*: the EDB clause for the magic predicate is

m_controlled_by(&1).                                                         (8.48)

*Basis*: clause 1 is the only basis clause, so the answer predicate is

a_controlled_by(Superior) :-                                           (8.49)
    m_controlled_by(Subordinate),
    reports_to(Subordinate, Superior).

*Answer*: the query predicate is

controlled_by(&1, Superior) :- a_controlled_by(Superior).              (8.50)

The completed right linear magic sets transformation is therefore

1. m_controlled_by(Intermediate) :-                                    (8.51)
    m_controlled_by(Subordinate),
    reports_to(Subordinate, Intermediate).
2. m_controlled_by(&1).
3. a_controlled_by(Superior) :-
    m_controlled_by(Subordinate),
    reports_to(Subordinate, Superior).
4. controlled_by(&1, Superior) :- a_controlled_by(Superior).

This should be compared with the magic sets transform of the same predicate in (8.38). Clause (8.51.1) is clause (8.38.2). Clause (8.51.2) is clause (8.38.1). Clauses (8.51.3) and (8.51.4) are clause (8.38.3). The unnecessary clause (8.38.4) does not appear in (8.51).

## 8.6  SUMMARY

We have in this chapter described the magic sets transformation which makes the semi-naive algorithm for bottom-up computation of deductive database queries a practical method. This transformation requires that a program first be transformed into a canonical form having subgoal rectification and the unique binding property, then further transformed into an equivalent program which requires much less computation to evaluate. There are common special cases where it is possible to do better than magic sets. We described in particular the improved transformation for right linear recursion.

There is much more to this topic than has been covered in this book. For example, there are extensions to magic predicate transformations for predicates containing function symbols and for constraints other than a query variable bound to a constant. There are adaptations for predicates containing negation or aggregation. Many of these, and other topics still the subject of active research, would be needed to construct a fully optimized deductive database query evaluation system.

## 8.7  FURTHER READING

The material in this chapter is based largely on Ullman (1989). Similar material is given in Ceri *et al.* (1990). There is a large and active literature in this area.

## 8.8   EXERCISES

8.1   Transform the rules below using the magic set algorithm:

   red_blue_path(X, Y) :- red(X, Y).
   red_blue_path(X, Y) :- red_blue_path(X, U), blue(U, V),
      red_blue_path(V, Y).

assuming a query with adornment *b f*

(Find paths in a coloured graph consisting of a red arc possibly followed by alternating blue and red arcs.)

8.2   Repeat Exercise 8.1 for the rules

   expression(plus(E, T)) :- expression(E), term(T).
   expression(E) :- term(E).

   term(times(T, F)) :- term(T), factor(F).
   term(T) :- factor(T).

   factor(parens(E)) :- expression(E).
   factor(F) :- identifier(F).

with the query goal bound (adornment *b*).

These rules represent the construction of arithmetic expressions with the operators + and ×, using parentheses.

8.3   Consider a system based on a suburban rail network. The EDB is

   station(Line, Station).   Station is a station on line Line.
   leg(Line, Station_1, Station_2).   Station_2 immediately follows Station_1
      on line Line.
   interchange(Station, Line_1, Line_2).   Station is a station at which one
      can transfer from line Line_1 to line Line_2.

   IDB: trip(Line, Start, End) is true if a trip is possible starting at station
      Start on line Line, ending at station End (possibly on another line). The
      first two arguments are bound, the last free.

   trip(Line, Start, End) :- station(Line, Start), Start = End.
   trip(Line, Start, End) :- leg(Line, Start, Int), trip(Line, Int, End).
   trip(Line, Start, End) :- interchange(Start, Line, Line_1), trip(Line_1, Start,
      End).

Perform the magic sets transform on this IDB, taking advantage of linear recursion if applicable.

## CHAPTER NINE

# Unfolding and folding

In this chapter we examine some techniques for simplifying IDBs.

## 9.1 UNFOLDING

Computing the perfect model for a deductive database consists of populating the IDB relations starting with the EDB and iterating until a fixed point is reached. Following the definitions in Chapter 2, the EDB relations are normally update types, and at least some of the IDB relations are query types. It is frequently the case that some of the IDB relations are neither update nor query types. We called these **intermediate** types.

Recall that update types are relations whose contents can be changed by the user, and that query types are relations whose contents may be queried by the user. Intermediate types are relations which can neither be updated nor queried: what use are they? Consider the following program, which is a magic sets transformation of the *ancestor* relation with binding pattern $f\ b$:

1. $m\_a(I) :- sup_{2,1}(D, I).$                                                  (9.1)
2. $sup_{1,0}(D) :- m\_a(D).$
3. $sup_{2,0}(D) :- m\_a(D).$
4. $sup_{2,1}(D, I) :- sup_{2,0}(D), par(I, D).$
5. $anc(A, D) :- sup_{1,0}(D), par(A, D).$
6. $anc(A, D) :- sup_{2,1}(D, I), anc(A, I).$
7. $m\_a(\&1).$

The update types are the EDB relations *par* and *m_a*. The former is also a query type. The latter is updated from the user-supplied constant in the query, so is an update type even though it is not a query type. The IDB relations are *anc* and the *sup* predicates. The former is a query type, while the latter are all intermediate types. The magic predicate $m\_a$ is both an EDB and IDB predicate, and is an update type.

In summary, the predicates added by the magic sets transformation to the $anc$ predicate are of no direct interest to the user. Why can't we just throw them away?

Consider DDB (9.1) with the definitions of the intermediate types discarded:

$$1.\ m\_a(I) :- sup_{2,1}(D, I). \tag{9.2}$$
$$5.\ anc(A, D) :- sup_{1,0}(D), par(A, D).$$
$$6.\ anc(A, D) :- sup_{2,1}(D, I), anc(A, I).$$
$$7.\ m\_a(\&1).$$

The $sup$ relations are all empty, so that we can compute no tuples for the $anc$ relation. The intermediate types convey bindings from the EDB predicates to the IDB query types, so they are essential to the computation of the perfect model and therefore essential to the operation of the deductive database.

On the other hand, since the function of the intermediate types is to convey bindings, the deductive database can sometimes be transformed to eliminate them. Consider

$$q(X) :- i(X). \tag{9.3}$$
$$i(X) :- u(X).$$

where $q$ is a query type, $u$ is an update type, and $i$ is an intermediate type. Bindings for $X$ are derived from $u$, and conveyed to $q$ through $i$. We can eliminate the middleman, replacing the DDB (9.3) with

$$q(X) :- u(X). \tag{9.4}$$

It should be clear that the perfect model for $q$ in DDB (9.4) is the same as the perfect model for $q$ in DDB (9.3).

This type of transformation is called **unfolding**. In general, unfolding can be applied in the following circumstance: we have a clause with head predicate $h$ and a predicate $a$ of intermediate type in its body

$$h( \ldots ) :- a( \ldots ), r( \ldots ). \tag{9.5}$$

where $r$ is a possibly empty conjunction of predicates. We will call (9.5) the **target** clause. The definition of $a$ is the clause group

$$1.\ a( \ldots ) :- b_1( \ldots ). \tag{9.6}$$
$$\ldots$$
$$n.\ a( \ldots ) :- b_n( \ldots ).$$

where the $b_i$ are possibly empty conjunctions of predicates.

Let $s_i$ be the most general unifier (mgu) between the predicate $a$ in the body of the target clause and the head of the $i$th clause in the definition of $a$. It is possible that some of the clauses in the definition of $a$ will not unify with the goal $a$ in the target clause. If none of them unify with the goal, then the target clause can never generate any tuples, since no tuple in the $a$ relation will ever be selected in the target clause. In this case the target clause can simply be removed from the DDB (more properly, the programmer should be informed, as this situation is a possible error). If clause $i$ in the definition of $a$ does not unify with the goal in the target clause, then the mgu $s_i$ does not exist. We will assume that at least one of the $s_i$ exists.

We will denote the $k$ mgus which exist by $s_{ij}$, $j = 1, \ldots, k$; where $1 \le k \le n$. To perform the unfolding transformation, we replace the target clause by $k$ clauses:

1. $h(s_{i1} \ldots)$ :- $b_{i1}(s_{i1} \ldots)$, $r(s_{i1} \ldots)$. (9.7)

...

k. $h(s_{ik} \ldots)$ :- $b_{ik}(s_{ik} \ldots)$, $r(s_{ik} \ldots)$.

where $s_{ij}, \ldots$ in a predicate is the result of applying the substitutions in the mgu $s_{ij}$ to the variables in that predicate.

For example, we can elaborate the DDB of (9.3)

q(X, Y) :- i(Z, X), r(X, Y). (9.8)
i(1, W) :- u(1, W).
i(2, W) :- u(2, W).

Here we have the mgus

s1 = {1/Z, W/X} (9.9)
s2 = {2/Z, W/X}

and the target clause becomes

q(W, Y) :- u(1, W), r(W, Y). (9.10)
q(W, Y) :- u(2, W), r(W, Y).

If DDB (9.8) were instead

q(X, Y) :- i(2, X), r(X, Y). (9.11)
i(1, W) :- u(1, W).
i(2, W) :- u(2, W).

we would have only one mgu

s2 = {2/Z, W/X} (9.12)

and the target clause becomes

q(W, Y) :- u(2, W), r(W, Y). (9.13)

Finally, if DDB (9.8) were

q(X, Y) :- i(3, X), r(X, Y). (9.14)
i(1, W) :- u(1, W).
i(2, W) :- u(2, W).

there would be no mgus and the target clause would not contribute to the computation of the perfect model.

The implication of (9.5)–(9.7) is that intermediate predicates can always be eliminated from a DDB by unfolding. This brings us to the question: when is it a good idea to unfold a predicate?

The major cost in a DDB computation is the evaluation of a join. We therefore need to be very careful about making transformations which increase the number of joins. The magic sets transformation itself increases the number of joins, but the benefit of the transformation is to reduce greatly the number of tuples generated, so the benefit outweighs the cost. When we unfold a predicate, we eliminate a step of copying bindings. DDB (9.4) is simpler than DDB (9.3) in that the binding for $X$ is passed directly from EDB predicate $e$ to the IDB predicate $q$ rather than being copied through the intermediate predicate $i$. Since the computational cost saving is low, we generally avoid creating additional joins when unfolding.

Rule of thumb: unfold only when the number of joins is not increased.

## 9.2  FOLDING

**Folding** is the opposite of unfolding. It is related to common subexpression elimination in arithmetic. Suppose we have the DDB

   1. p(X, Y) :- a(X, Z), b(Z, Y).                    (9.15)
   2. q(W, U) :- a(W, V), b(V, U).

Clauses 1 and 2 compute exactly the same join. It therefore makes sense to compute the join once and copy the result to the other clause, so that we get the equivalent DDB

   1. p(X, Y) :- a(X, Z), b(Z, Y).                    (9.16)
   2. q(W, U) :- p(W, U).

We need to be careful that the subexpressions are really the same. Consider the DDB

   1. p(X, Y) :- a(X, Z), b(Z, Y), c(Z).              (9.17)
   2. q(W, U) :- a(W, V), b(V, U).

In this case, the subexpression $a(X, Z), b(Z, Y)$ in clause 1 is different from that in clause 2 since there is an additional constraint on the bindings for the variable $Z$ coming from the predicate $c(Z)$, which are not constraints on the variable $V$ in clause 2.

In general, we consider folding if we have a DDB of the form

   1. a( . . . ) :- k( . . . ), r( . . . ).            (9.18)
   2. b( . . . ) :- k'( . . . ).

where $k$ and $k'$ are conjunctions of predicates with the same principal functors. In the example (9.15):

   k is a(X, Z), b(Z, Y),                              (9.19)
   k' is a(W, V), b(V, U).

These predicates will be called the **common predicates**. We will call clause 1 of (9.18) the **target** clause and clause 2 the **folding** clause. The predicate $r$ in the target clause is a conjunction of predicates, which may be empty, and is called the **remainder** of the target clause body. We can perform unfolding if additional conditions *F1–F3* are met:

**F1**: There must exist a most general unifier $s$ between the common predicates $k$ and $k'$. If, for example,

$$k(\dots) = a(1, Z), b(Z, Y). \qquad\qquad (9.20)$$
$$k'(\dots) = a(W, V), b(V, 2).$$

then the mgu $s$ is

$$s = \{W/1, Z/V, Y/2\} \qquad\qquad (9.21)$$

whereas if

$$k(\dots) = a(1, Z), b(Z, Y). \qquad\qquad (9.22)$$
$$k'(\dots) = a(2, V), b(V, 2).$$

there is no mgu.

**F2**: We have to consider the **internal variables** of the folding clause. These are the variables which occur in the clause body but not in the clause head. In DDBs (9.15) and (9.17), the only internal variable is $Z$. Generally, if $\{X_1, \dots, X_n\}$ is the set of internal variables of the folding clause, then we have two conditions on the set of internal variables *with the substitution s applied*, denoted $\{X_1 s, \dots, X_n s\}$. These conditions are:

- no $X_i s$ appear in either the head or the remainder of the target clause;
- the $X_i s$ are distinct.

Each of these conditions guards against one way in which extra constraints can be placed on the common part in the target clause. In DDB (9.17), clause 2 has the internal variable $V$ in the folding clause. It would unify with the internal variable $Z$ in the target clause, which has an additional constraint that $Z$ must satisfy $c(Z)$. This is an example of the first situation *F2* guards against. An example of the second is

$$1.\ p(X, Y) :- a(X, A), b(A, A), c(A, Z). \qquad\qquad (9.23)$$
$$2.\ q(W, U) :- a(W, B), b(B, C), c(C, U).$$

Clause 2 of (9.23) is the folding clause, while clause 1 is the target clause. The two arguments of $b$ in the target are the same, which is a constraint not present in the folding clause.

**F3**: If the clause group to which the folding clause belongs has more than one member, then the head of no other clause in the group unifies with the head of the folding clause with the substitution $s$ applied. In the example

$$1.\ p(X, Y) :- a(1, Z), b(Z, Y). \qquad\qquad (9.24)$$
$$2.\ q(W, U) :- a(W, V), b(V, 2).$$
$$3.\ q(1, T) :- a(T, T).$$

unfolding cannot be performed, since the head of clause 3 unifies with the head of the unfolding clause 2 under the substitution (9.21). On the other hand, in the example

1. p(X, Y) :- a(2, Z), b(Z, Y), c(Y, S).                                  (9.25)
2. q(W, U) :- a(W, V), b(V, U).
3. q(1, T) :- a(T, T).

the mgu between the common parts of clauses 1 and 2 is

$s' = \{2/W, Z/V, Y/U\}$                                                   (9.26)

The substitution $s'$ applied to the head of the folding clause gives

$q(W, U)s' = q(2, Y)$                                                      (9.27)

and the clause head (9.27) does not unify with the head of clause 3 from DDB (9.25).

If these three conditions hold, then the common part of the target clause can be replaced by the head of the folding clause with the substitution $s$ applied. DDB (9.15) transforms to

1. p(X, Y) :- q(X, Y).                                                     (9.28)
2. q(W, U) :- a(W, V), b(V, U).

while DDB (9.25) transforms to

1. p(X, Y) :- q(2, Y), c(Y, S).                                           (9.29)
2. q(W, U) :- a(W, V), b(V, U).
3. q(1, T) :- a(T, T).

Rule of thumb: Folding always reduces the number of joins to be computed, so can be performed whenever possible.

### 9.3   EXAMPLE OF FOLDING AND UNFOLDING

We can use unfolding and folding to simplify the magic sets transformation of the *ancestor* relation, with binding pattern *f b*:

anc(A, D) :- par(A, D).                                                    (9.30)
anc(A, D) :- par(I, D), anc(A, I).

where *par* is the EDB relation and *anc* is a query type. The magic sets transformation (9.1) is copied for convenience:

1. $m\_a(I) :- sup_{2,1}(D, I)$.                                           (9.31)
2. $sup_{1,0}(D) :- m\_a(D)$.
3. $sup_{2,0}(D) :- m\_a(D)$.
4. $sup_{2,1}(D, I) :- sup_{2,0}(D), par(I, D)$.
5. $anc(A, D) :- sup_{1,0}(D), par(A, D)$.
6. $anc(A, D) :- sup_{2,1}(D, I), anc(A, I)$.
7. $m\_a(\&1)$.

The magic predicate $m\_a$ is an update type, but not a query type; while the predicates $sup_{1,0}$, $sup_{2,0}$, $sup_{2,1}$ are intermediate types.

We first note that the predicates $sup_{1,0}$ and $sup_{2,0}$ in clauses 2 and 3 are intermediate, and have only one predicate in their bodies. We can therefore unfold clause 2 into clause 5 and unfold clause 3 into clause 4, resulting in the equivalent DDB:

1. $m\_a(I)$ :- $sup_{2,1}(D, I)$.                                        (9.32)
4. $sup_{2,1}(D, I)$ :- $m\_a(D)$, $par(I, D)$.
5. $anc(A, D)$ :- $m\_a(D)$, $par(A, D)$.
6. $anc(A, D)$ :- $sup_{2,1}(D, I)$, $anc(A, I)$.
7. $m\_a(\&1)$.

Clause 4 could be unfolded into clauses 1 and 6, but since clause 4 has two predicates in its body, unfolding it in this way would increase the number of joins, so we do not unfold it.

On the other hand, we notice that clauses 4 and 5 have identical bodies. Conditions *F1*, *F2* and *F3* are trivially satisfied, so we can fold clause 5 into clause 4, obtaining the equivalent DDB:

1. $m\_a(I)$ :- $sup_{2,1}(D, I)$.                                        (9.33)
4. $sup_{2,1}(D, I)$ :- $anc(I, D)$.
5. $anc(A, D)$ :- $m\_a(D)$, $par(A, D)$.
6. $anc(A, D)$ :- $sup_{2,1}(D, I)$, $anc(A, I)$.
7: $m\_a(\&1)$.

We could equally well have folded clause 4 into clause 5 in (9.32). We chose *anc* as the target clause since *anc* is a query type and must be computed in any case, while $sup_{2,1}$ is an intermediate type.

Clause 4 of (9.33) now has only one body predicate, so the unfolding proposed for DDB (9.32) can now be performed, resulting in the equivalent

1. $m\_a(I)$ :- $anc(I, D)$.                                        (9.34)
5. $anc(A, D)$ :- $m\_a(D)$, $par(A, D)$.
6. $anc(A, D)$ :- $anc(I, D)$, $anc(A, I)$.
7. $m\_a(\&1)$.

There are no more intermediate types, so there are no more opportunities for unfolding. There are no common subexpressions in the clause bodies, so therefore no more opportunities for folding.

Compare the transformation of this section to the transformation of (8.34) to (8.35). Note also that the example in this section is in fact right linear, so the right linear recursion specialization of magic sets from Chapter 8 is appropriate, and gives a better result.

### 9.4   SUMMARY

Folding and unfolding are transformation techniques which can be used to simplify IDB predicates by elimination of intermediate types or elimination of common subexpressions. We will see in Chapter 10 that unfolding is particularly productive when applied to propositional systems.

## 9.5　FURTHER READING

The further reading on this topic is unfortunately not very easy. The material in this chapter is taken largely from Seki (1989). A more complete, but much more abstract, treatment of the material is given by Sato (1992). A good exposition of the closely related topic of partial evaluation is given by Lakhotia and Sterling (1990).

## 9.6　EXERCISES

9.1　Use unfolding to simplify the magic sets transformation of the *same_generation* predicate from 7.32.

9.2　Use unfolding and folding (if possible) to simplify the magic sets transformation of the *expression* predicate from Exercise 8.2. (Work from the published solution.)

## CHAPTER TEN

# Propositional deductive databases

Unfolding is especially productive when applied to propositional deductive databases. There are other methods which can be applied to these systems, and which can also be used in first-order deductive databases in some cases.

## 10.1 PROPOSITIONAL SYSTEMS

We have so far considered propositional systems only in passing. In this chapter, we focus on these systems and see that they have some special properties. Recall from Chapter 4 that a propositional system has no variables, so that all clauses are ground; and that consequently there is no quantification. Using negation as failure, a proposition is regarded as *true* if it appears in the EDB, as *false* if it does not.

Many expert systems are essentially propositional Horn clause systems. We will use the following simple expert system as an example:

Example 10.1: Barbecue planner expert system

    rain_forecast → call_off
    bob → all_foods
    mary → vegetarian_fish
    jim → meat
    vegetarian_fish & not meat → lentil_burgers
    meat & not vegetarian_fish → steak
    meat & vegetarian_fish → fish
    all_foods → hot_dogs

The update types, with their intended interpretations, are

    *rain_forecast* – the weather forecast is rain
    *bob* – Bob has accepted an invitation to the barbecue

*mary* – Mary has accepted an invitation to the barbecue
*jim* – Jim has accepted an invitation to the barbecue

The query types, with their intended interpretations, are

*call_off* – the barbecue is to be called off
*lentil_burgers* – lentil burgers will be served
*steak* – steak will be served
*fish* – fish will be served
*hot_dogs* – hot dogs will be served

The intermediate types, with their intended interpretations, are

*vegetarian_ fish* – someone has been invited who is a vegetarian but will tolerate fish
*meat* – someone has been invited who prefers meat but will tolerate fish
*all_ foods* – someone has been invited who has no strong food preferences

The perfect model is intended to contain at most one of the query types other than *call_off*: in other words, the person planning the barbecue is expecting to serve only one type of food.


### 10.1.1   Recursion, stratification and indeterminacy

Propositional systems are simpler than first-order systems, so that some of the more problematic aspects of datalog either disappear or are reduced in importance.

Recursion as a concept does not apply to propositional systems. Apparently recursive formulas can be simplified. In particular, linear recursive formulas are tautologies. Consider

$$p :- q \ \& \ p. \tag{10.1}$$

Using the equivalence

$$p :- q = p + \sim q \tag{10.2}$$

formula (10.1) simplifies to

$$\begin{aligned} p :- q \ \& \ p &= p + \sim(q \ \& \ p) \\ &= p + \sim p + \sim q \\ &= \text{true} \end{aligned} \tag{10.3}$$

Mutual recursion is conditional equivalence. Consider

$$\begin{aligned} p &:- q \ \& \ r. \\ q &:- s \ \& \ p. \end{aligned} \tag{10.4}$$

Applying (10.2), the convention that all the clauses are true formulas, and the identity

$$(x \equiv y) = (x \ \& \ y) + (\sim x \ \& \ \sim y) \tag{10.5}$$

formula (10.4) becomes

$$(p + \sim q + \sim r) \ \& \ (q + \sim s + \sim p) = \qquad (10.6)$$

$$(p \ \& \ q) + (p \ \& \sim s) + \textit{false} +$$
$$\textit{false} + (\sim q \ \& \sim s) + (\sim q \ \& \sim p) +$$
$$(\sim r \ \& \ q) + (\sim r \ \& \sim s) + (\sim r \ \& \sim p) =$$

$$(p \equiv q) + \sim s \ \& \ (p + \sim q) + \sim r \ \& \ (q + \sim p) + \sim s \ \& \sim r$$

which says that if $s$ and $r$ are true, then $p$ and $q$ are equivalent. (If $s$ and $r$ have the value *true*, then all the disjuncts except $(p \equiv q)$ have the value *false*.)

This is an indeterminacy. If in the course of the semi-naive algorithm an alternative proof is found for either $p$ or $q$, then the formulas (10.4) will assign the same truth value to the other. If no other proof is found, then there is more than one model for the system.

Non-stratification leads to indeterminacy. From Chapter 4, a logic program is not stratified if its dependency graph has a cycle at least one edge of which is negative. In a propositional system, the general case of a cyclic dependency graph with one negative edge is

$$p :\text{-} \ q \ \& \ r. \qquad (10.7)$$
$$q :\text{-} \sim p \ \& \ s.$$

Applying identity (10.2), (10.7) becomes

$$p\&q + p + p\&\sim s + p\&\sim q + \sim q\&\sim s + q\&\sim r + p\&\sim r + \sim r\&\sim s = \qquad (10.8)$$
$$p + \sim q\&\sim s + q\&\sim r + \sim r\&\sim s$$

which is equivalent to $p$ if $r$ and $s$ are *true*, but to $p+q$ if $s$ is true and $r$ is false, and so forth. If both $r$ and $s$ are *true*, then the formulas (10.7) do not constrain $q$ at all, so that unless there is some other way of determining $q$, the system is indeterminate.

The point is that in propositional systems, recursion and non-stratification can be seen to be conditional indeterminacy. Recursive or non-stratified subsystems can be identified as errors and reported to the programmer. Alternatively, the propositions $r$ and $s$ in (10.6) and (10.8) define the conditions under which the formulas are well-behaved. The expressions deriving $r$ and $s$ therefore play the part of integrity constraints, and could therefore be removed from the expert system proper into a knowledge base which tests inputs for validity. Recursion and non-stratification are therefore eliminated, and therefore all the dependency graphs are acyclic.

We lose very little practical generality if we restrict our attention in propositional systems to Horn clause systems where the dependency graph is acyclic.

## 10.2 UNFOLDING APPLIED TO PROPOSITIONAL SYSTEMS

### 10.2.1 Application of unfolding

An important fact about propositional Horn clause systems where the dependency graph is acyclic is that they are equivalent to decision tables. No matter how many

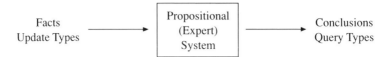

**Figure 10.1**   Functional view of propositional systems.

rules there are, and how many steps the semi-naive algorithm takes to compute the perfect model, the system is functionally dependent on the update types, and can be computed in a single step from a decision table. This relationship is a simple consequence of the truth-table method for evaluation of propositional expressions, and is illustrated in Figure 10.1. A propositional system of this type maps subsets of true facts into subsets of true conclusions.

Unfortunately, the simple truth-table method which shows the functional view to be valid does not provide a practicable method for computing the function, since the number of rows in the decision table is exponential in the number of facts in the update types. In this section, we show that unfolding provides a practicable method for computing the decision table equivalent to a propositional Horn clause system with an acyclic dependency graph.

In the general discussion about unfolding in Chapter 9, we gave the rule of thumb that unfolding might increase the number of joins, so should be used with caution. In propositional systems, the join is a very simple operation: namely the logical conjunction of two propositions, which can be implemented very cheaply. Therefore in propositional systems, there is no restriction on unfolding. If the propositional system is acyclic, then the propositions which are neither update nor query types can be eliminated by unfolding.

The transformed system has no intermediate types. If no IDB query type is in the antecedent of any rule (the user does not want to see intermediate results) then the resulting system is a set of rules whose antecedents are entirely facts. If no update type is the consequent of any rule (the user does not want to override intermediate results), then the resulting system is a set of rules whose consequents are entirely conclusions. The perfect model can be computed in a single step of the semi-naive algorithm. The resulting rules can be displayed in the form of a decision table with don't care conditions.

A **decision table** is an array whose column headings are attribute names. It is intended to classify cases. A **case** is an assignment of a single value to each attribute, corresponding to an EDB in the above. The rightmost column is the **conclusions**. Each cell contains a subset of the possible values for its attribute. This subset is called a **condition**. A case is said to **fire** a cell if the value of the cell's attribute in the case is a subset of the values in the cell. A row of the table is said to fire if all its cells fire. The conclusion in each row is an action to be performed if the row fires. A condition is called a **don't care condition** if it contains more than one value of the associated attribute. Conventionally, a cell whose condition is all possible values of the attribute is represented by a blank or a dash. In the following a blank cell will be used.

Example 10.2: Decision table equivalent of Example 10.1

| rain | bob | mary | jim | conclusion |
|------|-----|------|-----|------------|
| y    |     |      |     | call_off |
| n    |     | y    | n   | lentil_burgers |
| n    |     | n    | y   | steak |
| n    |     | y    | y   | fish |
| n    | y   | n    | n   | hot_dogs |

Note that propositional systems often reason about continuous measurements (e.g. the temperature of a boiler). The knowledge concerning the continuous measurement is usually expressed in qualitative terms, for example *temperature in the normal range*. There are generally rules which express the qualitative knowledge as a proposition, for example

(temperature < high_threshold) & (temperature > low_threshold) → temp_normal

These kinds of rules are often called **filter rules**.

## 10.2.2   Decision tables

The reader who verifies the decision table in Example 10.2 by unfolding the rules in Example 10.1 will notice that the unfolding process does not account for the n conditions in the *rain* column. The immediate justification of the n conditions is from the domain point of view: if the barbecue is to be called off on account of rain, there is no point in deciding on a menu.

More generally, it is very common in the construction of expert systems for the sequence of rules to be significant. If the system is evaluated depth-first by backwards chaining, we have seen in Chapter 2 that the earlier rules are tried before the later. The analogous depth-first approach to forward chaining (used by OPS-5 style interpreters) has a similar effect. In Chapter 4, the perfect model is evaluated breadth-first. All the consequents of the antecedents at each stage are computed before proceeding. In the depth-first systems, when a new proposition is given a value, the interpreter immediately attempts to evaluate rules which have that proposition in their antecedent. These interpreters are often programmed to stop as soon as a query type or conclusion proposition becomes *true*. In Example 10.1, the first rule, if it fires, establishes a conclusion. An interpreter of this type would therefore not attempt to execute any of the other rules. We can call this type of interpreter a **single-solution interpreter**.

It should be clear that a single-solution interpreter computes only part of the perfect model. It should also be clear that the sequence of rules can be preserved under unfolding. One strategy which achieves this effect is when an earlier rule is unfolded into a later rule, to move the later rule into the position of the earlier. If one rule is unfolded into several rules, the relative sequence of the rules is preserved. If the resulting decision table is evaluated one row at a time in the sequence given, then the conclusions are computed in the same sequence as the single-solution interpreter applied to the original rules, as shown in Example 10.2.

A decision table is said to be **ambiguous** if there is any assignment of truth-values to the update types which results in more than one query type having the value *true*. In other words, there is some input for which the expert system can come to more than one conclusion. It is easy to test a decision table for ambiguity: the table is ambiguous if the conditions in any row satisfy the conditions in any other row with a different conclusion. There are also procedures in the further reading for automatic elimination of ambiguity. The decision table arising from application of unfolding to Example 10.1 is ambiguous. The unambiguous table in Example 10.2 is derived from that of Example 10.1 by adding the negation of the condition for *call_off* to each of the other rows.

### 10.2.3   Decision trees

An unambiguous decision table can be transformed into a decision tree, which is simply a nested if-then statement. Figure 10.2 shows a decision tree equivalent of the table in Example 10.2.

A decision tree is formed from a decision table by recursively selecting a proposition as a node of the tree, then dividing the decision table into two: all rows where the condition is y are attached to the y arc of the tree, and all rows where the condition is n attached to the n arc. Rows with don't care conditions are put into both tables. The tree in Figure 10.2 was obtained from the table in Example 10.2 by selecting the propositions *rain*, then *mary*, then *jim* then *bob*. It is not necessary to select the same proposition in each of the sub-tables. There are algorithms given in the further reading for making selections of propositions which yield small trees.

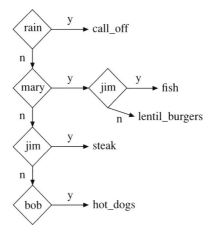

**Figure 10.2**   Decision tree equivalent of the table in Example 10.2.

## 10.2.4  Negation

In the discussion so far we have been treating negation from the logical point of view. Recall from Chapter 2 that a Horn clause cannot have a negated proposition as its head, so that a Horn clause system under the semi-naive algorithm can never prove a negation. Propositional datalog can therefore be seen to be weaker than the propositional calculus, since in the latter the truth-table decision procedure can be used to prove any theorem. In Prolog, we saw that negation was handled using the concept of negation-as-failure: a negated goal is defined to succeed if the unnegated goal fails.

Propositional datalog can make use of negation-as-failure. Its application here can be seen by considering identity (10.2), repeated here for convenience

$$p \text{ :- } q = p + \sim q$$

If $q$ is true then we can conclude $p$, but if $q$ is false, we cannot conclude anything about $p$. Using negation-as-failure, we assume $\sim p$ if we have $\sim q$: in other words a proposition is assumed false unless proven true.

Unfolding cannot in general be performed on negative subgoals. In propositional systems, however, we can unfold a negative subgoal using negation-as-failure. If we have $\sim p$ in a clause body and a definition of $p$

$$p \text{ :- } q_1. \tag{10.9}$$
$$p \text{ :- } q_2.$$
$$\ldots$$
$$p \text{ :- } q_n.$$

then we can replace $\sim p$ in clause bodies by the negation of (10.9), or

$$\sim p = \sim(q_1 + q_2 + \ldots + q_n) \tag{10.10}$$

This transformation has in fact been used in Examples 10.1 and 10.2.

There are situations where we can directly prove a negative proposition, so need not rely on negation-as-failure. Horn clause systems with the semi-naive algorithm do not allow the direct proof of negative propositions. However, if we wish to prove $\sim p$, we can define a new proposition $np = \sim p$ and use the new proposition in the clause head. We need the integrity constraint

$$p \equiv \sim np \tag{10.11}$$

With this tactic, we treat $p$ and $np$ as distinct propositions, with the stipulation that neither depends on the other. The consistency aspect of (10.11) is an integrity constraint, which can be enforced by checking that the unfolded definitions of the two are inconsistent:

$$p \text{ :- } qp. \tag{10.12}$$
$$np \text{ :- } qn.$$
$$qp \,\&\, qn \supset \textit{false}.$$

To check the completeness aspect of (10.11) we would also need to test

$$qp + qn \supset \textit{true}. \tag{10.13}$$

### 10.2.5    Uses of transformed systems

We have seen that, using unfolding and other techniques, propositional Horn clause systems can be transformed into decision tables and decision trees. Other transformations have been alluded to, for example extraction of integrity checks. The power of the method is that the transformations are automatic and provably maintain the behaviour of the system. The transformations permit the knowledge to be viewed in different ways, each of which has advantages.

The original Horn clause formulation of the knowledge base of an expert system may be a very convenient way for the human domain experts and knowledge engineers to understand the content of the knowledge. The decision table form can easily be tested for consistency, completeness and computational stability. The decision tree form is easily compiled into nested if-then statements for very fast execution, and can easily be analysed for consistency of dialog and the conditions under which expensive tests must be performed. In fact, the procedure for generating the decision tree from the decision table can be tailored to achieve consistency of dialog and postponement of expensive tests.

Computational stability is a property which is visible from the decision table form of the knowledge. Most expert systems reason from qualitative statements about measurements, such as whether a given measured variable is *low*, *normal* or *high*. If the variable is continuous, it can have a value which is just below normal. In the qualitative statement, the value is *low*, and not distinguished from a value which is much lower than normal. Propositional expert systems are used to make classifications, which are often qualitatively different. For example, an expert system used to monitor a power plant might identify some states of the plant which call for emergency shutdown, some states which call for immediate repair, and some which call for routine attention in the next maintenance shift.

Using the decision table view of the knowledge, it is not difficult to determine the minimum difference in the measured system state which would cause a change from one grade of classification to another. Ideally, a system designer would like several variables in the plant to change to make the difference between routine maintenance and emergency shutdown, for example.

More complete indications of how to perform these analyses can be found in the further reading section 10.5.

### 10.3    APPLICATIONS TO SEMI-PROPOSITIONAL PRODUCTION SYSTEMS

It frequently occurs that expert systems require more than the propositional calculus. These systems are often implemented in forward chaining expert system languages related to OPS-5, which was described in Chapter 4. An example of such a system, SIRATAC, is discussed in Chapter 1. Many of these systems (like SIRATAC) can be implemented as deductive databases, and (again like SIRATAC) they often have a large number of propositional subgoals as well as first-order subgoals. Many of the rules may be entirely propositional.

It is possible to factor propositional subgoals out of clauses. For example

r(X, Y) :- p, q, s(X, Y, Z), t(Z), u(Y).                                        (10.14)

is equivalent to

if p & q then                                                                   (10.15)
    r(X, Y) :- s(X, Y, Z), t(Z), u(Y).

The resulting proposition-free Horn clauses can be regarded as similar to a conclusion in a propositional system. The propositional system can be transformed into a decision table or a decision tree, so that each first-order clause is executed only if what might be called its **propositional guard** is true. The propositional guards might be thought of as situation descriptors which specify the conditions under which the first-order rule applies. If a system has a large number of propositional subgoals, and most of the first-order clauses contain one or more propositional subgoals, then a substantial reduction in execution time might be achieved by this strategy.

It is also the case that programs written in OPS-5 related languages frequently have propositional working memory elements which are updated, which are therefore non-monotonic and therefore not deductive databases (non-monotonic systems are discussed in Chapter 12). These updated propositions are generally used as state variables to section the rules so that fewer are considered at each stage of the recognize-act cycle. For example, a computation might have several stages (like SIRATAC). A wme called *<task>* might be used to control the stages. It would have several possible values, e.g. *stage_1*, *stage_2*, ... The initial value of *<task>* would be *stage_1*. When a rule is executed which knows that it concludes stage 1, part of its action would be to modify the value of *<task>* to *stage_2*.

Each state, identified by a combination of values of the updateable propositional wmes, selects a subset of the rules, which we will call the **program for that state**. The whole system can be regarded as a finite-state machine, whose action at any state is to execute its state program and whose transitions are determined by the program. If each state program is monotonic, then the methods of deductive databases can be applied to it.

### 10.4   SUMMARY

Our argument is that:

- most expert systems are either propositional or expressed in OPS-5 related languages;
- OPS-5 programs are similar to deductive databases; however, they sometimes contain non-monotonic actions, so are not always deductive databases;
- some of the non-monotonic actions are used to implement aggregation, as discussed in Chapter 4;
- other non-monotonic actions are state selectors, as discussed above;

■ many expert systems are therefore deductive databases, or at least collections of deductive databases, so that the methods described in this book can be applied;

■ many expert systems which are first-order deductive databases are largely propositional, so that the methods described in this chapter can be applied.

## 10.5 FURTHER READING

This chapter is drawn from a variety of sources. Most books on artificial intelligence describe at least propositional expert systems, for example Winston (1992), Genesereth and Nilsson (1987) or Rich and Knight (1991). A good introduction to first-order expert systems programmed in OPS-5 is Brownston *et al.* (1985). The application of unfolding to propositional expert systems is described by Colomb and Chung (1995), and an algorithm for transforming a decision table to a decision tree is given by Shwayder (1974). Various consistency and completeness tests for decision tables are given by Cragun and Steudel (1987), and the notion of computational stability in expert systems is described in Colomb (1992).

## 10.6 EXERCISES

10.1  Flatten the following set of propositional rules:

1. f1 & f2 → a1
2. ~f2 & f3 & f4 & ~f5 → a2
3. ~a1 & ~a2 → c2
4. a1 & a2 → c1
5. f5 & a1 → a2

where {f1, f2, f3, f4, f5} is the set of update types,
{c1, c2} is the set of query types,
and {a1, a2} is the set of propositions which are neither update nor query types.

Express the result as a decision table, and then as a decision tree written in Pascal, C or some other appropriate language. The result will look something like

if f1 then
    . . .
else
    . . .

**Hint**: you may need to simplify a boolean algebra expression using the identity x + x&y = x.

## CHAPTER ELEVEN

# Integrity constraints

In this chapter we consider the representation of integrity constraints and their integration into the deductive database.

## 11.1  UPDATES

We have seen in Chapter 4 that a deductive database can be divided into two parts, the EDB and the IDB. The EDB is the database of ground unit clauses, while the perfect model for the relations described by the predicates in a particular IDB is determined uniquely by the set of tuples comprising its associated EDB. We can therefore say that the perfect model is functionally dependent on the EDB.

Another partition of the deductive database we have seen in several chapters is into update, query and intermediate types. In particular, the update types are the predicates whose populations are allowed to be changed by the user, while the query types are those predicates whose populations are allowed to be viewed by the user. Note that the update and query types are relative to a class of user. Taking the University Calendar deductive database as an example, relative to the students the update types include enrolments, while relative to the Departments the update types include subjects offered and prerequisite structures, but not enrolments.

Therefore, from the point of view of a class of user, the population of the query types is functionally dependent on the population of the update types in the same way that the perfect model is functionally dependent on the EDB, assuming the remainder of the database is held constant. Further, for the given class of user, the entire state of the database is determined by the population of the update types. If we designate the population of the update types at a particular time by $U$, we can say that an update $u$ changes the population to a possibly different population $V$.

If we think in terms of populations of the update types, it makes sense to consider the set of possible populations, which we might call $S$. In other words, each member of the set $S$ is a possible population of the update types.

There are three kinds of elementary updates possible: we can

■ add a new clause;
■ delete an existing clause;
■ alter an existing clause.

We can alter a clause by first deleting the existing clause then adding the revised clause, so that all updates can be done by combinations of deletions and additions. An update transaction is therefore a collection of additions and deletions. Recall that a transaction is applied atomically, so that it does not make sense to add and delete the same clause. We can therefore assume that the clauses added are different from the clauses deleted. Since the clauses added differ from the clauses deleted, we can apply the additions and deletions in any order. We can express a transaction $T$ as a sequence of elementary updates

$$T = add(t_1), \ldots, add(t_k), delete(t_{k+1}), \ldots, delete(t_n) \tag{11.1}$$

Our intuition about updates is that the update transaction derives from a particular state of the database: the application generating the update usually performs a query, then constructs the update from the results of the query and additional inputs, perhaps from the user.

If we look a little deeper, we see that the update is actually relevant to many states of the database. Generally, there are many states of the database which give the same result to the query. For example, if a student wishes to change enrolment, the tuples recording the enrolment of other students are very rarely relevant. Since we want updates to apply to many states of the database, it will be easier if we consider that they apply to all states.

First consider the elementary update $add(t)$ to database state (population) $D \in S$. If clause $t$ is in $D$ already, the resulting state is $D$, otherwise the resulting state is $D \cup \{t\}$. Similarly, we can apply the elementary update $delete(t)$ to a database state $D$. If clause $t$ is in $D$, then the resulting state is $D / \{t\}$. If clause $t$ is not in $D$, then the resulting state is unchanged.

This allows us to view an update transaction as an operator on the set of update type states. In symbols, given a specific update transaction $T$, we have

$$T : S \to S \tag{11.2}$$

where the action of $T$ is the composition of the actions of its add and delete constituents.

## 11.2  INTEGRITY CONSTRAINTS

An integrity constraint is a description of allowed states of the database, i.e. both the domain and range of the transaction operator (11.2) are restricted by the integrity constraints. If a particular transaction $T$ maps a particular state $s$ in $S$ outside $S$, then $T$ is not allowed for database state $s$.

**Figure 11.1**  The NIAM uniqueness constraint.

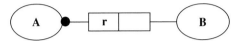

**Figure 11.2**  The NIAM mandatory constraint.

**Figure 11.3**  The NIAM subtype constraint.

Integrity constraints are frequently determined in the conceptual modelling phase of information systems development, and some kinds of constraints can be modelled using information systems modelling methods. Of particular interest to us is that most integrity constraints encountered in practice can be expressed as formulas in the first-order predicate calculus with aggregation. We will show below that these formulas can be translated automatically into normal Prolog programs, so that they integrate well with the deductive database theory we have encountered so far.

We will consider some examples of integrity constraints which can be modelled using the NIAM conceptual modelling method. Figure 11.1 shows the *uniqueness* constraint, which indicates that each entity in population $A$ participates in relation $r$ with at most one entity in population $B$.

This uniqueness constraint can be expressed in predicate calculus as

$$\forall X \ r(X, Z), r(X, Y) \rightarrow Y = Z \qquad (11.3)$$

Figure 11.2 shows the *mandatory* constraint, which indicates that each entity in population $A$ participates in relation $r$ with at least one entity in population $B$.

The mandatory constraint can be expressed in predicate calculus as

$$\forall X \exists Y \ a(X) \rightarrow r(X, Y). \qquad (11.4)$$

Figure 11.3 shows the *subtype* constraint, which indicates that every member of population $A$ is also a member of population $B$.

The subtype constraint can be expressed in predicate calculus as

$$\forall X \ a(X) \rightarrow b(X). \qquad (11.5)$$

There are many kinds of constraints which are not normally expressed in NIAM diagrams. Also, the integrity constraints may be expressed in terms of IDB predicates as well as EDB predicates. For example, suppose we have an application whose EDB consists of a graph, whose IDB consists of a transitive closure algorithm, and the integrity constraint is that the graph must be acyclic (directed acyclic graph from Chapter 3). The first-order expression of this situation is given in (11.6), where IC indicates the integrity constraint:

EDB:    arc(Source, Sink).                                    (11.6)
        $\forall X \forall Y(arc(X, Y) +$
            $\exists Z(arc(X, Z) \ \& \ path(Z, Y)))$
        $\rightarrow path(X, Y)$

IC:     not $\exists X \ path(X, X)$.

## 11.3    INTEGRITY CONSTRAINTS AS HORN CLAUSES

We now have the ability to express integrity constraints as formulas in the first-order predicate calculus. As we noted in Chapter 2, the logic programming language upon which the theory of deductive databases is built allows only Horn clauses, which are less general than the predicate calculus, so that we may not be able to represent our integrity constraints in our deductive database in the natural way. Later, we extended the theory to include negated predicates in the clause body using negation-as-failure, but these negated predicates cannot be used as conclusions. The essential character of Horn clause logic is thus retained: that only predicates occurring in clause heads can be derived.

However, we notice that the integrity constraints are used in a restricted way in databases and by extension in deductive databases. They are used only to test whether a database state is valid, i.e. we wish to be notified if a transaction puts the database in a state where at least one of the integrity constraint formulas is not satisfied.

Note that integrity constraints could in principle be used to derive conclusions. For example, if the population $B$ of the mandatory constraint example (11.4) had a single member, say $b$, then for every member $a$ of $A$, we would be able to conclude $r(a,b)$, since every member of $A$ must be in relation $r$ with at least one member of $B$, and $B$ has only the one member.

By limiting our use of integrity constraints to the detection of violations, giving up some of the power of first-order logic, we can use a trick to express them as Horn clauses. In terms of Chapter 5, we give up knowledge goal independence. Since we are interested in the absence of violations, we declare two special predicates, *bad* and *no_violations*. The predicate *bad* is true if at least one of the integrity constraints is violated, and *no_violations* is defined as

no_violations :- not bad.                                     (11.7)

If the integrity constraint theory consists of the $n$ formulas $W_i$, $i = 1, \ldots, n$, then the special predicate *bad* is defined:

bad :- not $W_1$.                                             (11.8)
. . .
bad :- not $W_n$.

| | | | |
|---|---|---|---|
| (a) | A :- not (V and W). | >> | A :- not V. |
| | | | A :- not W. |
| (b) | A :- ∀X W. | >> | A :- not ∃X not W. |
| (c) | A :- not∀XW. | >> | A :- ∃X not W. |
| (d) | A :- W → V. | >> | A :- V. |
| | | | A :- not W. |
| (e) | A :- not (W → V). | >> | A :- not V, W. |
| (f) | A :- V or W. | >> | A :- V. |
| | | | A :- W. |
| (g) | A :- not(V or W). | >> | A :- not V, not W. |
| (h) | A :- not W. | >> | A :- W. |
| (i) | A :- ∃X W. | >> | A :- W. |
| (j) | A :- not ∃X W(X, Y). | >> | A :- not p(Y). |
| | | | p(Y) :- ∃X W (X, Y). |
| (k) | A ≡ B | >> | A → B, B → A. |

**Figure 11.4**  Reduction rules for clause bodies.

If the integrity constraints (11.3)–(11.6) were applied to the same deductive database system, then the Horn clause representation would be (noting that $\forall X p(X) \equiv \sim\exists X \sim p(X)$):

bad :- ∃X not r(X, Z), r(X, Y) → Y = Z.    uniqueness          (11.9)
bad :- ∃X not ∃Y a(X) → r(X, Y).          mandatory
bad :- ∃X not a(X) → b(X).                subtype
bad :- not ∃X path(X, X).                 acyclic
no_violations :- not bad.

Expression of constraints as Horn clauses with first-order bodies has helped to a degree, in that we now have a clause head. However, the clause bodies in the deductive databases must be conjunctions of either positive or negative literals, i.e. they must not contain disjunction symbols or implication symbols, and certainly not quantifiers.

Fortunately, there is a procedure by which an arbitrary first-order predicate formula used as a clause body can be transformed into a *normal* program: a conjunction of positive and negative literals, so long as we make the closed world assumption and are willing to tolerate negation as failure.

Figure 11.4 shows the rewriting rules which suffice to transform an arbitrary first-order formula in the clause body into a normal program. The procedure is to find a clause of the form of one of the left-hand sides, then replace it with the right-hand side. The process continues until the program is normal. The process always terminates, and always produces a normal program. In using the rules, assume that the formula is of the form $A$ :- $W_1, W_2, \ldots, W_n$; where $W_i$ is a first-order formula with ~ replaced by *not*.

In rule (j), the body predicate is represented as $W(X, Y)$, to indicate that $W$ may have variables other than $X$. The predicate $p$ is introduced by the transformation. It should have a principal functor different from any other principal functor in the program. It has the same variables as $W$, excluding the variable $X$. The variable $X$

is not present in the new predicate's clause head, since the original predicate fails if the new predicate succeeds (see the material on negation-as-failure in Chapter 2). The new predicate has the other variables, designated $Y$, since its function is to communicate the variable bindings from the head, $A$, of the original clause to the body, $W$, of the new predicate.

We show below an example of the application of these rules. The predicate in (11.10) is based on the *ancestor* family of predicates from Chapter 2. It is true if none of a person's descendants are male.

    no_male_descendants(X) :-                                            (11.10)
        ∀Y(ancestor(X, Y) → female(Y)).

Applying (b), we get

    no_male_descendants(X) :-                                            (11.11)
        not ∃Y not (ancestor(X, Y) → female(Y)).

Applying (j), we get

    no_male_descendants(X) :-                                            (11.12)
        :- not male_descendant(X).
    male_descendant(X) :-
        ∃Y not (ancestor(X, Y) → female(Y)).

Note that the intermediate predicate *male_descendant* has the variable $X$, since this variable is present in the body of (11.11), but does not have the variable $Y$, since $Y$ is negatively existentially quantified in (11.11).

Applying (i), we get

    male_descendant(X) :-                                                (11.13)
        not (ancestor(X, Y) → female(Y).

Applying (e) we get

    male_descendant(X) :-                                                (11.14)
        not female(Y), ancestor(X, Y).

resulting in

    no_male_descendants(X) :-                                            (11.15)
        not male_descendant(X).
    male_descendant(X) :-
        not female(Y), ancestor(X, Y).

which is a normal program.


### 11.4  EFFECT OF UPDATES

As we have seen above, an update transaction consists of a series of *add* operations followed by a series of *delete* operations. These operations may be on either the

EDB, IDB or the integrity constraints. We assume that the database satisfied the integrity constraints before application of the update. The problem is to determine whether the database state resulting from the update satisfies the integrity constraints. Clearly, one way to do this is to re-evaluate the entire set of integrity constraints. Although it is sometimes necessary to perform a complete re-evaluation, it is frequently the case that the amount of computation can be reduced dramatically.

In particular, if the update is the removal of an integrity constraint, no computation need be done at all. If the database satisfies a set of constraints, it satisfies a less severe set of constraints. If the update is the addition of an integrity constraint, then only this new constraint must be evaluated: the database already satisfies the others.

An update to the EDB is the addition or deletion of a tuple from a relation. The EDB update may have additional effects on the perfect model, either the addition or deletion of tuples. An update to the IDB has the same result: it adds or deletes tuples from the perfect model, which may result in the addition or deletion of other tuples from other IDB predicates.

An integrity constraint is a first-order formula involving predicates which may be either in the EDB or the IDB. We observe that an update which does not affect any of the predicates in a particular integrity constraint cannot change the value of that constraint. If the database satisfied the constraint before the update, then it satisfies it afterwards. On the other hand, it may require partial evaluation of the perfect model to tell whether the update affects a particular IDB predicate involved in a particular integrity constraint.

Our first step in efficiently evaluating integrity constraints on updates is therefore to make a table of the relationship between update types and integrity constraints. We can unfold all the predicates in the integrity constraints (see Chapter 9) until we get all the update types upon which they depend directly or indirectly. This unfolding is a purely syntactic operation and does not affect the operation of the database. If we identify each constraint and each predicate, we can make an associative relation between the two sets of names which records the progress of unfolding. Given this associative relation and a list of predicates involved in an update, we can recover a list of integrity constraints which might be affected by the update. As well, we can recover a sequence of IDB predicates leading from the update to an affected constraint.

For example, suppose we have the following program:

icl :- idb1(X), edb1(X).                                      (11.16)
ic2 :- idb2(X), not idb3(X).
idb1(X) :- idb4(X, Y), edb2(X).
idb2(X) :- edb3(X), edb4(X).
idb3(X) :- not edb5(X), edb6(X).
idb4(X, Y) :- edb7(X, Y), not edb8(X).
otheridb(X) :- edb2(X), edb4(X), edb6(X), edb8(X).

Recall that for the system to satisfy the integrity constraints, neither *ic1* nor *ic2* may have any solutions. That is, for *ic1*, for any $X$, either *idb1* or *idb2* must fail to have a solution; and for *ic2*, either *idb2* must not have a solution or *idb3* must.

**Table 11.1**   Dependency table between predicates

| Constraint | Predicate | Constraint | Predicate |
|---|---|---|---|
| ic1 | idb1 | idb3 | edb5 |
| ic1 | edb1 | idb3 | edb6 |
| ic2 | idb2 | idb4 | edb7 |
| ic2 | idb3 | idb4 | edb8 |
| idb1 | idb4 | otheridb | edb2 |
| idb1 | edb2 | otheridb | edb4 |
| idb2 | edb3 | otheridb | edb6 |
| idb2 | edb4 | otheridb | edb8 |

The associative relation is a relational representation of the connectivity of the dependency graph of Chapter 4, which is essentially the same thing as the knowledge diagram of Chapter 5. The relational representation is a supertype of the *literal/calls* table of the CASE tool described in Chapter 6. Here, we will call it a **dependency table**. Its population for program (11.16) is given in Table 11.1.

The set of predicates leading to integrity constraints which are potentially affected by a change to an update predicate *p* is given by the transitive closure query *affected* defined as

affected(Affected_Predicate, Update_Predicate) :-        (11.17)
    dependency(Affected_Predicate, Update_Predicate).
affected(Affected_Predicate, Update_Predicate) :-
    dependency(Intermediate_Predicate, Update_Predicate),
    affected(Affected_Predicate, Intermediate_Predicate).

If the EDB relation *edb2* is updated, then the predicates *idb1*, *ic1* and *otheridb* are potentially affected. However, the *affected* query on the dependency table tells us that only *idb1* and *ic1* need be considered. We therefore do not need to perform any computations in *otheridb*, nor on any of the other predicates or integrity constraints. Constraint *ic2* will be satisfied after the update to *edb2* no matter what that update is. The model for *otheridb* will possibly change, but it is not relevant to any integrity constraint.

Furthermore, whether an update can change the value of an affected predicate depends on whether the updated predicate occurs positively or negatively in the body of an affected integrity constraint. Consider constraint *ic2* in (11.16). If this constraint is true in the original state of the database, then there must either not be a solution for subgoal *idb2* in that database state, or there must be a solution for *idb3*. If we delete a tuple from *idb2*, the constraint must still be satisfied since there either was no solution, or a solution existed which was also a solution for *idb3*. Similarly, if we add a tuple to *idb3*, the constraint must still be satisfied, since adding a tuple to the predicate defining a negative literal can never make the negative literal true.

In order to use this observation we need to know whether an update affects a particular predicate positively or negatively. Since IDB predicates may appear in integrity constraints, and there may be a long chain of inference involving both positive and negative predicates between the updated predicate and the constraint, we need a procedure to propagate the update through the IDB.

This algorithm will collect in set $P$ all the clauses which involve adding tuples to the perfect model, and in the set $N$ all the clauses which involve deleting tuples from the perfect model. Recall that an elementary update either adds or deletes clauses. We begin by collecting all the clauses added in the set $P$, and all the clauses deleted in the set $N$, and by identifying the IDB and integrity constraint clauses affected by the updates as the subprogram $R$. Let $preds(P)$ be the predicate names represented by clauses in $P$, and $preds(N)$ be the predicate names represented by clauses in $N$.

### 11.4.1   Update propagation procedure

**Step 1**: Collect in the subprogram $R^+$ all the clauses in $R$ which have a predicate from $preds(P)$ occurring positively in the body or a predicate from $preds(N)$ occurring negatively in the body. This subprogram contains all the clauses which could possibly generate new tuples in the perfect model as a direct result of the updates.

Collect in the subprogram $R^-$ all the clauses in $R$ which have a predicate from $preds(N)$ occurring positively in the body or a predicate from $preds(P)$ occurring negatively in the body. This subprogram contains all the clauses which could possibly remove tuples in the perfect model as a direct result of the updates.

**Example**: if the update added clauses to $edb5$ and $edb7$, and deleted clauses from $edb6$ and $edb8$, then we would have $preds(P) = \{edb5, edb7\}$ and $preds(N) = \{edb6, edb8\}$. $R^+$ would contain $idb4$, while $R^-$ would contain $idb3$.

**Step 2**: Generate additional clauses $P^+$ from $P$ and $N$ by taking in turn each clause from $P$ and $N$ and unifying it in turn with each clause body predicate in $R^+$. The clause in $P^+$ arising from each step in this process has possibly some of its variables instantiated to constants, but these clauses may contain variables. Generate $P^-$ from $P$, $N$ and $R^-$ in the same way. This step is essentially the same as one step of the semi-naive algorithm from Chapter 4.

**Example**: If the clause added was $edb7(a, b)$, and the clause deleted was $edb8(a)$, then $R^+$ contains only $idb4$, while $R^-$ is empty. The clause $edb7(a, b)$ generates the clause $idb4(a, b)$; while the clause $edb8(a)$ generates the clause $idb4(a, Y)$. $P^+$ therefore contains $\{idb4(a, b), idb4(a, Y)\}$. $P^-$ is empty.

**Step 3**: compare the clauses in $P^+$ with each other. If one clause is more general than another, discard the less general. (Clause $p$ is more general than clause $q$ if $p$ has variables where $q$ has constants, but $q$ has constants everywhere $p$ does.) Then compare the remaining clauses with those in $P$. If a clause in $P^+$ is more general than a clause in $P$, discard the less general clause from $P$. Finally replace $P$ with the union of the reduced $P$ and $P^+$. Similarly, replace $N$ by a reduced $N$

and $P^-$. This step attempts to retain as many as possible of the constant arguments from the updated clauses. We are computing the queries which must be evaluated to check the integrity constraints, and the more constant arguments, the easier it is to evaluate queries.

**Example**: $P^+$ is $\{idb4(a, b), idb4(a, Y)\}$, $P$ is $\{edb7(a, b)\}$, $N$ is $\{edb8(a)\}$. The clause $idb4(a, Y)$ is more general than $idb4(a, b)$, and none of the clauses in $P$ unify with any in $P^+$, so the resulting $P$ is $\{edb7(a, b), idb4(a, Y)\}$.

Repeat steps 1–3 until no new clauses are added to either $P$ or $N$.

**Example**: continuing the example from steps 2 and 3, the final $P$ contains $\{edb7(a, b), idb4(a, Y), idb1(a), ic1\}$, while the final $N$ contains only $\{edb8(a)\}$.

We now know how the predicates used in the integrity constraints are affected by the update. In fact, we know that the integrity constraint predicate $ic1$ needs to be evaluated. We know that its first subgoal $idb1$ has the solution $a$ arising from the update. We can now test whether the new state of the database satisfies the integrity constraints by evaluating the query $edb1(a)?$, since if this subgoal returns a solution, then the constraint $ic1$ has a solution, and therefore the system is inconsistent.

Note that we have not only discovered that constraint $ic2$ is not affected by the update, but have also discovered that only one subgoal in constraint $ic1$ needs to be evaluated, and only for the argument $a$.

## 11.5   DISCUSSION

The main point of this chapter is that it is possible to express a wide variety of integrity constraints as first-order predicate calculus formulas, and that these formulas can be represented for integrity checking as Horn clause programs. A secondary point is that an update is proposed from a state of the database which already satisfies the integrity constraints. In many cases we can take advantage of this fact to reduce the amount of computation we must do to check whether the state of the database resulting from the update also satisfies the constraints.

In particular, we can identify constraints which are irrelevant to the update since they do not involve predicates which depend on the updated predicates. We can eliminate further constraints by considering whether the updated predicates appear negatively or positively. Finally, using the update propagation procedure, we can sometimes propagate the constants in the updated clauses into the constraint predicates, reducing the scope of the computation.

The update propagation algorithm has other uses. For example, if the perfect model has been evaluated eagerly, it can detect which predicates must be re-computed as a result of the update. It thus allows incremental change in the perfect model, with possibly a great reduction in computation over re-computing the perfect model from the new database state.

In practice, aggregation functions are important both in the perfect model and in integrity constraints. Aggregation functions such as *SUM* or *COUNT* which admit

**Table 11.2**  Additions to $P$ and $N$ for (11.18) and (11.19)

| Round | $P$ | $N$ |
|---|---|---|
| 0 | mother(mary, bill) | {} |
| 1 | parent(mary, bill) [4] | {} |
| 2 | ancestor(mary, Y) [3] and [4], [4] more general | {} |
| 3 | ancestor(X, Y) [3] more general than ancestor(mary, Y) | {} |
| 4 | male_descendant(X) [1.2] | {} |
| 5 | {} | no_male_descendant(X) [1.1] |

incremental updates can take advantage of the update propagation algorithm to identify incremental change in their inputs. The output of an aggregation function is a binding of a variable in a tuple of the perfect model. The old tuple can be deleted and the new added, adding to both $P$ and $N$.

It is important to recognize that the integrity constraint problem is far from solved in general. In particular, if the IDB is recursive, the update propagation algorithm tends not to result in constraint variables bound to particular constants appearing in the updated clauses. Consider the example:

1. no_male_descendants(X) :- $\forall Y(\text{ancestor}(X, Y) \rightarrow \text{female}(Y))$.  (11.18)
2. ancestor(X, Y) :- parent(X, Y).
3. ancestor(X, Y) :- parent(X, Z), ancestor(Z, Y).
4. parent(X, Y) :- mother(X, Y).
5. parent(X, Y) :- father(X, Y).

EDB predicates mother, father, female

The first predicate in (11.18) is shown in the sequence (11.10)–(11.15) to translate into

1.1 no_male_descendants(X) :- not male_descendant(X).  (11.19)
1.2 male_descendant(X) :- not female(Y), ancestor(X, Y).

Consider the update

add(mother(mary, bill)).  (11.20)

The update propagation algorithm gives Table 11.2, showing $P$ and $N$ at the completion of each round (the clause of (11.18/11.19) responsible is indicated for each clause in [ ... ]).

Notice that the constants *mary*, *bill* are eliminated from the recursive clause [4] of (11.18) in rounds 2 and 3. This is because the integrity constraint relates to the transitive closure of a recursive predicate, which is equivalent to a property of the transitive closure of a graph. Addition of a new link may add many more tuples to the transitive closure.

On the other hand, there is clearly further room for optimization. By inspection, the reader should be able to conclude that the update (11.20) should be rejected. We can expect better and more practicable results in this area in the future.

A second point for discussion is that not all constraints expressed in first-order predicate calculus make sense. The language is extremely powerful, so that it is possible to express constraints which require an exponential amount of computation, or which are not computable at all.

## 11.6  SUMMARY

In this chapter, we have examined the problem of formulation and evaluation of integrity constraints in deductive databases. We have shown that any integrity constraint expressed as a first-order formula can be represented in a natural way, and also that there is potential for optimization in the evaluation of integrity constraints upon updates to the deductive database. The optimizations have practical utility in many cases.

## 11.7  FURTHER READING

The material in this chapter is drawn largely from Lloyd (1987).

## 11.8  EXERCISES

11.1  Integrity constraints as formulas:

   (a)  Transform the first-order formulas in the text for uniqueness, mandatory, and subtype to definite clauses.

   (b)  Put those first-order formulas into Horn clause integrity constraints, and perform the transform to definite clauses on the resulting clause bodies.

   (c)  Formulate referential integrity in the relational model as a first-order formula, then transform the corresponding Horn clause integrity constraint clause body to definite clause form.

11.2  Consider the conceptual schema given in Chapter 6 for the relational model (information model). In the text and in the exercises you have seen the relational schema for at least some of this model.

   Show in first-order predicate calculus a few of the integrity constraints between the schemes *pred/role*, *tuple/role*, *literal/calls*, *literal/argument*, *supertype* and *labels*.

## CHAPTER TWELVE

# Non-monotonic reasoning

In this chapter, we look at what happens when we use integrity constraints to propagate updates rather than restrict them. We first consider a general approach which has not yet found a fully practicable formulation, then a very restricted but effectively implementable approach.

## 12.1 THE PROBLEM OF NON-MONOTONICITY

As we saw in Chapter 11, integrity constraints in an information system are normally thought of as restricting the possible updates which can be applied to a given database state: if a proposed update transaction would result in a database state which violates the integrity constraints, then the update is rejected. There are, however, many applications in which the user wishes the update to stand, regardless of the integrity constraints. In these systems, the integrity constraints largely govern information which is somehow subsidiary to the part of the database which was changed, and what the user desires is that the subsidiary parts be "fixed up" as automatically as possible, so that the integrity constraints can hold with the nominated update in place. This is called **update propagation**.

For example, consider a personnel information system in an organization. Some of the other applications in the organization might be the telephone directory, membership in a tea club, and what items of furniture and equipment are under the person's care. Each of these other applications would have in its database a referential integrity constraint to the employee table. If a person leaves the organization, these referential integrity constraints will prevent that person's record from being deleted from the employee table. This is not a reasonable restriction, since the personnel department, which is responsible for the employee table, may not even be aware of some of these other systems, much less be authorized to make updates in them. What we ideally want is for the deletion from the employee table to stand, and for the other applications to adjust themselves automatically so that referential integrity is preserved.

This kind of situation is common. Users of information systems often want to remove products from a catalog, cancel an invoice, allow a student to withdraw enrolment or to obsolete a sub-assembly. In the University Catalog Major Exercise in Chapter 5, a Department may wish to withdraw a subject which is on the schedule for several courses offered by other faculties. Following Chapter 6, software engineers may wish to remove a module definition from the repository of their CASE tool. (This last example is discussed in detail below.)

In the expert system world, planning applications often need to change state. Planning how to move a robot from one place to another to perform some action generally involves many intermediate stages. Identification of a medical condition may depend on a sequence of laboratory tests: the result of a test may invalidate many possible hypotheses. A design system may produce a candidate design which the user may reject: it therefore must undo part of the design and try another alternative.

Clearly, it is possible to write an application program to do any of these sorts of adjustments. This text, however, is concerned with replacing *ad hoc* application programs with a sound deductive framework based in logic. The problem we have is that logic is a system of mathematics in which updates do not occur. The logical systems we have drawn upon are **monotonic**, i.e. once a conclusion is derived it is never invalidated. A logical system is concerned with derivation of theorems from a fixed set of axioms. These theorems are conceptually all derived at once in zero time. The derivation of one theorem cannot invalidate the proof of another unless the logical system is inconsistent, in which case any formula is a theorem and the system is useless. The main results in Chapters 2 and 4 are of this kind.

The primary purpose of the present chapter is to show how the logical systems can be adapted to deal with updates. Section 12.2 looks at a formulation of the general problem in terms of **belief revision**. This provides a framework to describe the problem of non-monotonic deductive systems, although there is as yet no general satisfactory solution. Section 12.3 looks at a specialized subproblem, for which excellent solutions exist.

## 12.2  BELIEF REVISION

It is convenient for our present purpose to describe the tuples in the EDB, the tuples in the perfect model, and the rules in the IDB as **beliefs**; and the entire assemblage as a **belief system**. We consider that some of these beliefs are more strongly held than others. When we propose an update, we consider that the immediately updated beliefs are held very strongly. Should our belief system be inconsistent (our database violates its integrity constraints), what we want to do is to find some other, less strongly held, beliefs which we can change to allow the database to be consistent and for our new beliefs to hold. This process is called **belief revision**.

There are two main processes in belief revision: first we must identify the existing beliefs which conflict with the update, then we must decide which beliefs to change.

### 12.2.1 Identification of conflicts

The first process, identification of conflicting beliefs, follows on from the identification of affected integrity constraints from Chapter 11. After the constraint queries are identified, they must be evaluated. In order for a query to be successful, we saw in Chapter 2 that there must be a successful proof tree. A successful proof tree contains a success subtree. In order for the integrity constraint to be satisfied, its clauses must generate no success subtrees. To remove a success subtree, thereby allowing the integrity constraint to be satisfied, all of its branches must be cut. A positive branch can be cut by deleting beliefs, while a negative branch can be cut by adding beliefs.

Consider example (11.16). We showed that if the update transaction consisted of

    add(edb7(a, b))                                                    (12.1)
    delete(edb8(a))

then the integrity constraints can be checked by the query

    ic1?                                                               (12.2)

Assume that the original state of the database was

    edb1(a).                                                           (12.3)
    edb2(a).
    edb8(a).

so that the proposed update state after applying (12.1) is

    edb1(a).                                                           (12.4)
    edb2(a).
    edb7(a, b).

The integrity constraint fails because query (12.2) has a solution. The proof tree for this solution is given in Figure 12.1.

This proof tree can be made to fail by one of four possible actions to the EDB:

- deleting edb1(a);
- deleting edb2(a);
- deleting edb7(a, b);
- adding edb8(a).

It can also be made to fail by removing rules from the IDB, namely the definitions of *idb4*, *idb1* and *ic1*.

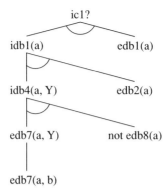

**Figure 12.1**   Proof tree for integrity constraint query *ic1?*.

### 12.2.2   Resolving the conflict: the concept of entrenchment

In cutting the proof tree in Figure 12.1, either of the actions *delete(edb7(a, b))* or *add(edb8(a))* would reverse part of the update transaction (12.1). We prefer not to do that, as we consider these beliefs to be strongly held. Our problem is how we decide between the remaining possibilities.

One way is to explain the situation to the user, present the user with the possibilities, and get the user to choose. This can be quite acceptable. In effect, we are asking the user to evaluate the strength of their belief for each possibility, and to choose a combination of actions which changes the weakest held of these beliefs.

We would like to minimize the amount of work we ask the user to perform, however. What we would ideally like is for the user to evaluate all the beliefs in advance, either by assigning a strength to each belief, or perhaps providing rules whereby the relative strength of beliefs can be calculated. These predetermined strengths, expressed as numbers, are called **entrenchments**. A strongly-held belief is said to be strongly entrenched, a weakly-held belief is said to be weakly entrenched. Since entrenchments are numbers, they can easily be compared. All the conflict resolution program has to do is to compute all the possibilities and to choose the least entrenched one.

The problem, of course, is to assign the entrenchments. There is no general way known to do this. It may not even be generally possible. There are, however, some useful special cases where belief revision can be automated, at least partially.

Consider weak entities. A **weak entity** is an entity which has no independent identification: it depends on another identity for its existence. For example, in an accounting application, an invoice might be a weak entity dependent on the customer entity. Further, a line-item entity might be a weak entity depending on the invoice entity, and therefore indirectly on the customer entity. This structure was described in Chapter 3.

There would be referential integrity constraints preventing the deletion of an invoice instance if it had any line-items, and preventing the deletion of a customer instance if it had any invoices. The system could have a rule that invoices were less entrenched than customers, and that line-items were less entrenched than invoices. If the user wished to delete a customer instance, the belief revision system would resolve the integrity constraint violation by automatically deleting all the invoice instances referring to that customer, and all the line-item instances referring to each invoice deleted.

The entrenchments could be conditional. The rule could state that by default unpaid invoices were more entrenched than customers, while paid invoices were less entrenched. In this way, if the user wished to delete a customer who had unpaid invoices, they would have to make a decision as to what to do about them, while deletion of a customer all of whose invoices were paid would proceed and automatically propagate so that the resulting state of the database would be consistent.

Associative relations can often be treated the same way. A relation containing the association between employees and projects constrains both tables. If it were less entrenched than either, then when a tuple was deleted from either the project or employee tables, the belief revision system would delete the relevant tuples from the associative relation. Conditional entrenchment also makes sense for associative relations.

Mandatory constraints can also be supported by belief revision. For example, if a new instance is added to a type participating in mandatory roles, the belief revision system could either prompt the user for the necessary facts or could insert default values into them.

We have seen that it is often practical to assign entrenchments to beliefs and to maintain database integrity by belief revision. Entrenchments are not, however, completely arbitrary. A derived belief must be more entrenched than at least one of the beliefs needed to derive it. This is why in the customer/ invoice/ line-item example, we had customers more entrenched than invoices, and invoices more entrenched than line-items.

Our discussion of belief revision has been solely in terms of adding or deleting facts in the EDB. Recall that the proof tree of Figure 12.1 can be cut equally well by removing one of the IDB definitions *idb4*, *idb1* or *ic1*. From the perspective of database systems, this might seem like a strange thing to do, but there are applications where it makes sense to have IDB predicates less entrenched than EDB predicates. For example, in the field of machine learning, one often attempts to derive general rules from a database of facts. These rules are tested against the evolving database, and are sometimes invalidated. It therefore makes sense that they should be less entrenched than the EDB. The *no_male_descendants* example (11.11) could be an application of this type. It should be clear that the newly added fact *mother(mary, bill)* violates the integrity constraint regardless of the remainder of the EDB. In order for the update to be accepted, one of the IDB predicates must go, and the intuitively most plausible predicate to remove is *no_male_descendants* itself.

### 12.2.3 Example: software maintenance as belief revision

In Chapter 6, we demonstrated a tool to help build deductive database systems which was itself based upon a deductive database (the repository). When the specification of a system changes, it is necessary to update its representation in the repository. Since the repository has a rich set of integrity constraints, we might expect that belief revision would be important to keep the specification internally consistent. Recall from Chapter 7 that the whole purpose of knowledge maintainability quality principles is to make it possible to revise a specification correctly by following the structural links which are represented in the repository by integrity constraints.

Assume that we have the hierarchical thesaurus example of Chapter 5 stored in the repository as described in Chapter 6. (We will augment the definition of some of the repository predicates.) Our users decide that the predicate *has-ingredient* should be removed. This task is achieved by removing the information about that predicate from the tables from which Table 6.2 is derived, and which were not shown in Chapter 6. We will call the central of these tables *valid-predicate*.

Referential integrity constraints now come into play. The definition of a predicate is contained in the two tables *literal/calls* and *literal/argument*. Both the *literal/calls* and *literal/argument* predicates have referential integrity constraints from the name of the group defined to the table of valid predicate labels. These constraints are

$$\text{bad :- not } \forall \text{Group (literal/calls(Group, ... )} \rightarrow \tag{12.5}$$
$$\text{valid-predicate(Group, ... ))}$$

$$\text{bad :- not } \forall \text{Group (literal/argument(Group, ... )} \rightarrow \tag{12.6}$$
$$\text{valid-predicate(Group ... ))}$$

Both the populations of *literal/calls* and *literal/argument* must be less entrenched than the population of *valid-predicate*, so that the repository can remove the definitions of *has-ingredient* from both tables. This situation is analogous to the relationship between customers, invoices and line-items described above.

The predicate *has-ingredient* we have removed is a special class of predicate which turns a label into a predicate (in this case the label *ingredient-of* playing the *type* role in the predicate *typed-broader* stored in the repository table *tuple/role*, Table 6.5). Assume that this class of predicate is identified in the repository via the tuple *(ingredient-of, has-ingredient)* in the predicate *label/predicate(Label, Enforcing-predicate)*, and that there is a constraint that the predicate is defined only if the label is valid. A label is valid for a given predicate if it is in the table *valid-populations* associated with that predicate. This constraint would look something like

$$\text{bad :- not } \forall \text{Label } \forall \text{Enforcing-Predicate } \exists \text{Predicate} \tag{12.7}$$
$$\text{label/predicate(Label, Enforcing-Predicate)} \rightarrow$$
$$\text{valid-populations(Predicate, Label).}$$

$$\text{bad :- not } \forall \text{Enforcing-Predicate (label/predicate(\_, Enforcing-Predicate)} \rightarrow$$
$$\text{valid-predicate(Enforcing-Predicate ... ))}$$

The predicates *label/predicate* and *valid-populations* were not included in the repository in Chapter 6. The former identifies predicates of the special class which turns labels into predicates, while the latter records the labels which can occur in any population which has defined population constraints (Table 6.1). Before the

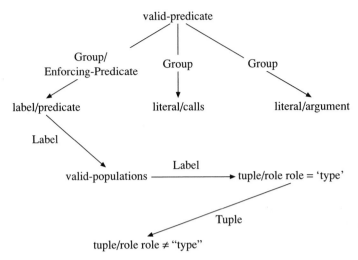

**Figure 12.2**  Propagation of a deletion of a valid-predicate.

proposed update, formula (12.7) was satisfied by the substitution *Predicate = typed-broader*. In other words, the label *ingredient-of* was a label in the defined population constraint of the predicate *typed-broader*.

If the populations of *label/predicate* and *valid-populations* are equally entrenched and less entrenched than *valid-predicate*, then the belief revision system can automatically remove the tuple causing the constraint violation from *label/predicate* and then from *valid-populations*. The latter is the tuple containing the label "ingredient-of"

Another referential integrity constraint is now violated: that between the *instance* role of *tuple/role* and *valid-populations*. The population of *tuple/role* must be less entrenched than that of *valid-populations*, so that the offending tuples can be automatically removed from *tuple/role*. These are all the tuples whose *instance* role is the label *ingredient-of*.

Finally, we would have a constraint on *tuple/role* that every mandatory role must have an instance in the role *role* for each instance in the role *tuple*. The update propagation should remove the entire relational tuple from the predicate *tuple/role*, i.e. in this case, all tuples in the population of Table 6.5 where the *predicate* role is *typed-broader* and the *tuple* role is *onion soup/onion*. The sample population of the application has a number of other examples where the broader term is of type *ingredient-of*, which would be represented in *tuple/role* by tuples having the *tuple* role *onion soup/butter* and *onion soup/water*.

Propagation of the removal of *has-ingredient* is summarized in Figure 12.2. The propagation is via referential integrity constraints as shown by arrows between predicates. The arrows are labelled with the names of the variables indicating the roles linked. Note that the population of *tuple/role* is in fact the entire population of all of the EDB predicates. In practice, these populations would probably be stored as they would be in a conventional database, so that *tuple/role* would be implemented as a sort of view of the EDB from the repository.

The integrity constraints we have been following so far are constraints of the repository. The repository also stores constraints of the application, either as formulas in *literal/argument* or in special-purpose tables such as might be used to record referential integrity and the other kinds of constraints indicated on the information model. From these tables, the repository would find that the tuples from *typed-broader* with type *has-ingredient* must be included in the population of *broader*.

That this last constraint is not violated should be intuitively reasonable, since the population of *broader* is the superset in the inclusion constraint. These application constraints require that some tuples in *tuple/role* are more entrenched than others. In particular, all tuples where *predicate* is *typed-broader* are less entrenched than all tuples where *predicate* is *broader*.

So far, the belief revision system attached to the repository has allowed us to propagate the deletion of the predicate *has-ingredient* downward. We now consider its propagation upward, to the predicates which call *has-ingredient*. From the knowledge diagram in Figure 5.8, we see that removal of *has-ingredient* affects both *source-of-ingredient* and *possible-use-for*. The repository makes these conclusions from referential integrity constraints on *literal/calls* and *literal/argument*. In these two cases, it is hard to see how the repository could have enough information to propagate the update automatically. The CASE tool would therefore inform the user that these two predicates are affected, and ask for instructions. Assume that the user requests the CASE tool to remove *source-of-ingredient* but modifies the definition of *possible-use-for* by replacing *has-ingredient* in the body of the single clause in its definition by *instance-of*.

Removal of *source-of-ingredient* propagates downward similarly to *has-ingredient*. In particular, the definition of *source-of-ingredient* contains a call to *one-of*. This last predicate was introduced to normalize the definition of *source-of-ingredient*, and it is called by no other predicate. This fact can be derived by the repository using a query on *literal/calls*. The repository could have a dynamic entrenchment rule saying that the definition of a predicate of this kind is less entrenched than the definition of its calling predicate, so that the definition of *one-of* would be automatically removed by the belief revision system in the repository.

In this way, a belief revision system can assist the knowledge engineer in maintaining the specification of a knowledge-based system: making automatic revisions where it can and asking for decisions from the knowledge engineer where it needs to. This same principle applies to any CASE tool which is supported by such a repository.

### 12.2.4   Discussion

We have described the general problem of propagating updates in deductive databases as a process of belief revision, where integrity constraint violations are corrected not by withdrawing proposed updates but by adding or deleting sufficient other beliefs that the integrity constraints are satisfied by a database state which includes the proposed update. We have described this process through the concept of entrenchment: that the beliefs removed are less entrenched than the beliefs which are retained.

Although the general problem of assigning entrenchments *a priori* so that a belief revision system can operate unaided is not solved, and is quite probably not solvable, we have seen that there are practical situations where automatic belief revision is possible. Further, we have seen that belief revision can sometimes be carried out cooperatively between a human user and an incomplete system of entrenchments.

## 12.3 ASSUMPTION-BASED TRUTH MAINTENANCE

### 12.3.1 Motivation

In Chapter 11 we have seen that we can consider the perfect model to be functionally dependent on the EDB, and also that we can consider the population of the query types to be functionally dependent on the population of the update types. We also looked at an algorithm for propagating the results of changes in update types into the perfect model computation, which was intended as a mechanism for determining which integrity constraints needed to be evaluated to determine the validity of the proposed changes to the update types.

In some applications, it is convenient to compute the population of the query types eagerly. In this case, if a change is made to the populations of the update types, this change must be propagated to the populations of the query types. The update propagation algorithm of Chapter 11 can be used for this purpose, but there is an important class of application where a different algorithm, called **assumption-based truth maintenance**, or **ATMS**, is appropriate.

Consider the problem of planning a motoring trip: say, a trip from Brisbane to Townsville and back, 1400 km each way, taking three days in each direction. There are a large number of considerations, for example:

■ inland or coast road?

■ where to stay overnight?

■ side trips, points of interest?

■ leave late or early?

■ arrive late or early?

■ OK to duplicate portions of trip?

and there are a large number of choices. The choices interact with each other, for example:

■ take inland road back if leave Townsville early

■ visit Lisa if overnight at Gladstone and Lisa available

■ overnight at Gladstone if leave Brisbane early

■ overnight at Gladstone if coast road back and arrive Brisbane late

The actual construction and evaluation of specific plans is outside the domain of deductive database theory. It could be done with the assistance of planning software, based perhaps on a constraint satisfaction approach, or could be done by hand. In either case, there are a few absolute constraints: say

- first leg of trip starts from Brisbane
- arrive Townsville before 6:00 pm Friday 10th
- second leg of trip starts from Townsville
- arrive Brisbane before 10:00 pm Monday 21st
- drive no more than 600 km each day

and a large number of possibilities which are more or less desirable, for example:

- will we visit Lisa?
- will we pass through Mount Morgan?
- will we have to drive after 4:00 pm?

These latter possibilities (which we will call *contingent possibilities*) are used to evaluate the relative desirability of different plans, and are analogous to the query types in deductive databases. As we change plans, we want to keep track of the query types. The process of determining the values of the query types can be expensive. Therefore as we make changes in the plan, we want to compute the effect of the changes in the query types with a minimum of computation. This is an example of the class of situation for which ATMS was developed.

### 12.3.2   The ATMS system

An ATMS system is seen as a companion to a problem solver of some kind, as shown in Figure 12.3. The problem solver makes changes in the query types and their interdependencies, while the ATMS keeps track of the relationships between the query types, and is able to answer questions about the current status of any of the contingent possibilities.

An ATMS is essentially a propositional deductive database, with integrity constraints but without negation. However, ATMS has its own vocabulary, which derived

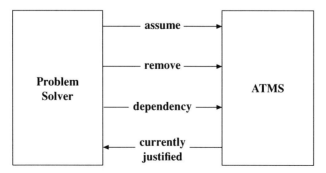

**Figure 12.3**   Overview of an ATMS.

from its first implementations as companions to problem solvers in the Artificial Intelligence field.

The contingent possibilities are called **nodes** or **atoms**. In deductive database terms, they are ground facts. Relationships between nodes are called **informants**. An informant is a propositional Horn clause, where each of the predicates is one of the nodes. For example, we might have three nodes:

visit_lisa (12.8)
overnight(gladstone)
lisa_available

related by the informant

visit_lisa :- overnight(gladstone), lisa_available. (12.9)

The informant is usually expressed in production rule form (see Chapter 4), where the nodes in the clause body are the antecedents and the node in the clause head is the consequent. The clause (12.9) would be expressed as

overnight(gladstone), lisa_available $\rightarrow$ visit_lisa (12.10)

We divide the set of nodes into two classes: those which appear as the consequent of at least one informant, and those which do not appear as the consequent of any informant. A member of the latter class is called an **assumption**. The intuition is that assumptions are independent variables while the other nodes are dependent variables. (This distinction is not essential, and will be relaxed below.)

A set of assumptions is called an **environment**. As an assumption is a proposition, an environment is interpreted as the conjunction of the propositions which are its members. In other words, an environment is an assertion that all of its assumption members hold.

A node is **believed** if it is associated with an environment. The association between a node and an environment is called a **justification**. The justification for an assumption is an environment consisting solely of that assumption. We use the symbol $\Rightarrow$ to indicate that an environment and a node are related by a justification. For example,

{overnight(gladstone)} $\Rightarrow$ overnight(gladstone) (12.11)

expresses that *overnight(gladstone)* is believed because it is an assumption, while

{overnight(gladstone), lisa_available} $\Rightarrow$ visit_lisa (12.12)

expresses that *visit_lisa* is believed because both of the assumptions *overnight(gladstone)* and *lisa_available* are believed. Justifications for nodes other than assumptions are derived from informants. If we have the justification $E \Rightarrow a$, then we say that *node a is believed in environment E*.

A node can have more than one justification. The collection of justifications for a node is called that node's **label**. A node is believed if its label is not empty. For example, we might stay overnight at Gladstone either if we leave Brisbane early on the way to Townsville, or on the way back take the coast road and plan to arrive in Brisbane late. If all three assumptions hold, we might stay in Gladstone twice. The label for *overnight(gladstone)* in this case would contain two justifications:

$$\{\text{leave\_brisbane\_early}\} \Rightarrow \text{overnight(gladstone)} \qquad (12.13)$$
$$\{\text{return(coast\_road), arrive\_brisbane\_late}\} \Rightarrow \text{overnight(gladstone)}$$

Finally, the equivalent to integrity constraints are sets of assumptions which cannot be contained in any environment, called **nogoods**. We can have nogoods arising from logical inconsistencies such as

$$\text{nogood: } \{\text{leave\_brisbane\_early, leave\_brisbane\_late}\} \qquad (12.14)$$

from policy, such as

$$\text{nogood: } \{\text{go(inland\_road), return(inland\_road)}\} \qquad (12.15)$$

expressing the policy that the inland road will be taken only once, or from impossibility of meeting constraints. For example, it is not possible to overnight at Bowen, Proserpine and Mackay since any solution with all three requires a drive longer than 600 km on one day. The nogood would be

$$\text{nogood: } \{\text{overnight(bowen), overnight(proserpine), overnight(mackay)}\} \qquad (12.16)$$

Nogoods (12.14) and (12.15) are *a priori*. The former is a logical property and the latter could be a matter of policy given as a constraint to the planning process. Nogood (12.16) could have been computed dynamically by the problem solver. It could have concluded that no possible plan meeting the policy and logical constraints could contain those nodes.

Remember that the ATMS is a deductive database, so has no semantic knowledge. It simply accepts assumptions, nogoods and informants from some other system, and maintains labels computed from them. Assumptions can be deleted as well as added. (Nogoods and informants can in principle be deleted as well, but since changes of this kind require considerable computation, they are normally not allowed.)

Initially, the set of nodes is empty. The possible inputs to the ATMS, with their associated actions, are:

**Add an informant** $a_1, a_2, \ldots, a_n \rightarrow c$

- create a label with node $c$, if none exists already
- if all the antecedents $a_i$ are believed, then the ATMS creates some new justifications for $c$ by the following process:

  There must be a set of environments $E_{ij}$, $i = 1, \ldots, n$; $j = 1, \ldots, n_i$; where all $n_i > 0$; and the label for $a_i$ contains the justifications $E_{ij} \Rightarrow a_i$.

  Select one of the $E_{ij}$ for each $i$, and compute the union

  $$E = \cup_i E_{ij}$$

  If $E$ contains none of the nogoods, and none of the existing environments in which $c$ is believed are a subset of $E$, then add the justification $E \Rightarrow c$ to the label for $c$. The requirement that none of the existing environments be a subset of $E$ prevents adding redundant environments. If there is an existing environment

$V$ such that $E \supseteq V$, then whenever the assumptions in $E$ hold, so do the assumptions in $V$. $V$ is said to *subsume* $E$.

Repeat the process for every combination of selections for the $E_{ij}$.

Example 12.1: if the ATMS contains the labels

1. $\{x, y\} \Rightarrow a$
2. $\{z, w\} \Rightarrow a$
3. $\{q, r\} \Rightarrow b$
4. $\{s, t\} \Rightarrow b$

and the nogood

   nogood: $\{w, r\}$

then addition of the informant $a, b \rightarrow c$ results in the additional labels, obtained by the union of the environments indicated. Environment $2 + 3$ contains the nogood, so is excluded.

| | |
|---|---|
| $\{q, r, x, y\} \Rightarrow c$ | $1 + 3$ |
| $\{s, t, x, y\} \Rightarrow c$ | $1 + 4$ |
| $\{s, t, w, z\} \Rightarrow c$ | $2 + 4$ |

If $c$ appears in the antecedent of any informant, and if the other antecedents are believed, then it is necessary to propagate the update. Follow the procedure described below.

**Add an assumption** $a$:

- create a label with node $a$ if one does not exist, and add the justification $\{a\}$ $\Rightarrow a$

- if $a$ appears as an antecedent in an informant $a_1, a_2, \ldots, a_n \rightarrow c$, and all the other antecedents are believed, then create additional justifications in the label associated with the consequent of the informant by the following procedure, which is closely related to the procedure for adding an informant.

  There must be a set of environments $E_{ij}$, $i = 2, \ldots, n$; $j = 1, \ldots, n_i$; where all $n_i > 0$; and the label for $a_i$ contains the justifications $E_{ij} \Rightarrow a_i$. Also, there is a set of environments $E_{1j}$, $j = 1, \ldots, n_1$ in which $a$ is believed. As $a$ is an assumption, $n_1 = 1$ and $E_{11} = \{a\}$.

  Select one of the $E_{ij}$ for each $i$, and compute the union

  $$E = \cup_i E_{ij}$$

  If $E$ contains none of the nogoods, and none of the existing environments in which $c$ is believed are a subset of $E$, then add the justification $E \Rightarrow c$ to the label for $c$.

  Repeat the process for every combination of selections for the $E_{ij}$.

  **Update propagation**: If the consequent $c$ appears as the antecedent of another informant, repeat the entire process with each new environment which was added to the label for $c$.

Example 12.2: if the ATMS contains the labels

$\{w, x\} \Rightarrow c$
$\{x\} \Rightarrow x$
$\{w\} \Rightarrow w$
$\{y\} \Rightarrow y$
$\{\} \Rightarrow b$

and the informants

$y, z \rightarrow a$
$a, c \rightarrow b$

then if we add the assumption $z$, we get the additional labels

$\{y, z\} > a$
$\{w, x, y, z\} > b$

Note that the intermediate node $c$ is removed in the process of propagation of the update through the justifications. This update propagation algorithm is a specialization of the update propagation algorithm described in Chapter 11.

**Delete an assumption** $a$:

■   remove all environments containing $a$.

**Add a nogood** $N$:

■   remove all environments of which $N$ is a subset.

### 12.3.3   Discussion

When the planner adds an assumption to the ATMS, that assumption is believed. If that assumption triggers any informants, and all the other antecedents of the informant are believed, then there is reason to believe the consequent. The reason is possibly in addition to existing reasons to believe the consequent. If, in turn, there are informants with the consequent of the first as antecedent, there is reason to believe the new consequent, again possibly in addition to existing reasons for believing it. The reasons for believing any node are always assumptions, so that as the update propagates through the informants, the justifications of the consequents are always assumptions. If there are alternative reasons for believing a node, then each of the reasons must be reflected in the justifications of nodes connected to that node via informants. This is reasonable since adding an assumption should increase the number of things believed, and as some beliefs depend on others, one would expect the new assumption to have a cascade of consequences.

Similarly, when an informant is added, all possible combinations of assumptions in which its consequent is believed must be computed. If its consequent is the antecedent of another informant, then the update must propagate. Again, this is reasonable since a new informant suggests additional grounds for believing something.

Since the process of adding an assumption or informant results in justifications for nodes containing only assumptions, when an assumption is removed it is simply necessary to delete any justifications whose environment contains it. This may make some labels empty, so that their nodes are no longer believed. This is reasonable, since removing assumptions should reduce what is believed. (Recall that ATMS does not include negation, so it is impossible to have a node justified by the absence of an assumption. This ensures that removal of an assumption does not increase the beliefs.)

Similarly, adding a nogood adds a new constraint to the system, so that some combinations of assumptions can no longer be held at the same time. This reduces the range of things believed. Again, as the justifications for the nodes have been constructed in terms of assumptions only, addition of a nogood simply removes the reason to believe some nodes.

### 12.3.4   ATMS and deductive databases

ATMS is a highly specialized deductive database. It has, however, a close relationship with the general deductive database. Both the EDB and the perfect model of a deductive database are sets of ground tuples, and there is a functional relationship given by the fixed point operator $T \uparrow \omega$ from the set of possible EDBs to the set of possible perfect models. For a definite program, this functional relationship can be decomposed into a relation between sets of EDB tuples and sets of perfect model tuples. This relation is computed in the course of application of the $T \uparrow \omega$ operator. An ATMS can be used to make this relation explicit.

Consider the $T \uparrow \omega$ computation to be a problem solver to which an ATMS is attached. The ATMS is first asked to assume each of the EDB tuples. The problem solver then makes one application of the $T$ operator. Some of the clause bodies in the IDB have solutions, generating tuples for the relation defined by their clause heads. Each solution for the first application of $T$ must be a combination of tuples from the EDB. For each solution, the problem solver gives the ATMS an informant whose antecedents are the tuples in the solution and whose consequent is the tuple generated for the head predicate.

The problem solver continues to apply the $T$ operator, giving the ATMS further informants whose antecedents are tuples from the EDB and previously computed perfect model tuples, and whose consequents are the corresponding head predicate tuples. From these assumptions and informants, the ATMS maintains justifications for each of the perfect model tuples. Each environment is a set of EDB tuples from which that perfect model tuple can be derived. Clearly, one perfect model tuple can be derived from many sets of EDB tuples, and equally one set of EDB tuples can be used to derive many perfect model tuples.

For example, consider the *ancestor* predicate from Example 4.1. The tuple *ancestor(bill, sue)* is derived from the tuples *parent(bill, paul)* and *parent(paul, sue)*. The tuple *ancestor(bill, eva)* is derived from the tuples *parent(bill, paul)*, *parent(paul, sue)* and *parent(sue, eva)*. The ATMS would contain the labels

{parent(bill, paul)} ⇒ ancestor(bill, paul)                                    (12.17)
{parent(paul, sue)} ⇒ ancestor(paul, sue)
{parent(sue, eva)} ⇒ ancestor(sue, eva)
{parent(bill, paul), parent(paul, sue)} ⇒ ancestor(bill, sue)
{parent(bill, paul), parent(paul, sue), parent(sue, eva)} ⇒
    ancestor(bill, eva)

When a tuple of the perfect model is computed, the ATMS creates a non-empty label for it. The fixed point of the $T$ operator is therefore reached when there is a non-empty label for each head predicate tuple generated in its latest application.

We would like to use the ATMS to maintain the materialized perfect model under changes in the EDB, i.e. under addition and deletion of tuples from the EDB. It should be clear that when a tuple is added to the EDB, the problem solver must be run to generate additional perfect model tuples, and therefore give additional informants to the ATMS. When a tuple is deleted from the EDB, the effect can be determined directly from the ATMS, by deleting all environments containing that tuple and examining the resulting labels. Tuples deleted from the perfect model will have empty labels.

The only difficulty is that under the stopping rule for $T \uparrow \omega$, the problem solver stops when every tuple in the perfect model has been computed, and consequently when every perfect model tuple has a non-empty label in the ATMS. The environment in a particular justification is essentially a record of a particular derivation of the associated perfect model tuple. When an EDB tuple is deleted, the ATMS can determine whether any derivations have been invalidated. However, the fact that a perfect model tuple no longer has a derivation on record does not prove that no derivation exists for it. In order for the ATMS to have a complete record of all possible derivations for all perfect model tuples, the problem solver would have to be run until no new environments were created, rather than stopping when no new labels are generated. This is essentially the problem of finding all paths in a graph, taking cycles into account, as was discussed in Chapter 3.

### 12.3.5  Propositional expert systems

In Chapter 10 we considered a special case of a deductive database where all the IDB predicates are propositional, which we called a propositional expert system. The EDB is the set of propositions which are input to the expert system, and a perfect model includes all propositions which can be derived from the input, including the conclusions of the expert system.

Application of the ATMS to the perfect model calculation therefore results in a label for each derived proposition whose justifications have environments which are the combinations of input propositions which must hold if the conclusion is to be derived. This is exactly the same result as produced by the rule flattening unfolding procedure described in Chapter 10. The resulting decision table is equivalent to the set of labels produced by the ATMS.

## 12.3.6   Differences between ATMS and deductive databases

An ATMS is a deductive database. A definite deductive database is an ATMS in the sense that the perfect model can be represented in a natural way. If the deductive database is propositional, the correspondence is exact. Otherwise, the ATMS must represent the universally quantified clauses by sets of ground tuples.

We have seen in Chapter 4 that deductive databases may include negative predicates in clause bodies: these predicates are not dealt with in a direct way by the ATMS system. Specific solutions can be found for specific applications, but there is no general theory.

A further difference is that in an ATMS the distinction between update types and query types is not so defined as it is in a deductive database. The ATMS was developed to keep track of partial solutions to constraint satisfaction problems. A node represents the assignment of a specific value to a specific variable. An informant is interpreted as a statement that if each of the assignments represented by an antecedent node is made, then the assignment represented by the consequent satisfies some constraints. Even though a node may be the consequent of an informant, so long as its label is empty it makes sense to introduce it as an assumption. For example, the label for *overnight(gladstone)* in (12.13) is the result of informants described in the preceding paragraph and the assumptions in the environments in (12.13). If those assumptions had not been made, then the label for *overnight(gladstone)* would be empty. The problem solver is free to give the ATMS the assumption *overnight(gladstone)*.

Thus any node can in principle be an assumption, even if it appears as the consequent of an informant, so long as its label is empty. This is a dynamic constraint, which must be maintained at run time by the ATMS. Some complication in the implementation of the ATMS system results from maintenance of this constraint.

### 12.4   SUMMARY

In this chapter we have examined the general problem of updating deductive databases using the framework of belief revision, and have then looked at a particular special case of belief revision, Assumption-Based Truth Maintenance. The theory of belief revision is much more general than that underlying ATMS, but is not sufficient to derive implementations, except in special cases. ATMS obtains its implementability from its extremely weak logic (propositional Horn clauses with integrity constraints but without negation).

### 12.5   FURTHER READING

The material on belief revision is based on Gardenfors (1988), while the specific formulation of update propagation is based on, for example, Guessoum and Lloyd (1990). The material on ATMS is drawn largely from de Kleer (1986).

### 12.6  EXERCISES

12.1   Consider the conceptual schema given in Chapter 6 for the relational model (information model). In the text and in the exercises for that Chapter you have seen the relational schema for at least some of this model.

(a)   Consider the schema of Exercise 5.2. Where in the repository would we look to determine the validity of the population *product class*?

(b)   Consider removing the population *product class*. How might this change propagate?

12.2   Consider the possibility of an automatic solution to Exercise 12.1(b). What alternatives might the program consider in propagating the change, what choice would you program it to make, and why would you instruct it to make that choice?

12.3   Consider the solution to Exercise 12.1(b) and the alternatives from Exercise 12.2. How might you assign entrenchments so that the propagation of the change would be automatic?

12.4   Consider the following model of a power plant control system. There are indicators:

      fuel_exhausted
      temperature_too_high
      cooling_valve_stuck_shut
      temperature_too_low
      cooling_valve_stuck_open

two alarms, yellow and red

and the following informants:

      fuel_exhausted → red
      temperature_too_high → yellow
      cooling_valve_stuck_shut → yellow
      temperature_too_low → yellow
      cooling_valve_stuck_open → yellow
      temperature_too_high and cooling_valve_stuck_shut → red
      temperature_too_low and cooling_valve_stuck_open → red

Assume that the following sequence of indicator events occurs:

    1. temperature_too_high on
    2. cooling_valve_stuck_open on
    3. temperature_too_high off
    4. temperature_too_low on
    5. cooling_valve_stuck_open off
    6. temperature_too_low off
    7. fuel_exhausted on

Record the state of the indicators at times 1 through 7 as an ATMS, with their justifications.

12.5 Consider the following sequence of inputs to an ATMS. At the end, what nodes are believed, and what is their justification?

| | |
|---|---|
| assume a | informant x & y → z |
| assume b | informant r & s → t |
| informant a & b → c | informant t & z → w |
| assume d | informant x & b → f |
| assume e | assume r |
| informant a & e → f | assume s |
| informant f & d → g | assume y |
| nogood a, d | assume x |
| informant g & w → u | |

12.6 Sketch how an ATMS could be used to help a student plan a valid program for a course such as the Postgraduate Diploma in Information Technology, as described in the major Exercise from Chapter 5.

# Solutions to exercises

1.1  The schema is A B C

| | A | B | C |
|---|---|---|---|
| Population | a1 | b1 | c1 |
| | a1 | b1 | c2 |
| | a2 | b1 | c1 |
| | a2 | b1 | c2 |
| | a3 | b2 | c1 |

1.2  The schema is A B C

| | A | B | C |
|---|---|---|---|
| Population | a1 | b1 | c1 |

**Refresher on joins**

In case Exercises 1.1 and 1.2 found a gap in your memory, the following is a discussion of joins which may help.

A natural join is a combination of the attributes and populations of two relations, which we will call R1 and R2, each of which has a schema consisting of a set of attributes. In Exercise 1.1, R1 has the schema A B, and R2 has the schema B C.

Each of the relations contributes attributes to the join. The join has a set of attributes, called the join attributes, which determine which tuples from the two relations will contribute to tuples in the join relation. In Exercise 1.1, the set of join attributes has a single member, B.

Besides the join attributes, each relation may have other attributes. In Exercise 1.1, R1 has a set of other attributes with a single member, A; while R2 has a set of other attributes with a single member, C.

The join is a relation with a schema consisting of

■   the join attributes;
■   the other attributes from R1;
■   the other attributes from R2.

In Exercise 1.1, the join relation has the schema A B C.

The population of the join relation is derived from the populations of R1 and R2. The following procedure for computing the join population is closely related to how a typical Prolog interpreter would do it.

Each tuple of R1 is compared with each tuple of R2. If the values of the join attributes differ between the two tuples, no action is taken. If, however, the two tuples have the same values for all the join attributes, then a new tuple is generated for the join relation. The value of the join attribute in the join relation is the common value; the value of the other attributes from R1 is the value of those attributes in the tuple from R1; and similarly, the value of the other attributes from R1 is the value of those attributes in the tuple from R2.

We illustrate the procedure from Exercise 1.1:

| Step | R1 | | R2 | | R1 join R2 | | |
|------|----|----|----|----|----|----|----|
|      | A  | B  | B  | C  | A  | B  | C  |
| 1    | a1 | b1 | b1 | c1 | a1 | b1 | c1 |
| 2    | a1 | b1 | b1 | c2 | a1 | b1 | c2 |
| 3    | a1 | b1 | b2 | c1 | fails to match | | |
| 4    | a2 | b1 | b1 | c1 | a2 | b1 | c1 |
| 5    | a2 | b1 | b1 | c2 | a2 | b1 | c2 |
| 6    | a2 | b1 | b2 | c1 | fails to match | | |
| 7    | a3 | b2 | b1 | c1 | fails to match | | |
| 8    | a3 | b2 | b1 | c2 | fails to match | | |
| 9    | a3 | b2 | b2 | c1 | a3 | b2 | c1 |

It may happen that one of the relations R1 and R2 has no other attributes. This situation occurs in Exercise 1.2. In this case, R1 is the result of Exercise 1.1, which has the schema A B C, and R2 has the schema A C. The join attributes are A C, the other attribute from R1 is B, and the set of other attributes from R2 is empty. The schema of the join is therefore A B C. The population is derived as in Exercise 1.1, as follows:

| Step | R1 | | | R2 | | R1 join R2 | | |
|------|----|----|----|----|----|----|----|----|
|      | A  | B  | C  | A  | C  | A  | B  | C  |
| 1    | a1 | b1 | c1 | a1 | c1 | a1 | b1 | c1 |
| 2    | a1 | b1 | c1 | a3 | c2 | fails to match | | |
| 3    | a1 | b1 | c2 | a1 | c1 | fails to match | | |
| 4    | a1 | b1 | c2 | a3 | c2 | fails to match | | |
| 5    | a2 | b1 | c1 | a1 | c1 | fails to match | | |

| 6  | a2 | b1 | c1 | a3 | c2 | fails to match |
| 7  | a2 | b1 | c2 | a1 | c1 | fails to match |
| 8  | a2 | b1 | c2 | a3 | c2 | fails to match |
| 9  | a3 | b2 | c1 | a1 | c1 | fails to match |
| 10 | a3 | b2 | c1 | a3 | c2 | fails to match |

It is also possible for the set of join attributes to be empty. Consider the example with two relations:

| A  | B  | C  | D  |
|----|----|----|----|
| a1 | b1 |    | c1 | d1 |
| a2 | b2 |    | c2 | d2 |

Their natural join has the schema A B C D, and has the population

| A  | B  | C  | D  |
|----|----|----|----|
| a1 | b1 | c1 | d1 |
| a1 | b1 | c2 | d2 |
| a2 | b2 | c1 | d1 |
| a2 | b2 | c2 | d2 |

In this situation, the natural join is a cartesian product, associating each tuple of R1 with each tuple of R2.

Finally, it is possible for both relations to consist entirely of join attributes, so that the set of other attributes is empty for both R1 and R2. For example, both R1 and R2 have the schema A B, so that the join relation also has the scheme A B. Suppose the populations are

| R1 |    | R2 |    |
|----|----|----|----|
| A  | B  | A  | B  |
| a1 | b1 | a1 | b2 |
| a2 | b1 | a1 | b2 |
| a2 | b2 | a2 | b1 |

The population of the join is

R1 join R2

| A  | B  |
|----|----|
| a2 | b1 |

## CHAPTER 2

Data consist of several extensional predicates:

male(Person) : true if Person is male.
female(Person) : true if Person is female.
parent(Parent, Child) : true if Parent is a parent of Child.
married(Husband, Wife) : true if Husband is married to Wife.
        Implicitly male(Husband), female(Wife).

2.1   person(P) :- male(P).
      person(P) :- female(P).

      same_generation(Person, Person) :- person(Person).
      same_generation(Person1, Person2) :-
         parent(Parent1, Person1),
         parent(Parent2, Person2),
         same_generation(Parent1, Parent2).

2.2   great_grandparent(Ancestor, Child) :-
         parent(Ancestor, Int1),
         parent(Int1, Int2),
         parent(Int2, Child).

2.3   mother(M, C) :- parent(M, C), female(M).
      % Note that the use of the variable name *Female_ancestor* does not guarantee
         that the ancestor is female. It requires the type predicate *female(Female_
         ancestor)* to do so.
      1. ancestors(Child, [Female_ancestor]) :-
            mother(Female_ancestor, Child).
      2. ancestors(Child, [Intermediate| Rest]) :-
            mother(Intermediate, Child),
      ancestors(Intermediate, Rest).

      nearer_cousin(Person1, Person2) :-
         grandparent(Ancestor, Person1),
         grandparent(Ancestor, Person2).

      % Shared ancestors less than grandparent not needed since the shared parents
      must extend to the great_grandparent level.

      Given the database

         parent(a, b).      parent(b, c).      parent(c, d).
         female(a).         female(b).         female(c).

      the query

         ancestors(d, [c, b])?

      will succeed, as well as the queries

         ancestors(d, [c])?      ancestors(d, [c, b, a])?

      If the query is *ancestors(d, L)?*, the solution first generated is *[c]*, from clause
      1. To get the second solution, we bypass clause 1 to clause 2, which generates
      *ancestors(c, L)?* and constructs the solution *[c, b]*. The third solution bypasses
      clause 1 in this second subgoal, so that clause 2 is used twice to generate the
      subgoal *ancestors(b, L)?*, which clause 1 solves as *L = [a]*, and the two execu-
      tions of clause 2 construct first *L = [b, a]* then *L = [c, b, a]*, the third solution.
      The request to generate a fourth solution fails, as clause 3 is executed three
      times to generate the query *ancestors(a, L)?*, clause 1 can find no solution to
      *mother(M, a)*, and for the same reason, neither can clause 2.

2.4   second_cousin(Person1, Person2) :-
      great_grandparent(Ancestor, Person1),
      great_grandparent(Ancestor, Person2),
      not nearer_cousin(Person1, Person2).

2.5   different_sex(Child1, Child2) :-
      male(Child1),
      female(Child2).

      same_sex_children(Woman) :-
      female(Woman),
      parent(Woman, Child1),
      parent(Woman, Child2),
      Child1 <> Child2,
      not different_sex(Child1, Child2).

2.6   most_children(Parent, Number_of_children) :-
      num_children(Parent, Number_of_children),
      not more_children(Number_of_children).

      num_children(Parent, Number_of_children) :-
      bagof(Child, parent(Parent, Child), Children),
      length(Children, Number_of_children).

      more_children(Number_of_children) :-
      num_children(Parent, N),
      N > Number_of_children.

2.7   A problem involving all of anything usually requires *bagof* or one of its
      derivatives, like *all_solutions*. We can use *mother/2* to create a specialization
      of *ancestor*

      fem_anc(F, C) :- mother(F, C).
      fem_anc(F, C) :- mother(F, I), fem_anc(I, C).

      then collect the ancestors

      ancestors(C, L) :- all_solutions(F, fem_anc(F, C), L).

      It is possible to adapt the solution to Exercise 2.3 (call it program 3) to solve
      Exercise 2.6 without the use of *all_solutions*. Program 3 generates successively
      longer partial solutions. It fails when it gets to a person who has no mother
      recorded in the database. If we think of the generate-and-test paradigm for
      problem-solving, program 3 generates successively longer possible solutions
      on backtracking, so if we could test each successive solution, we could stop
      when the test succeeds:

      ancestors(Child, List) :- partial solution(Child, List),
            successful_solution(List).

      The test will succeed when the furthest female ancestor fails to have an ancestor.
      If the variable *T* could somehow be bound to that ancestor, then the test is

            not mother(_, T).

The difficulty with program 3 is that the furthest female ancestor is deeply buried in the list. We can adapt program 3 to make the top of the list available, so the generate-and-test approach will work in a simple way:

    1. anp(C, [M], M) :- mother(M, C).

    2. anp(C, [M|R], T) :- mother(M, C), anp(M, R, T).

    ancestors(C, L) :- anp(C, L, T), not mother(_, T).

The new predicate *anp* is a variation of the original *ancestors* (program 3). The third argument of *anp* is the top of the list, which is put in place by clause 1. Clause 2 simply transmits the variable binding through from the recursive call to the clause head.

### CHAPTER 3

3.1  (a)  occupies(Emp, Room) :-
          academic(Emp, _, _, _, Ext, _),
          phone(Ext, Room).

3.1  (b)  response(Emp, Name, Degree) :-
          department(Dept, _, _, _, Fax),
          Fax != null,
          academic(Emp, Name, Dept, _, _, _),
          Name != "Cantor",
          award(Emp, Degree, _, Year),
          Year $\Leftarrow$ 1985, Year $\Rightarrow$ 1965.

3.1  (c)  response(Dept, Name, Degree) :-
          academic(Emp, Name, Dept, professor, _, _),
          award(Emp, Degree, uq, _).
       response(Dept, Name, "nil") :-
          academic(Emp, Name, Dept, professor, _, _),
          not award(Emp, _, uq, _).

3.2  (a)  SELECT emp# empname deptname ext# room FROM
          academic, phone
       WHERE academic.ext# = phone.ext#

3.2  (b)  SELECT a1.emp# FROM
          academic a1, academic a2, phone p1, phone p2
       WHERE a1.ext# = p1.ext#
         AND a2.ext# = p2.ext#
         AND p1.room = p2.room
         AND a1.emp# NOT = a2.emp#

3.3  path(h, d, [], [h]).
     path(h, e, [], [h, d]).
     path(h, f, [], [h, d]).

3.4  path(h, d, [], [h]).
     path(h, e, [], [h, d]).

path(h, f, [], [h, d]).
path(h, a, [], [h, d, f]).
path(h, d, [], [h, d, f, a]).
path(h, e, [], [h, d, f, a, d]).
etc.   .

There are an infinite number of paths, since the graph has cycles.

3.5   path(h, d, [], [h]).
path(h, e, [], [h, d]).
path(h, f, [], [h, d]).
path(h, a, [], [h, d, f]).
path(h, d, [], [h, d, f, a]).

3.6   One solution is shown in Figure S3.6(a). The main structure is a directed acyclic graph, whose nodes are of type *unit*, whose arc is named *made-up-of* and whose derived-arc is named *component-of*. Note that the fact type *needed* applies to both *made-up-of* and (as a derived fact), to *component-of*.

A somewhat more detailed solution is shown in Figure S3.6(b). Breaking out the subtype *assembly* shows that some units are assemblies and some may not be. (An assembly is a unit which participates as the source node in a *made-up-of* fact.) A part may be the target of a *made-up-of* fact through its supertype *unit*.

(a)

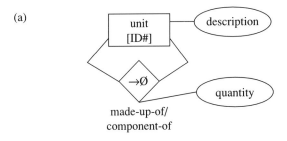

(b)

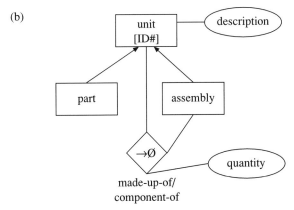

**Figure S3.6**  (a) Adequate conceptual model. (b) Better conceptual model.

## CHAPTER 4

4.1   The perfect model of the ancestor relation is:

        ancestor(jim, jimmy).            ancestor(christine, jake).
        ancestor(heather, christine).     ancestor(jimmy, jake).
        ancestor(christine, adam).       ancestor(jim, jake).
        ancestor(heather, adam).        ancestor(heather, jake).

4.2   (a)

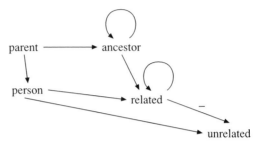

**Figure S4.2**   Dependency diagram.

    parent(jim, jimmy).           parent(christine, jake).
    parent(heather, christine).    parent(jimmy, jake).
    parent(christine, adam).

      person(P) :- parent(P, _).

      person(P) :- parent(_, P).

    ancestor(Older, Younger) :- parent(Older, Younger).
    ancestor(Older, Younger) :- parent(Older, Intermediate),
                         ancestor(Intermediate, Younger).

    related(P, P) :- person(P).
    related(P1, P2) :- ancestor(P2, P1).
    related(P1, P2) :- ancestor(P1, P2).

    related(P1, P2) :- ancestor(A1, P1), ancestor(A2, P2), related(A1, A2).

_ _ _ _ _ _ _ _ _ _ _ _ _ _ _ _ _ _ _ _ _ _ _ _ _ _ _ _ _ Stratum 0

     unrelated(P1, P2) :- person(P1), person(P2), not related(P1, P2).
                                       Stratum 1

  (b)   All tuples for *ancestor*, *person* and *related*

        unrelated(jim, heather).
        unrelated(christine, jim).
        unrelated(jimmy, heather).
        unrelated(christine, jimmy).
        unrelated(jim, adam).
        unrelated(jimmy, adam).

    as well as the reverse of these.

  (c)   All pairs are in the interpretation. The interpretation is not a model.

4.3

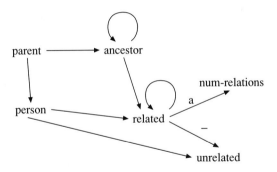

**Figure S4.3** Dependency diagram.

(a) The program is aggregation stratified.

(b) num-relations(jim, 3).

4.4 The dependency graph for Example 4.10 is shown in Figure S4.4(a) and for Example 4.11 is shown in Figure S4.4(b). Example 4.10 has a loop involving aggregation between *cost-to-mfg* and *cost-contribution*. Example 4.11 has broken that loop by removing the arc *cost-to-mfg* → *cost-contribution*. The former is not aggregation stratified, while the latter is.

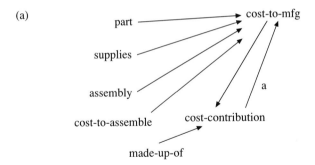

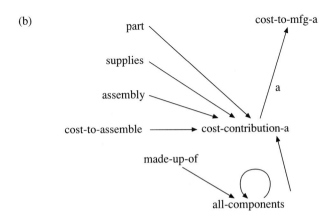

**Figure S4.4** (a) Dependency diagram for Example 4.10. (b) Dependency diagram for Example 4.11.

4.5   Bottom-up evaluation of *successor*:

    successor(s(0), 0).
    successor(s(s(0)), s(0)).
    successor(s(s(s(0))), s(s(0))).

and so on. The model is infinite.

CHAPTER 5

5.1   Barbecue planner expert system: The data analysis is the tabulation of query, update and intermediate types from the problem definition. The information analysis is null, since there are only the predicate names. A knowledge diagram is given in Figure S5.1.

Notice that the outcome *hot_dogs* depends on the intermediate types *vegetarian_fish* and *meat* as well as *all_foods*. These relationships come from the conflict resolution mechanism in OPS-5. If *rain_forecast*, then none of the menu conclusions can fire. The outcome *hot_dogs* can only occur if none of the other menu outcomes can fire.

Horn clause representation of the knowledge:

call_off :- rain_forecast.
all_foods :- bob.
vegetarian_fish :- mary.
meat :- jim.
lentil_burgers :- vegetarian_fish, not meat, not rain_forecast.
steak :- meat, not vegetarian_fish, not rain_forecast.
fish :- meat, vegetarian_fish, not rain_forecast.
hot_dogs :- all_foods, not meat, not vegetarian_fish, not rain_forecast.

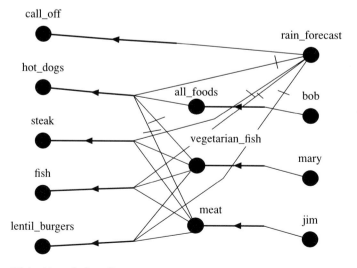

**Figure S5.1**   Knowledge diagram.

5.2   Application model:

There are products, product identifiers, retail prices, wholesale prices, list prices, product classes.

Product is identified by product identifier, and has the properties retail price, wholesale price, list price, product class.

There are customers, customer identifiers, boutique customers, department store customers, customer classes, customer types.

Customer is identified by customer identifier, and has the properties customer class, customer type.

"boutique" and "department_store" are labels, making up the population customer type.

Boutique customers are customers whose customer type property has the value "boutique".

Department store customers are customers whose customer type property has the value "department store".

There are discount rates and discounts.

Discount is identified by customer class and has the property discount rate.

There are sales tax and sales tax rates.

Sales tax is identified by product class and has the property sales tax rate.

There are invoice, quantities ordered, costs, sales tax amounts, total sales tax amounts, total wholesale prices, total costs.

An invoice is an association between customer and product, distinguished by invoice number.

For boutique customers, invoice has the properties customer identifier, product identifier, quantity ordered, retail price, list price, discount rate, cost, sales tax rate, sales tax amount, total sales tax amount, total wholesale price, total cost.

For boutique customers, sales tax amount is a percentage of wholesale price determined by sales tax rate from sales tax depending on product class.

For boutique customers, wholesale price is the list price of the product less a percentage given by discount rate from discount depending on customer class.

For boutique customers, cost is the total of wholesale price and sales tax.

For department stores, cost is the retail price of the product less a percentage given by discount rate from discount depending on customer class.

For department stores, wholesale price depends on the cost and the sales tax rate from sales tax identified by product class (wholesale price = cost/(1 + sales tax rate)).

For department stores, sales tax amount is the cost less the wholesale price.

Total wholesale price is the wholesale price times the quantity ordered.

Total sales tax is the sales tax amount times the quantity ordered.

Total cost is the cost times the quantity ordered.

For department store customers, invoice has the properties customer identifier, product identifier, quantity ordered, retail price, discount rate, cost, sales tax rate, sales tax amount, total sales tax amount, total wholesale price, total cost.

Information model:

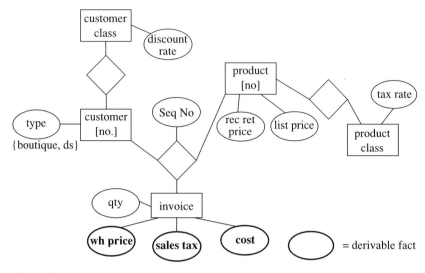

**Figure S5.2**  (a) Information model.

EDB schema

    customer(Customer id, Customer_class, Customer_type)
    product(Product id, Retail_price, List_price, Product_class)
    invoice_id(Customer id, Product id, Seq no, Quantity_ordered)
    sales_tax(Product class, Sales_tax_rate)
    discount(Customer class, Discount_rate)

Knowledge

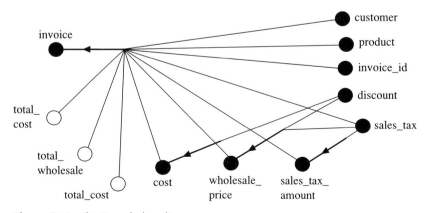

**Figure S5.2**  (b) Knowledge diagram.

Horn clause representation

sales_tax_amount(boutique, Sales_tax_amount, Wholesale_price,
    Product_class) :-
    sales_tax(Product_class, Sales_tax_rate),
    Sales_tax_amount is Wholesale_price * Sales_tax_rate /100.
sales_tax_amount(ds, Sales_tax_amount, Cost, Wholesale_price) :-
    Sales_tax_amount is Cost − Wholesale_price.

wholesale_price(boutique, Wholesale_price, List_price, Customer_class) :-
    discount(Customer_class, Discount_rate),
    Wholesale_price is List_price * (100 − Discount_rate)/100.
wholesale_price(ds, Wholesale_price, Cost, Product_class) :-
    sales_tax(Product_class, Sales_tax_rate),
    Wholesale_price = Cost/((100 + Sales_tax_rate)/100).

cost(boutique, Cost, Wholesale_price, Sales_tax) :-
    Cost is Wholesale_price + Sales Tax.
cost(ds, Cost, Retail_price, Customer_class) :-
    discount(Customer_class, Discount_rate),
    Cost is Retail_price * (100 − Discount_rate)/100.

total_wholesale(Total_WP, Wholesale_price, Quantity_ordered) :-
    Total_WP is Wholesale_price * Quantity_ordered.

total_stax(Total_ST, Sales_tax_amount, Quantity_ordered) :-
    Total_ST is Sales_tax_amount * Quantity_ordered.

total_cost(Total_cost, Cost, Quantity_ordered) :-
    Total_cost is Cost * Quantity_ordered.

invoice(Customer_id, Product_id, Seq_no, Quantity_ordered,
        Retail_price, List_price, Discount_rate, Cost,
        Sales_tax_rate, Sales_tax_amount,
        Total_ST, Total_WP, Total_cost) :-
    customer(Customer_id, Customer_class, boutique),
    invoice_id(Customer_id, Product_id, Seq_no, Quantity_ordered),
    product(Product_id, Retail_price, List_price, Product_class),
    wholesale_price(boutique, Wholesale_price, List_price, Customer_class),
    sales_tax_amount(boutique, Sales_tax_amount, Wholesale_price,
        Product_class),
    cost(boutique, Cost, Wholesale_price, Sales_tax_amount),
    total_stax(Total_ST, Sales_tax_amount, Quantity_ordered),
    total_wholesale(Total_WP, Wholesale_price, Quantity_ordered),
    total_cost(Total_cost, Cost, Quantity_ordered).

invoice(Customer_id, Product_id, Seq_no, Quantity_ordered,
        Retail_price, "NA", Discount_rate, Cost,
        Sales_tax_rate, Sales_tax_amount,
        Total_ST, Total_WP, Total_cost) :-
    customer(Customer_id, Customer_class, ds),

invoice_id(Customer_id, Product_id, Seq_no, Quantity_ordered),
product(Product_id, Retail_price, _, Product_class),
cost(ds, Cost, Retail_price, Customer_class),
wholesale_price(ds, Wholesale_price, Cost, Product_class),
sales_tax_amount(ds, Sales_tax_amount, Cost, Wholesale_price),
total_stax(Total_ST, Sales_tax_amount, Quantity_ordered),
total_wholesale(Total_WP, Wholesale_price, Quantity_ordered),
total_cost(Total_cost, Cost, Quantity_ordered).

5.3   *Broader term*, *narrower term*, *is-a* are profitably considered transitive. The
others are not.

1   Information model

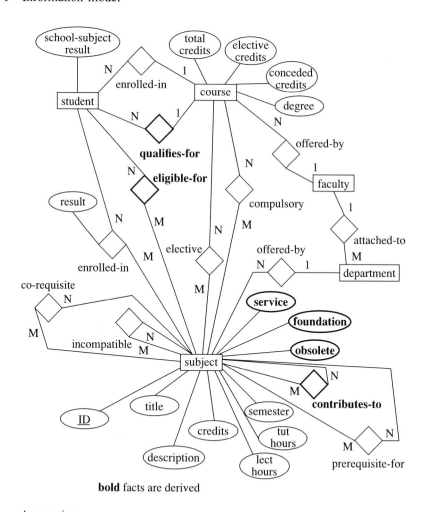

**bold** facts are derived

Assumptions
    Course and degree are in one-to-one correspondence
    A student may be enrolled in only one course

## 2 Knowledge Diagram

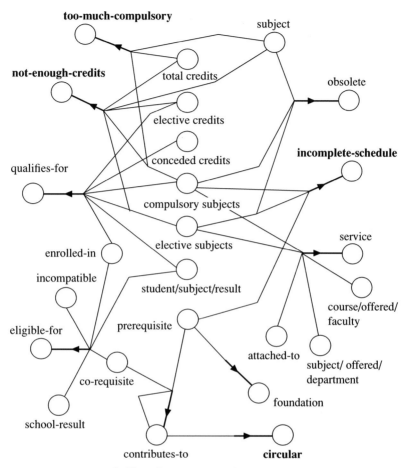

**bold** predicates are integrity constraints

## 3 Horn clause expression

### Relevant EDB

subject(Code, Credits, ... )
course(Code, Faculty, Degree, Total_credits, Elective_credits,
   Conceded_credits)
compulsory(Course, Subject)
elective(Course, Subject)
student/subject/result(Student#, Code, Result)
subject/offered/department(Code, Dept)
department(Dept, Faculty)
enrolled_in(Student#, Course_id)
prerequisite(Subject, Pre_Subject)
co-requisite(Subject, Co_Subject)

incompatible(Subject, Inc_Subject)
school_result(Student#, Subject, Result)
IDB
predicates in bold are intermediate types
obsolete(Code) :- subject(Code),
   notschedule(_, Code).
schedule(Course, Code) :- compulsory(Course, Code).
schedule(Course, Code) :- elective(Course, Code).
foundation(Code) :- subject(Code, _, . . . ), not prerequisite(Code, _).
contributes_to(Subject, Pre_Subject) :-
   prerequisite(Subject, Pre_Subject).
contributes_to(Subject, Co_Subject) :-
   co-requisite(Subject, Co_Subject).
contributes_to(Subject, Pre_Subject) :-
   prerequisite(Subject, Int_Subject),
   contributes_to(Int_Subject, Pre_Subject).
contributes_to(Subject, Co_Subject) :-
   co-requisite(Subject, Int_Subject),
   contributes_to(Int_Subject, Co_Subject).
service(Code) :- subject/offered/department(Code, Dept),
   schedule(Course, Code),
   course(Code, Faculty, _, _, _, _),
   department(Dept, D_Faculty),
   Faculty ≠ D_Faculty.
qualifies_for(Student#, Course) :-
   enrolled_in(Student#, Course),
   course(Code, _, _, _, Elective_credits, Conceded_credits),
   not missed_any_compulsory(Course, Student#),
   not failed_compulsory(Course, Student#),
   elective_credits(Student#, Course, S_E_credits),
   S_E_credits ≥ Elective_credits,
   conceded_credits(Student#, S_C_credits),
   S_C_credits ≤ Conceded_Credits.
missed_any_compulsory(Course, Student#) :-
   compulsory(Course, Code),
   student/subject/result(Student#, Code, not_available).
failed_compulsory(Course, Student#) :-
   compulsory(Course, Subject),
   student/subject/result(Student#, Code, fail).
elective_credits(Student#, Course, S_E_credits) :-
   aggregate(sum(Credits),
      elective_cr(Student#, Course, Credits),
      S_E_credits).

elective_cr(Student#, Course, Credits) :-
   elective(Course, Code),
   student/subject/result(Student#, Code, Result),
   pass(Result),
   subject(Code, Credits, . . . ).

pass(pass).
pass(conceded_pass).

conceded_credits(Student#, S_C_credits) :-
   aggregate(sum(Credits),
      conceded_cr(Student#, Course, Credits),
      S_C_credits).

conceded_cr(Student#, Course, Credits) :-
   schedule(Course, Code),
   student/subject/result(Student#, Code, conceded_pass),
   subject(Code, Credits, . . . ).

eligible_for(Student#, Subject) :-
   el_for(Student#, Subject),
   not passed_incompatible(Student#, Subject).

el_for(Student#, cs317) :-
   enrolled_in(Student#, b_inf_tech)
   student/subject/result(Student#, cs214, pass),
   student/subject/result(Student#, cs225, pass).
el_for(Student#, cs317) :-
   enrolled_in(Student#, Course),
   course ≠ b_inf_tech,
   student/subject/result(Student#, cs214, pass),
   conjunct(1,Student#, cs317).
conjunct(1,Student#, cs317) :-
   student/subject/result(Student#, cs225, pass).
conjunct(1,Student#, cs317) :-
   student/subject/result(Student#, cs102, pass),
   student/subject/result(Student#, cs226, pass).
el_for(Student#, cs214) :-
   student/subject/result(Student#, cs213, pass).
el_for(Student#, cs213) :-
   conjunct(1,Student#, cs213),
   conjunct(2,Student#, cs213).
conjunct(1,Student#, cs213) :-
   student/subject/result(Student#, cs113, pass).
conjunct(1,Student#, cs213) :-
   student/subject/result(Student#, cs115, pass).
conjunct(2,Student#, cs213) :-
   student/subject/result(Student#, me205, pass).

```
conjunct(2,Student#, cs213) :-
    student/subject/result(Student#, mp104, pass).
conjunct(2,Student#, cs213) :-
    student/subject/result(Student#, mp108, pass).
conjunct(2,Student#, cs213) :-
    student/subject/result(Student#, mp173, pass).
conjunct(2,Student#, cs213) :-
    student/subject/result(Student#, mp178, pass).
conjunct(2,Student#, cs213) :-
    student/subject/result(Student#, mt108, pass).
el_for(Student#, cs115) :-
    student/subject/result(Student#, cs114, pass).
el_for(Student#, cs115) :-
    school_result(Student#, ipt, ha).
el_for(Student#, cs114) :-
    enrolled_in(Student#, ba),
    conjunct(1,Student#, cs114).
el_for(Student#, cs114) :-
    enrolled_in(Student#, Course),
    Course ≠ ba.
conjunct(1,Student#, cs114) :-
    student/subject/result(Student#, ec131, pass).
conjunct(1,Student#, cs114) :-
    student/subject/result(Student#, mp107, pass).
conjunct(1,Student#, cs114) :-
    school_result(Student#, sen_math_1, Result),
    good_enough(Result).

passed_incompatible(Student#, Subject) :-
    incompatible(Subject, Inc_subject),
    student/subject/result(Student#, Inc_subject, pass).

bad :- course(Code, _), too_much_compulsory(Code).
bad :- course(Code, _), not_enough_credits(Code).
bad :- course(Code, _), incomplete_schedule(Code).
bad :- circular.

too_much_compulsory(Code) :-
    course(Code, _, _, Total_credits, _, _),
    total_compulsory(Course, Total_C),
    Total_C > Total_credits.

total_compulsory(Course, Total_C) :-
    aggregate(sum(Credits),
        (compulsory(Course, Subject), subject(Subject, Credits, ... )),
        Total_C).
```

```
not_enough_credits(Code) :-
    course(Code, _, _, Total_credits, _, _),
    total_compulsory(Course, Total_C),
    total_elective(Course, Total_E),
    Total_C + Total_E < Total_credits.

total_elective(Course, Total_E) :-
    aggregate(sum(Credits),
        (elective(Course, Subject), subject(Subject, Credits, ... )),
        Total_E).

incomplete_schedule(Code) :-
    compulsory(Code, Subject),
    prerequisite(Subject, Pre),
    not compulsory(Code, Pre).
incomplete_schedule(Code) :-
    elective(Code, Subject),
    prerequisite(Subject, Pre),
    not elective(Code, Pre).

circular :- contributes_to(X, X).
```

4 Population

```
subject(cs317, 8, ... ).
subject(cs225, 8, ... ).
subject(cs214, 8, ... ).
subject(cs213, 8, ... ).
subject(cs115, 8, ... ).
subject(cs114, 8, ... ).

course(b_inf_tech, science,
    b_inf_tech, 288, 144, 30).

compulsory(b_inf_tech, cs100).
compulsory(b_inf_tech, cs102).
compulsory(b_inf_tech, cs114).
compulsory(b_inf_tech, cs115).
compulsory(b_inf_tech, cs162).
compulsory(b_inf_tech, cs163).
compulsory(b_inf_tech, cs164).
compulsory(b_inf_tech, cs200).
compulsory(b_inf_tech, ec150).
compulsory(b_inf_tech, en153).
compulsory(b_inf_tech, mt108).
compulsory(b_inf_tech, cs202).
compulsory(b_inf_tech, cs210).
compulsory(b_inf_tech, cs213).
compulsory(b_inf_tech, cs261).

compulsory(b_inf_tech, co211).
compulsory(b_inf_tech, cs381).
compulsory(b_inf_tech, cs383).

elective(b_inf_tech, ec101).
elective(b_inf_tech, ec110).
elective(b_inf_tech, mt100).
elective(b_inf_tech, mp105).
elective(b_inf_tech, mt101).
elective(b_inf_tech, ms101).
elective(b_inf_tech, ms112).
elective(b_inf_tech, ms113).
elective(b_inf_tech, py102).
elective(b_inf_tech, cs205).
elective(b_inf_tech, cs214).
elective(b_inf_tech, cs215).
elective(b_inf_tech, cs223).
elective(b_inf_tech, cs225).
elective(b_inf_tech, cs231).
elective(b_inf_tech, e3277).
elective(b_inf_tech, gn238).
elective(b_inf_tech, gn242).
elective(b_inf_tech, ic210).
elective(b_inf_tech, ic220).
```

elective(b_inf_tech, ma212).
elective(b_inf_tech, mn212).
elective(b_inf_tech, pd211).

subject/offered/
  department(cs317, cs).
subject/offered/
  department(mt108, math).
subject/offered/
  department(e3277, ee).
subject/offered/
  department(ic210, inter).
subject/offered/
  department(gn242, earth).
subject/offered/
  department(ec101, econ).
subject/offered/
  department(py102, psych).
subject/offered/department
  (co211, commerce).
subject/offered/department
  (en153, english).
subject/offered/department
  (pd211, philosophy).

department(cs, science).
department(math, science).
department(inter, science).
department(earth, science).
department(econ, commerce/econ).
department(psych, science).
department(commerce, commerce/
  econ).
department(english, arts).
department(philosophy, arts).
department(ee, engineering).

prerequisite(cs317, cs214).
prerequisite(cs317, cs225).
prerequisite(cs317, cs226).
prerequisite(cs317, cs102).
prerequisite(cs214, cs213).
prerequisite(cs213, cs115).
prerequisite(cs115, cs114).
prerequisite(cs213, me205).
prerequisite(cs317, mp104).
prerequisite(cs317, mp108).

## 5 Exceptions in application of quality principles

Principle I.2 is violated by *prerequisite* and *eligible_for*, since in principle *prerequisite* can be derived from the clauses in *eligible_for*. However, the theorem proving techniques required to do so are beyond the scope of this subject. An alternative, probably better than the one presented, strategy would be to represent the prerequisite structure for a subject as an and/or tree. Both *eligible_for* and *prerequisite* could be derived from this tree. However, structured data is not allowed by strict datalog, so is beyond the material expected of the student at this stage.

The intermediate predicates shown in the solution are all in response to principles K.3 and K.4.

Several clauses have multiple derivations (principle G.2). The predicates *contributes_to* and *service* are both projections onto non-key attributes. The integrity constraint *bad* has many derivations, but for the system to be consistent, there should be no tuple *bad* in the perfect model. Similarly, *missed_any_compulsory* and *failed_compulsory* have multiple derivations, but only contribute to the perfect model if they have no solutions.

There are several instances of labels appearing in definitions. In all cases, the clause in which a label appears is functionally dependent on the label.

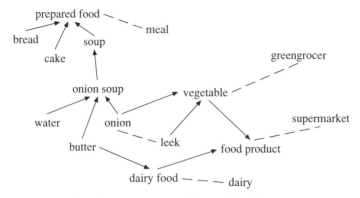

**Figure S5.3**   Graphical representation of hierarchical thesaurus.

CHAPTER 6

6.1   predicate definition has name
        population is subtype of population
        population is domain of predicate definition has role
        tuple has role stores instance
        instance instance-of population

6.2   All valid labels
          Label(<u>Text</u>, Predicate?, Population?, Instance?).

      Labels used as predicate definitions
          Has-definition(<u>Name</u>, Predicate).

      Labels in a subtype/supertype relation
          Subtype(<u>Supertype, Subtype</u>).

      Labels which are populations of roles in predicates.
          Domain-of(<u>Predicate, Role</u>, Population).

      Labels which are instances of roles in tuples
          Stores(<u>Tuple, Role</u>, Instance).

      Labels which are instances of populations
          Instance-of(<u>Instance, Population</u>).

6.3   SQL
          SELECT Name FROM Has-definition
              UNION
          SELECT Supertype FROM Subtype
              UNION
          SELECT Subtype FROM Subtype
              UNION
          SELECT Population FROM Domain-of
              UNION

SELECT Instance FROM Stores
  UNION
SELECT Instance FROM Instance-of
  UNION
SELECT Population FROM Instance-of

Datalog

label(T) :- has-definition(T, _).
label(T) :- subtype(T, _).
label(T) :- suptype(_, T).
label(T) :- domain-of(_, _, T).
label(T) :- stores(_, _, T).
label(T) :- instance-of(T, _).
label(T) :- instance-of(_, T).

| 6.4 | Group | Clause | Literal# | Arg# | Label | Called_Predicate | Role |
|---|---|---|---|---|---|---|---|
| | ancestor | 1 | 0 | 1 | Older | — | — |
| | ancestor | 1 | 0 | 2 | Younger | — | — |
| | ancestor | 1 | 1 | 1 | Older | parent | older |
| | ancestor | 1 | 1 | 2 | Younger | parent | younger |
| | ancestor | 2 | 0 | 1 | Older | — | — |
| | ancestor | 2 | 0 | 2 | Younger | — | — |
| | ancestor | 2 | 1 | 1 | Older | parent | older |
| | ancestor | 2 | 1 | 2 | Intermediate | parent | younger |
| | ancestor | 2 | 2 | 1 | Intermediate | ancestor | older |
| | ancestor | 2 | 2 | 2 | Younger | ancestor | younger |

6.5   sg(X, X).
      sg(X, Y) :- parent(P, X), parent(Q, Y), sg(P, Q).

6.6   A join in *literal/argument* occurs when a label occurs in two different literals
      with literal# greater than 0 in the same clause and the same group.

6.7   SELECT DISTINCT Domain FROM pred/role, literal/argument l1, literal/
           argument l2
             WHERE l1.group = l2.group
               AND l1.clause = l2.clause
               AND l1.literal# > 0
               AND l2.literal# > l1.literal#
               AND l1.label = l2.label
               AND pred/role.predicate = l1.called_predicate
               AND pred/role.role = l1.role

      join-attribute(Population) :-
          literal/argument(G, C, Lit1, _, Lab, Called1, Role1),
          literal/argument(G, C, Lit2, _, Lab, Called2, Role2),
          Lit1 > 0, Lit2 > Lit1,
          pred/role(Called1, Role1, Population, _).

% we are assuming that the join attributes are join compatible,
and further that the domains are the same.

Two attributes are join compatible if their domains are non-disjoint subtypes of the same population. They at least have a common ancestor in the transitive closure *subtype-of* predicate. Further, they are not disjoint subtypes of their nearest common ancestor.

## CHAPTER 7

A natural enhancement to a system is to add queries using the existing data, for example: *find all items whose source is X*; for example, *what items are obtainable from a greengrocer*. We want only the most specific items: if an item has subtypes or instances, it should be excluded.

    items-obtainable-from(Supplier, Item) :-
        source-of(Item, Supplier), most-specific(Item).
    items-obtainable-from(Supplier, Item) :-
        source-of(Type, Supplier),
        one-of(Type, Item),
        most-specific(Item).

    most-specific(Item) :- not instance-of(Item, _), not subtype-of(Item, _).

Re-uses the predicates *source-of*, *one-of*, *instance-of* and *subtype-of*.

Another natural enhancement is to add similar sorts of data: for example a new narrower term type *significant source of allergen* requires adding terms which are allergens, such as *lactose*, *gluten*, and adding the new narrower term to existing terms (*lactose* to *butter*, *gluten* to *bread*). New queries would be needed to support the new data, for example *preparations containing a given allergen* or *class of product generally safe from allergen*.

    preparation-containing-allergen(Prep, Allergen) :-
        significant-source-of-allergen(Ingredient, Allergen),
        has-ingredient(Prep, Ingredient).

    class-generally-safe(Class, Allergen) :-
        class-of-preparations(Class),
        not class-possibly-unsafe(Class, Allergen).

    class-of-preparations(Class) :-
        one-of(Class, Instance),
        has-ingredient(Instance, _).

    class-possibly-unsafe(Class, Allergen) :-
        one-of(Ingredient, Class),
        preparation-containing-allergen(Ingredient, Allergen).

Re-uses *has-ingredient* and *one-of*. Note new knowledge has introduced new intermediate predicates.

A third kind of change is to generalize existing structures. For example, we could declare that some of the narrower or related term types were **transitive**, like *is-a*. (Note that of the other narrower or related term types in the original system, only *ingredient of* is plausibly transitive, although it has not been recognized as such in the application.) This allows us to introduce new types such as *owned-by*, which serve perhaps a new set of data which are particular companies that are instances of *supermarket*, *dairy*, *greengrocer*, etc. This would be implemented by first modifying the existing *subtype of*

    subtype-of(Supertype, Subtype) :- transitive-closure(Supertype, Subtype, is-a).

    transitive-closure(Supertype, Subtype, Arc) :- Arc(Supertype, Subtype).
    transitive-closure(Supertype, Subtype, Arc) :-
        Arc(Supertype, Intermediate),
        transitive-closure(Intermediate, Subtype, Arc).

then adding, say,

    owned-by(Owner, Owned) :- transitive-closure(Owner, Owned, owned-by).

Here, what we have done is to apply principle K.4 to the definition of *subtype-of* to extract the transitive closure predicate. We can easily make *has-ingredient* transitive as well:

    rename *has-ingredient* to say *contains*.

    replace *has-ingredient* with
        has-ingredient(Product, Ingredient) :-
            transitive-closure(Product, Ingredient, contains).

The main principles directly involved in these changes are K.3 and K.4. This is because the changes proposed have been in terms of the existing universe of discourse, and structurally and semantically similar extensions. However, the general lack of redundancy achieved by following the set of principles has made the changes less troublesome than they otherwise would have been, since we have been confident that the obvious changes have no hidden side-effects.

## CHAPTER 8

8.1   red_blue_path(X, Y) :- red(X, Y).
     red_blue_path(X, Y) :- red_blue_path(X, U), blue(U, V), red_blue_path(V, Y).
     *bf*

     red_blue_path is subgoal-rectified and has the unique binding property.

     Using the magic set algorithm:

     Magic predicates
        m_p(X) :- $sup_{2,0}(X)$.
        m_p(V) :- $sup_{2,2}(X, V)$.

Zeroth supplementary

$sup_{1,0}(X) :- m\_p(X).$
$sup_{2,0}(X) :- m\_p(X).$

Other supplementary

$sup_{2,1}(X, U) :- sup_{2,0}(X), red\_blue\_path(X, U).$
$sup_{2,2}(X, V) :- sup_{2,1}(X, U), blue(U, V).$

IDB predicates

$red\_blue\_path(X, Y) :- sup_{1,0}(X), red(X, Y).$
$red\_blue\_path(X, Y) :- sup_{2,2}(X, V), red\_blue\_path(V, Y).$

Initialization

$m\_p(\&1).$

8.2 Magic predicates

$m\_e(E) :- sup_{1,0}(E, T).$
$m\_e(E) :- sup_{5,0}(E).$
$m\_t(T) :- sup_{1,1}(E, T).$
$m\_t(T) :- sup_{2,0}(T).$
$m\_t(T) :- sup_{3,0}(T, F).$
$m\_f(F) :- sup_{3,1}(T, F).$
$m\_f(F) :- sup_{4,0}(F).$

Zeroth supplementary

$sup_{1,0}(E, T) :- m\_e(plus(E, T)).$
$sup_{2,0}(T) :- m\_e(T).$
$sup_{3,0}(T, F) :- m\_t(times(T, F)).$
$sup_{4,0}(T) :- m\_t(T).$
$sup_{5,0}(E) :- m\_f(parens(E)).$
$sup_{6,0}(F) :- m\_f(F).$

Other supplementary

$sup_{1,1}(E, T) :- sup_{1,0}(E, T), expression(E).$
$sup_{3,1}(T, F) :- sup_{3,0}(T, F), term(T).$

IDB predicates

$expression(plus(E, T)) :- sup_{1,1}(E, T), term(T).$
$expression(T) :- sup_{2,0}(T), term(T).$
$term(times(T, F)) :- sup_{3,1}(T, F), factor(F).$
$term(T) :- sup_{4,0}(T), factor(T).$
$factor(parens(E)) :- sup_{5,0}(E), expression(E).$
$factor(F) :- sup_{6,0}(F), identifier(F).$

Initialization

$m\_e(expression\_to\_be\_parsed).$

8.3 Adornment: bbf

Linear recursion:

*Max 1 recursive*: clause 1 has no IDB subgoals, while clauses 2 and 3 have one IDB subgoal, *trip*.

*Recursive last*: *trip* in clauses 2 and 3 can be last without violating the unique binding property.

*Recursively computed output*: *End* is the free variable in the head of clauses 2 and 3, is also the free variable in the subgoal *trip* in both clauses, and occurs nowhere else in the two clauses.

Therefore the predicate is right linear recursive.

Magic predicates

    m_t(Line, Int) :- m_t(Line, Start), leg(Line, Start, Int).
    m_t(Line_1, Start) :- m_t(Line, Start), interchange(Start, Line, Line_1).

Magic EDB tuple    m_t(&1, &2).

Answer predicates    a_t(End) :- m_t(Line, Start), station(Line, Start), Start = End.

Query answer    trip(&1, &2, End) :- a_t(End).


## CHAPTER 9

9.1    1. m_sg(Xp) :- supp2,1(X, Xp).
    2. sup1,0(X) :- m_sg(X).
    3. sup2,0(X) :- m_sg(X).
    4. sup2,1(X, Xp) :- sup2,0(X), par(Xp, X).
    5. sup2,2(X, Yp) :- sup2,1(X, Xp), sg(Xp, Yp).
    6. sg(X, X) :- sup1,0(X), person(X).
    7. sg(X, Y) :- sup2,2(X, Yp), par(Yp, Y).
    8. m_sg(&1).

Unfold 2 into 6, 3 into 4

    1. m_sg(Xp) :- supp2,1(X, Xp).
    4. sup2,1(X, Xp) :- m_sg(X), par(Xp, X).
    5. sup2,2(X, Yp) :- sup2,1(X, Xp), sg(Xp, Yp).
    6. sg(X, X) :- m_sg(X), person(X).
    7. sg(X, Y) :- sup2,2(X, Yp), par(Yp, Y).
    8. m_sg(&1).

Unfold 5 into 7

    1. m_sg(Xp) :- supp2,1(X, Xp).
    4. sup2,1(X, Xp) :- m_sg(X), par(Xp, X).
    6. sg(X, X) :- m_sg(X), person(X).
    7. sg(X, Y) :- sup2,1(X, Xp), sg(Xp, Yp), par(Yp, Y).
    8. m_sg(&1).

Could unfold 4 into 1 and 7, but do not as it increases the number of joins which must be computed.

9.2
m.1 $\quad$ m_e(E) :- $\sup_{1,0}$(E, T).
m.2 $\quad$ m_e(E) :- $\sup_{5,0}$(E).
m.3 $\quad$ m_t(T) :- $\sup_{1,1}$(E, T).
m.4 $\quad$ m_t(T) :- $\sup_{2,0}$(T).
m.5 $\quad$ m_t(T) :- $\sup_{3,0}$(T, F).
m.6 $\quad$ m_f(F) :- $\sup_{3,1}$(T, F).
m.7 $\quad$ m_f(F) :- $\sup_{4,0}$(F).
z.1 $\quad$ $\sup_{1,0}$(E, T) :- m_e(plus(E, T)).
z.2 $\quad$ $\sup_{2,0}$(T) :- m_e(T).
z.3 $\quad$ $\sup_{3,0}$(T, F) :- m_t(times(T, F)).
z.4 $\quad$ $\sup_{4,0}$(T) :- m_t(T).
z.5 $\quad$ $\sup_{5,0}$(E) :- m_f(parens(E)).
z.6 $\quad$ $\sup_{6,0}$(F) :- m_f(F).
s.1 $\quad$ $\sup_{1,1}$(E, T) :- $\sup_{1,0}$(E, T), expression(E).
s.2 $\quad$ $\sup_{3,1}$(T, F) :- $\sup_{3,0}$(T, F), term(T).
r.1 $\quad$ expression(plus(E, T)) :- $\sup_{1,1}$(E, T), term(T).
r.2 $\quad$ expression(T) :- $\sup_{2,0}$(T), term(T).
r.3 $\quad$ term(times(T, F)) :- $\sup_{3,1}$(T, F), factor(F).
r.4 $\quad$ term(T) :- $\sup_{4,0}$(T), factor(T).
r.5 $\quad$ factor(parens(E)) :- $\sup_{5,0}$(E), expression(E).
r.6 $\quad$ factor(F) :- $\sup_{6,0}$(F), identifier(F).
i.1 $\quad$ m_e(expression_to_be_parsed).

Unfold z.1 into m.1 and s.1; z2 into m4, r2; z3 into m5, s2; z4 into m7, r4; z5 into m2, r5; z6 into r6; giving:

m.1 $\quad$ m_e(E) :- m_e(plus(E, T)).
m.2 $\quad$ m_e(F) :- m_f(parens(F)).
m.3 $\quad$ m_t(T) :- $\sup_{1,1}$(E, T).
m.4 $\quad$ m_t(T) :- m_e(T).
m.5 $\quad$ m_t(T) :- m_t(times(T, F)).
m.6 $\quad$ m_f(F) :- $\sup_{3,1}$(T, F).
m.7 $\quad$ m_f(T) :- m_t(T).
s.1 $\quad$ $\sup_{1,1}$(E, T) :- m_e(plus(E, T)), expression(E).
s.2 $\quad$ $\sup_{3,1}$(T, F) :- m_t(times(T, F)), term(T).
r.1 $\quad$ expression(plus(E, T)) :- $\sup_{1,1}$(E, T), term(T).
r.2 $\quad$ expression(T) :- m_e(T), term(T).
r.3 $\quad$ term(times(T, F)) :- $\sup_{3,1}$(T, F), factor(F).
r.4 $\quad$ term(T) :- m_t(T), factor(T).
r.5 $\quad$ factor(parens(E)) :- m_f(parens(F)), expression(E).
r.6 $\quad$ factor(F) :- m_f(F), identifier(F).
i.1 $\quad$ m_e(expression_to_be_parsed).

None of the other candidates for unfolding are desirable, since they increase the number of joins. There are no candidates for folding.

## CHAPTER 10

10.1     f1 & f2 & f5 → c1
             f1 & ~f2 → c2
         ~f1 & ~f3 → c2
         ~f1 & ~f4 → c2
          ~f1 & f5 → c2
         ~f2 & ~f3 → c2
         ~f2 & ~f4 → c2
          ~f2 & f5 → c2

Note that there is a lot of cancellation, due to

p & ~p = false
p + p & q = p

As a decision table:

| f1 | f2 | f3 | f4 | f5 | Action |
|----|----|----|----|----|--------|
| y  | y  |    |    | y  | c1     |
| y  | n  |    |    |    | c2     |
| n  |    | n  |    |    | c2     |
| n  |    |    | n  |    | c2     |
| n  |    |    |    | y  | c2     |
|    | n  | n  |    |    | c2     |
|    | n  |    | n  |    | c2     |
|    | n  |    |    | y  | c2     |

The table is unambiguous, so can be converted into a decision tree.

    if f1 then
        if f2 then
            if f5 then c1
            else fail
        else c2
    else
        if not f3 or not f4 or f5 then c2
        else fail

There are other alternatives.

## CHAPTER 11

11.1   (a)   Uniqueness: $\forall X\ r(X, Z), r(X, Y) \rightarrow Y = Z$.

            $\sim\exists X\sim(r(X, Z), r(X, Y) \rightarrow Y = Z)$.
            $p(Y, Z) :- \sim(r(X, Z), r(X, Y) \rightarrow Y = Z)$.
            $\sim p(Y, Z)$.
            $p(Y, Z) :- r(X, Z), r(X, Y), Y\ != Z$.

Mandatory: $\forall X \exists Y \ a(X) \rightarrow r(X, Y)$.

$\sim\exists X \sim\exists Y \ a(X) \rightarrow r(X, Y)$.
$p(Y) :- \sim\exists Y \ a(X) \rightarrow r(X, Y)$.
$\sim p(Y)$.
$q(X) :- a(X) \rightarrow r(X, Y)$.
$p(Y) :- \sim q(X)$.
$q(X) :- r(X, Y)$.
$q(X) :- \sim a(X)$.

Subtype: $\forall X \ a(X) \rightarrow b(X)$.

$\sim\exists X \sim a(X) \rightarrow b(X)$.
$p :- \sim a(X) \rightarrow b(X)$.
$\sim p$.
$p :- a(X), \sim b(X)$.

(b)   Uniqueness: $bad :- \sim\forall X \ r(X, Z), r(X, Y) \rightarrow Y = Z$.

$bad :- \exists X \sim(r(X, Z), r(X, Y) \rightarrow Y = Z)$.
$bad :- \sim((r(X, Z), r(X, Y)) \rightarrow Y = Z)$.
$bad :- r(X, Z), r(X, Y), (Y \ != Z)$.

Mandatory: $bad :- \sim\forall X \exists Y \ a(X) \rightarrow r(X, Y)$.

$bad :- \exists X \sim\exists Y \ a(X) \rightarrow r(X, Y)$.
$bad :- \sim\exists Y \ a(X) \rightarrow r(X, Y)$.
$p(X) :- a(X) \rightarrow r(X, Y)$.
$bad :- \sim p(X)$.
$p(X) :- r(X, Y)$.
$p(X) :- \sim a(X)$.

Subtype: $bad :- \sim\forall X \ a(X) \rightarrow b(X)$.

$bad :- \exists X \sim a(X) \rightarrow b(X)$.
$bad :- \sim (a(X) \rightarrow b(X))$.
$bad :- a(X), \sim b(X)$.

(c)   Referential integrity: The set of entities in a particular attribute of relation $A$ is a subset of the set of entities in the corresponding attribute in relation $B$. This is the same as the subtype constraint.

11.2   There are many constraints. These are some:

Every tuple is an instance of its scheme and every instance label is of the correct type

$\forall$Tuple $\forall$Predicate $\forall$Role $\forall$Instance (
   tuple/role(Predicate, Tuple, Role, Instance) $\rightarrow$
   ($\exists$Pred $\exists$R $\exists$Domain
      pred/role(Pred, R, Domain, Type) &
      Pred = Predicate & R = Role &
      $\exists$I $\exists$D (labels(I, D) & I = Instance & D = Domain)))

Every scheme has a key

∀Predicate ∀Role ∃Type
  pred/role(Predicate, Role, Domain, Type) &
  Type = "key"

Every subgoal calls a defined predicate

∀Group ∀Clause ∀Literal# ∀Called_Predicate
  literal/calls(Group, Clause, Literal#, Called_Predicate, Negative) →
  (∃C_P pred/role(C_P, Role, Domain, Type) &
    C_P = Called_Predicate)

A literal is a defined predicate

∀Group ∀Clause ∀Literal# ∀Called_Predicate
  literal/argument(Group, Clause, Literal#, Argument#, Label,
    Called_Predicate, Role) →
  (∃C_P pred/role(C_P, Role, Domain, Type) &
    C_P = Called_Predicate)

A clause head literal is its own predicate

∀Group ∀Clause ∀Literal#
  ((literal/argument(Group, Clause, Literal#, Argument#, Label,
    Called_Predicate, Role) & Literal# = 0) →
  Called_Predicate = null)

A clause body literal is a called predicate

∀Group ∀Clause ∀Literal# ∀Called_Predicate
  (literal/argument(Group, Clause, Literal#, Argument#, Label,
    Called_Predicate, Role) and Literal# > 0) →
  ∃Group ∃Clause ∃Literal# ∃C_P
    (literal/calls(Group, Clause, Literal#, C_P, Negative) &
    C_P = Called_Predicate)

### CHAPTER 12

12.1  (a)  Probably the most reasonable place to find out whether the population
           *product_class* is valid is in the table *pred/role*, with the query *pred/
           role(_, _, product_class, _)?*

      (b)  If the population *product_class* were removed, we would need to identify
           in *pred/role* all those predicates which have *product_class* as a domain.
           In this case: *product, sales_tax, sales_tax_amount, wholesale_price,*
           and *invoice*.

           It would be imprudent to delete these automatically, so they would
           be referred to the programmer. Assume that the programmer decides to
           modify *product* and *invoice*, and to delete the others. These predicates
           would have to be removed from *pred_role, literal/calls, literal/argument,*
           and *tuple/role* via referential integrity constraints. These all propagate

to *invoice* and via join attributes in *literal/argument* to *total_wholesale*, *total_stax*, and *total_cost*. The programmer decides to modify *invoice*, to retain *total_wholesale*, and remove *total_stax* and *total_cost*.

12.2 ■ The first decision is whether to delete each of *product*, *sales_tax*, *sales_tax_amount*, *wholesale_price*, and *invoice*, or to modify them to remove the domain *product_class*.

■ *product_class* is a non-key domain of *product*, so the domain only can be removed.

■ *product_class* is a key domain of *sales_tax*, so it makes sense to delete the whole predicate.

■ Both *product_class* and *sales_tax* have been deleted. *sales_tax_amount* is a computational predicate based on *sales_tax*, so can be deleted.

■ The same is true of *wholesale_price*.

■ *product_class* is not a key of *invoice*, the predicates removed are only a small part of *invoice*, so it is not safe to delete *invoice*. The program can delete argument *Product_class* from *product*, and the subgoals *sales_tax_amount* and *wholesale_price* from both clauses of *invoice*.

■ *total_wholesale* is affected by the join variable *Wholesale_price*. It is a computational predicate for which *Wholesale_price* is an input, so can be deleted, and its subgoal deleted from both clauses of *invoice*. Similarly for *sales_tax_amount* via the join variable *Sales_tax_amount*.

■ There is no more propagation in the second clause of *invoice*, but in the first clause the subgoal *cost* is connected by both join variables to deleted subgoals. *cost*, however has two clauses, the first dependent on *boutique* and the second on *ds*. The first clause of *invoice* is dependent on *boutique* and the second on *ds*. The first clause of *cost* is a computational predicate taking deleted arguments as input, so could be deleted.

■ The output of *cost* is an output of *invoice*, and is not deleted in the second clause, so at this point the automatic propagation would probably have to stop and refer to the programmer. (What the programmer would probably do is realize that with the absence of sales tax, cost and list price are the same, and amend the program accordingly.)

12.3 ■ A predicate definition is less entrenched than its key domains.

■ A predicate definition is more entrenched than its non-key domains.

■ We need to have some way of identifying essential parameters of computational predicates. If we could, then a computational predicate definition is less entrenched than its essential parameters, but more entrenched than its non-essential parameters. Certainly the only input parameter is essential.

■ Similarly, we need some way of identifying essential subgoals (as in *invoice*). Computational subgoals are probably inessential, as are lookup predicates, which we might be able to define as predicates based directly or indirectly on predicates having two arguments, the key argument of which is deleted.

12.4    Notation:

Label of node n in set of environments is <{environments} node>

| | | |
|---|---|---|
| 0. <{ } yellow> <{ } red> | | neither on |
| 1. <{{temperature_too_high }} yellow> <{ } red> | | yellow on |
| 2. <{{temperature_too_high },{cooling_valve_stuck_open }} yellow> | | |
|     <{ } red> | | yellow on |
| 3. <{{cooling_valve_stuck_open }} yellow> | | |
|     <{ } red> | | yellow on |
| 4. <{{cooling_valve_stuck_open }{temperature_too_low }} yellow> | | |
|     <{{cooling_valve_stuck_open, temperature_too_low }} red> both on | | |
| 5. <{{temperature_too_low }} yellow> | | |
|     <{ } red> | | yellow on |
| 6. <{ } yellow> <{ } red> | | neither on |
| 7. <{ } yellow> <{{fuel_exhausted}} red> | | red on |

12.5    {a} → a
{b} → b
{a, b} → c
{d} → d
{e} → e
{a, e} → f
{x, b} → f
{} → g
{r} → r
{s} → s
{r, s} → t
{y} → y
{x} → x
{x, y} → z
{r, s, x, y} → w
{} → u

g is not believed because the only environment in which it could be believed is {a, e, d}, which contains the nogood {a, d}. u is not believed because g is not believed.

12.6    An ATMS could be used by a student planning a program for keeping track of subjects selected not because of their intrinsic interest but because they are prerequisites for subjects of intrinsic interest or are fillers to gain enough credits in a particular category. Justifications might be of the form subject_1 → subject_2

if subject_2 were chosen as a prerequisite for subject_1, and

need_credits_in_category_x → subject

if *subject* were selected to fill credits in category *x*. Main subjects would be assumptions. Querying the labels would identify all subjects currently selected. Those with empty justifications could be removed with no loss of intrinsic interest.

# References

BATINI, C., S. CERI and S.B. NAVATHE (1992) *Conceptual Database Design*. Benjamin Cummings. Redwood City, CA.

BRATKO, I. (1986) *Prolog Programming for Artificial Intelligence*. Addison Wesley. Reading, MA.

BROWNSTON, L., R. FARRELL, E. KANT and N. MARTIN (1985) *Programming Expert Systems in OPS-5*. Addison Wesley. Reading, MA.

CERI, S., G. GOTTLOB and L. TANCA (1990) *Logic Programming and Databases*. Springer-Verlag. Berlin.

CLOCKSIN, W.F. and C.S. MELLISH (1987) *Programming in Prolog*. 3rd edn. Springer-Verlag. Berlin.

COLOMB, R.M. (1990) *Implementing Persistent Prolog*. Ellis Horwood. Chichester, England.
(1992) 'Computational stability of expert systems'. *Expert Systems with Applications* **5** (2/3), 411–419.
and C.Y. CHUNG (1995) 'Strategies for building propositional expert systems'. *International Journal of Intelligent Systems* **10** (3), 295–328.

CRAGUN, B.J. and H.J. STEUDEL (1987) 'A decision-table-based processor for checking completeness and consistency in rule-based expert systems'. *International Journal of Man-Machine Studies* **26** (5), 633–648.

DAS, S.K. (1992) *Deductive Databases and Logic Programming*. Addison Wesley. Reading, MA.

DEBENHAM, J.K. (1989) *Knowledge Systems Design*. Prentice-Hall. Englewood Cliffs, NJ.
and C.A. LINDLEY (1990) The knowledge analyst's assistant: a tool for knowledge systems design. In 'Proceedings 4th Australian Joint Conference on Artificial Intelligence'. World Scientific. Singapore. pp. 343–354.

DE KLEER, J. (1986) 'An assumption-based TMS'. *Artificial Intelligence* **28** (2), 127–162.

ELMASRI, R. and S.B. NAVATHE (1994) *Fundamentals of Database Systems*. 2nd edn. Benjamin Cummings. Redwood City, CA.

GARDENFORS, P. (1988) *Knowledge in Flux*. MIT Press. Cambridge, MA.

GENESERETH, M.R. and N.J. NILSSON (1987) *Logical Foundations of Artificial Intelligence*. Morgan Kaufmann. San Mateo, CA.

GUESSOUM, A. and J.W. LLOYD (1990) 'Updating knowledge bases'. *New Generation Computing* **8**, 71–89.

HALPIN, T.A. (1994) *Conceptual Schema and Relational Database Design.* 2nd edn. Prentice-Hall. Englewood Cliffs, NJ.

LAKHOTIA, A. and L. STERLING (1990) 'ProMiX: a Prolog partial evaluation system'. In L. STERLING (Ed.). *The Practice of Prolog.* MIT Press. Cambridge, MA. pp. 137–179.

LI, D. (1984) *A Prolog Database System.* Research Studies Press. Letchworth, England.

LINDLEY, C.A. (1990) An integrated conceptual model for data, information and knowledge. In Proceedings of the 13th Australian Computer Science Conference, *Australian Computer Science Communications* **12** (1), 226–235.

and J.K. DEBENHAM (1990) A software tool for the design and maintenance of knowledge systems. In *Proceedings Australian Software Engineering Conference*, May 22–25, The Institute of Engineers. pp. 165–170.

LLOYD, J.W. (1987) *Foundations of Logic Programming.* 2nd edn. Springer-Verlag. Berlin.

NIJSSEN, G.M. and T.A. HALPIN (1989) *Conceptual Schema and Relational Database Design.* Prentice Hall. Englewood Cliffs, NJ.

RAMAKRISHNAN, R. and J. ULLMAN (1995) 'A survey of deductive database systems'. *Journal of Logic Programming* **23** (2), 125–149.

RICH, E. and K. KNIGHT (1991) *Artificial Intelligence.* 2nd edn. McGraw-Hill. New York.

SATO, T. (1992) 'Equivalence-preserving first order unfold/fold transformation systems'. *Theoretical Computer Science* **105**, 57–84.

SEKI, H. (1989) Unfold/fold transformations of stratified programs. In G. LEVI and M. MARTELLI (Eds). *Logic Programming: Proceedings of the Sixth International Conference (Lisbon).* MIT Press. Cambridge, MA. pp. 554–568.

SHETH, A.P. and J. LARSEN (1990) 'Federated database systems for managing distributed, heterogeneous and autonomous databases'. *Computing Surveys* **22** (3), 183–236.

SHWAYDER, K. (1974) 'Extending the information theory approach to converting limited-entry decision tables to computer programs'. *Communications of the ACM* **17** (9), 532–537.

STERLING, L. and E. SHAPIRO (1986) *The Art of Prolog.* MIT Press. Cambridge, MA.

ULLMAN, J.D. (1988) *Principles of Database and Knowledge-base Systems*, Vol. 1. Computer Science Press. Rockville, MD.

(1989) *Principles of Database and Knowledge-base Systems*, Vol. 2. Computer Science Press. Rockville, MD.

WINSTON, P.H. (1992) *Artificial Intelligence.* 3rd edn. Addison Wesley. Reading, MA.

YOURDON, E. and L. CONSTANTINE (1978) *Structured Design: Fundamentals of a Discipline of Computer Program and Systems Design.* Prentice Hall. Englewood Cliffs, NJ.

# Index